WITHDRAWN
UTSA LIBRARIES

THE JAPANESE MIRACLE
and Peril

BOOKS BY WILLARD PRICE:

The Japanese Miracle
Odd Way Round the World
America's Paradise Lost
Rivers I Have Known
The Amazing Mississippi
Incredible Africa
Roaming Britain
Adventures in Paradise
Journey by Junk
The Amazing Amazon
I Cannot Rest from Travel
Roving South
Key to Japan
Japan and the Son of Heaven
Japan's Islands of Mystery
Japan Rides the Tiger
Barbarian
Children of the Rising Sun
Pacific Adventure
Ancient Peoples at New Tasks
The Negro Round the World
America's Influence in the Orient

FOR BOYS:

Diving Adventure
Gorilla Adventure
Lion Adventure
Safari Adventure
Elephant Adventure
African Adventure
Whale Adventure
Volcano Adventure
Underwater Adventure
South Sea Adventure
Amazon Adventure

THE JAPANESE

WILLARD PRICE

MIRACLE and PERIL

THE JOHN DAY COMPANY   New York

Copyright © 1971 by Willard Price

All rights reserved. No part of this book may be reprinted, or reproduced or utilized in any form or by any electronic, mechanical or other means, now known or hereafter invented, including photocopying and recording, or in any information storage and retrieval system, without permission in writing from the Publisher.

The John Day Company, 257 Park Avenue South, New York N.Y. 10010
An Intext Publisher

Published on the same day in Canada by Longman Canada Limited.

Library of Congress Catalogue Card Number: 76-135277
Printed in the United States of America
Designed by The Etheredges

CONTENTS

1 *History Can Be Exciting* 1
2 *Conceit* 6
3 *Humility* 24
4 *250 Guns Opened Japan* 37
5 *Romance of the First Consul* 54
6 *Okichi* 61
7 *The Proudest Moment* 69
8 *Blood and Tears* 79
9 *Death of Okichi* 94
10 *War* 100
11 *Fever of Goodwill* 107
12 *Go West, Young Man* 118
13 *The Hate Campaign* 127
14 *How to Use an Emperor* 131

15 *"Move Over, God, It's Mac"* 162
16 *Desperation but Not Despair* 177
17 *The Uses of Adversity* 189
18 *Up from the Ashes* 203
19 *Creators or Copycats?* 218
20 *First in the Twenty-first Century?* 221
21 *Women, Progress, and Problems* 229
22 *From Witch to M.D.* 253
23 *Birth Control* 266
24 *Greek Japan* 277
25 *Nipponese Babylon* 294
26 *Old Japan Endures* 298
27 *The Peril* 321
    Index 339

THE JAPANESE MIRACLE
and Peril

1

HISTORY CAN BE EXCITING

"You like octopus tentacles?" asked the geisha on my right.

"*Dozo*, please, have more raw fish," said the geisha on my left.

A girl behind refilled my sake cup.

It was a business conference. I was an innocent bystander (more accurately, bykneeler). The business was between representatives of two firms. One wanted to sell and the other was thinking about buying.

But there was not a word about either selling or buying. The geisha party was a warming-up process. The deal, if there was a deal, would come some days later.

We rose after a three-hour kneel, the foreigner's cracking bones sounding like firecrackers on the Fourth of July. Our host taxied me back to my hotel.

"Wonderful party," I said. "Six of the prettiest geishas I ever saw. And enough food and sake to sink a ship. I wonder if you will think me rude if I ask you how much it cost."

"No," he said. "It's a natural question, since you don't do

things that way in America. It really didn't cost too much. I am not a big executive in my firm. My expense account is modest. The party cost about $300 in your money."

And in New York a minor executive who spent more than thirty dollars on a dinner appointment with a prospect would find himself on the carpet before his boss's desk the next morning.

I questioned my friend on this point a few days later.

"About that party—what did your superior say when he got the bill?"

"He said I should have spent more. This prospect can give us a million-dollar order. If we spend one percent of that in entertaining him, it is good business."

"But can't you just walk into his office and tell him about your product?"

"Not if he is a Japanese. We can't go at him. We have to go around him. It comes down from feudal times. Samurai considered merchandising beneath them. They would not discuss money. Instead, they bargained with courtesies. One gave the other a party or a valuable gift. The other was bound by custom to reciprocate the *giri*, obligation. We still do it that way—backwards. The seller doesn't do the selling. He waits for the buyer to beg the privilege of buying. American or European firms with something to sell must go at it in the same indirect way. No *giri*, no sale."

"It must be good business," I said, "for the geisha house."

"It is. At the better restaurants a geisha party will cost from $50 to $100 for each guest. If your prospect is not so important you may take him to a bar or *boîte*. There you will have drinks and pretty hostesses but no food. I did this recently. The bill was about $48 for forty-eight minutes. It would have been triple that if we had taken a couple of the hostesses back to our rooms. That can usually be arranged. The law has closed the Yoshiwara [red light district] and the void has been filled by many of the hostesses of Tokyo's hundred thousand bars, restaurants, and night clubs. A top-grade 'semi-pro' will cost some $60 a night."

How can Japanese industrialists stand it?
It is the least of their worries. No nation has had a more sensational rise to prosperity. In one lifetime Japan has risen from feudalism to industrial dominance.

The Japanese ninety-year-old can remember when Japan was a babe in the world's arms, just learning to suck nourishment from other civilizations, imitating crudely the products of industrial revolutions that had already taken place elsewhere.

Her goods were shoddy and flimsy, just as Germany's had been when she began to copy the industrialization of Britain. Japan was a child among giants, and the giants were very patronizing, believing they had nothing to fear from the fumbling fingers of this juvenile.

•

Today Japan is the world's third greatest producer. She may be destined to be first. Her exports are expanding at twice the world rate. Her output grows five times as fast as that of the United States (15 percent a year against 3 percent). At the present rate of increase, her per capita income will soon be the world's highest.

Before the 70's are over she will, at this rate, have a larger gross national product than all European nations combined; and in the 80's will overtake and pass both Russia and the United States.

She already has many firsts to her credit:
She leads the world in shipbuilding.
She stands first in the manufacture of motorcycles, second in number of automobiles.

She is far and away first in fishing.
First in farm yield per acre.
First in electronics.
First in production of radios, second in television sets.
First in sewing machines.
First in cameras, superseding Germany.
First in watches, Switzerland in second place.
First in production of motion pictures.
Her Tokyo–Osaka train is one of the world's fastest (125 miles per hour).
Her chief city, Tokyo, is the world's largest, nearly 12 million. Runners-up are London, 8 million, and New York, about the same.
Her literacy is the world's highest, 99.8 percent.
Per head, she publishes more books than any other country.
Her Expo 70 was the biggest exposition the world has seen.

•

Now, instead of imitating, she is imitated. Her many inventions are eagerly investigated and duplicated in other industrial nations.

Teddy Roosevelt was one of the few who saw it coming. He wrote in his autobiography, "I have the heartiest admiration for the Japanese. They can teach us much. Their civilization is in some respects higher than our own."

What he saw in the future has been substantiated. As for the farther future, Japanese and foreign observers expect Japan to continue riding high and higher on the tide of affluence.

It will not be smooth sailing. The problems of abundance already worry thoughtful Japanese. Says leading economist Kiichi Miyazawa, "For years, our people learned to cope with poverty. We do not yet know how to cope with plenty."

Japan's history is punctuated by explosions. Each explosion, like those in the engine of a motorcar, has propelled her forward. Even disasters have spurred her progress.

Some of the reasons for her meteoric advance are the iron in her blood, colossal self-conceit, humility in learning from others, microscopic devotion to details, and, not least, astounding good luck.

This story of her rise does not pretend to be a history in the ordinary sense. It is no complete chronicle of Japanese events. It will leap over the troughs of the waves and concern itself only with the crests—the surges that have put Japan today in first place in many categories, and made her a breathless runner-up in all others.

2

CONCEIT

The primal push toward greatness came when Japan convinced herself that she was divinely appointed to lead the world.

According to the sacred books, in the beginning there was only vapor. The god Izanagi and goddess Izanami stood in the swirling mists on the high bridge of heaven. Izanagi thrust his spear into the mists. The dampness condensing on the spear made drops which fell to form the first land on the surface of the globe.

Japanese schoolchildren learn in their geographies that this island was Awaji which lies at the entrance of the Inland Sea. It is sometimes called The Island of the Congealed Drop. The new land floated in the water like a jellyfish.

The delighted gods descended and started around their island in opposite directions. When they met, the lady exclaimed, "How lovely to meet a handsome male!"

These gods have been called by Lamott "the deities of sex appeal." The name Izanagi means The-Male-Who-Invites, and Izanami, The-Female-Who-Invites. It was destined that they should invite each other, but it was most unfitting that the woman should take the initiative. So the male insisted that they circle the island again and when they met this time he got in the first word: "How lovely to meet a joyful female!"

That was good so far as it went but there seems to have been some uncertainty as to what to do next.

Fortunately two birds were lovemaking nearby. Japanese art still depicts the two deities thoughtfully studying the birds. The result of this research was a son who, by a slight error, was born from the father rather than the mother.

But they quickly got into the swing of things and were divinely able to beget not only gods, but islands. The first was the island of Hirugo, but since it was a miscarriage they put it in a boat of bulrushes and let it drift away. The others were healthy and thus the eight large islands of Japan came into existence.

For endless ages these islands were the only lands in the world. Gradually the scum and mud in the waters of the sea solidified to form other islands and continents. Thus Japan is the only holy land; the rest of the world is made from the leavings.

We may skip the many obscenities of the legend which parades as true history in Japan's ancient books and note only that after Izanami was burned to death in the act of giving birth to the god of fire, her husband was compelled to do his begetting alone.

From each of his garments as he cast it off a god was born. From the dirt that was washed from him as he bathed in the sea, evil gods were formed.

But his greatest achievement, quite unequaled by his wife who had given birth only to lesser gods, was the begetting of three of the chief deities in Japan's pantheon of eight million gods. Amaterasu, the sun goddess, was born from his left eye. Tsuki-no-kami, the moon goddess, came from his right eye. When he blew his nose, Susanoo, literally "The Impetuous Male," was born.

We might properly call Susanoo the god of rape. He was a violent and lusty despoiler. His cruel practical jokes and his deeds of unbridled passion are still quoted with gusto. Soldiers who ravage and rape conquered peoples find justification in the example of their god Susanoo. The Japanese government honored him by engraving his portrait on paper money.

He is the god of the Japanese sword. Wishing to make indiscriminate love to a group of maidens, he was much annoyed when a dragon ate them. His chivalry was somewhat different from that of the knights of King Arthur. He fought the dragon, not to protect his ladies-fair from insult, but in vengeance because he had not had a chance to insult them himself.

He slew the dragon and from its tail extracted a sword. It became one of the three imperial treasures to be preserved to the present day. It is the father of all Japanese swords.

Of course the sword is deeply revered in Japan. It has always been regarded as a living spirit and has been called "the soul of the samurai." The god of the sword, Susanoo, is therefore deeply respected and his exploits are considered worthy of emulation. This psychological background may explain certain aspects of the behavior of the Japanese fighting man.

Susanoo violated his sister, Amaterasu, and from this violation sprang the line of Japan's emperors. The indignant Amaterasu fled into a cave, closing the entrance with a stone. Since she was the sun goddess, the universe was now in complete darkness. The distressed gods pled with her to come forth but she refused. Then they resorted to stratagem. They had a goddess dance what seems to have been the world's first striptease, flinging aside one garment after another while the gods roared with laughter.

The sun goddess, who had expected all to be plunged in

sorrow upon her departure, pushed away the stone slightly and asked the cause of the merriment.

She was told that a new and more beautiful goddess had taken her place. In proof, the world's first mirror was held before her face. Having never seen herself before, she was insanely jealous of the beauty of the face looking out at her and was readily persuaded to resume her duties on condition that this lovely rival be banished.

There are many variations of these legends. But they all agree in making Amaterasu the ancestress of the Japanese emperors. Her son, born of incest, had a son, Ninigi, whom Amaterasu commanded to descend to the earth and rule it. He did as ordered and his great grandson was Jimmu, Japan's first emperor, who is supposed to have ascended the throne in 660 B.C. His mother was a crocodile eight fathoms long.

Don't laugh. All this has been accepted as history in Japan.

Then the two great "historical" books of Japan proceed to give the story of the emperors. This is necessarily almost pure fabrication since during the ages concerned the Japanese were unable to read or write and therefore had no way of recording the facts of history. Any stories passed down verbally would soon be so changed in the telling as to bear no resemblance to the facts. The *Kojiki* and *Nihongi* were not written until A.D. 712 and A.D. 722, respectively, yet they attempt to give a minute record of events from 660 B.C. onward.

When we reflect upon our difficulty in remembering a date a year or so old, we stand in amazement before these doughty chroniclers who can give not only the year, but the month and the day of an event that supposedly took place thirteen hundred years previously. There are pages of items such as these:

"This was the year Kinoye Tora, eleventh month, ninth day. The emperor arrived at the harbor of Oka. . . .

"Twelfth month, twenty-seventh day. He arrived at the province of Aki.

"Third month, tenth day. Proceeding upwards against the stream. . . ."

And so on, in great detail.

And the modern journalist who knows how difficult it is to set down on paper exactly what was said in an interview only an hour or so past will raise his eyebrows over the *Nihongi's* verbatim reports of conversations a thousand years old.

How seriously these records have been considered may be gathered from the fact that one leading scholar has written a commentary of forty-five volumes on the *Kojiki.*

That he found so long an apologia necessary is significant. Certainly there is plenty in the *Kojiki* that needs explaining. For example, how about the colossal "ground-spiders" and the "eight-headed serpents" which had to be conquered by the troops of the Emperor Jimmu?

Well, says the commentator, they were the aborigines who opposed the children of the gods. Their descendants are the Ainu who live in areas like Indian reservations in Hokkaido.

But if we admit that there were human beings in the land before Jimmu, where did they come from?

That is an easy one for the commentator. The aborigines were also children of the gods Izanagi and Izanami, but, as in every family there are apt to be a few mistakes, these were misshapen and evil offspring cast aside by their divine parents as worthless. Another commentator finds authority in the holy word that the Ainu were born of the excreta of the mother-goddess.

It is harder to explain the phenomenal ages of the early emperors. Their exact birthdays are given and the span of years attained by each.

The ages of the first seventeen add up to 1,853 years, an average of 109 years for each emperor. The age of Jimmu is stated as 127 years; of Koan, 137 years; of Korei, 128 years; of Keiko, 143 years; of Nintoku, 110 years. Nor is the longevity limited to emperors. The Prime Minister Prince Take-no-uchi is said to have lived 380 years.

It is notable that when Japan at last learned to read and write in the seventh century A.D. the ages of emperors from then on averaged only sixty-one years.

Of course, while Japan was illiterate, China and Korea were keeping historical records not only of their own affairs but of those of Japan. These records flatly contradict the *Kojiki* and *Nihongi*. Therefore they are rejected and suppressed by Japanese scholars.

There are many anachronisms in the Japanese holy books. Sansom notes that "the gods are described as possessing swords and mirrors, things unknown to the Japanese before they came under the influence of the metal culture of the Chinese." And he expresses the opinion that "these chronicles, in their early parts at least, are works compiled with a political aim, in which fact and fancy are combined in such a way as to justify retrospectively the supremacy of the leading clans over other families or tribes."

Says the scholarly investigator William Bramsen, concerning the *Kojiki*, "It is hardly too severe to style this one of the greatest literary frauds ever perpetrated."

It is on this basis of fraud and fantasy that Shinto is built. Since its gods are amoral when not immoral, it can have no code of ethics or decency without offending such divine sinners as Susanoo.

"The Shinto gods," wrote Rein, one of the earliest foreign students of Shinto, "are by no means the pure and exalted forms which Buddhism presents to us—no saints through the overcoming of sensuous pleasures—but affected by all human feelings and weaknesses, and taking pleasure in everything that adds enjoyment and amusement to existence. Accordingly their worshipers seek to delight them on their festivals not only with meat and drink, but also by theatrical processions, pantomimes, and so on, and do not think it objectionable that the road from the town of Yamada, in Ise, to the largest Shinto shrine in the country leads through a street in which many houses are dedicated to the worship of Aphrodite. Of the servant of the gods, purity of the body is required rather than purity of the heart. . . ."

Scholars are agreed on this point. Writes Sansom, "The early religion is almost entirely deficient in abstract ideas of morality. Its code is not ethical but customary and ceremonial."

Admitting that Shinto was a religion without morals, Motoori, the eighteenth century's greatest defender of the faith, wrote:

"Morals were invented by the Chinese because they were an immoral people, but in Japan there was no necessity for any system of morals, as every Japanese acted rightly if he only consulted his own heart."

We have here one key to the cockiness of the Japanese. They are not humbled by a sense of sin. Whatever they do is, according to Shinto, entirely right, provided only that they themselves think so.

Moreover it does not much matter whether an action be right. The gods are not finicky.

True, Japanese who become entangled in Christianity or Buddhism must take account of sin. But even they have a way out. Religions in Japan are not watertight compartments. One may be a Buddhist or Christian and still be a Shintoist. And if at any moment the tenets of one of the sterner faiths press down too severely, one may invoke the easier creed of Shinto and do as one pleases.

Instead of being peculiarly Japanese, as claimed, the belief called Shinto may be found among primitive and barbaric tribes anywhere in the world. It is usually called animism. Every rock, bush, tree, hill, cloud, wind, is supposed to be animated by a spirit. In the course of some ethnological studies made during fairly extensive travels I have found the same thing, without any significant difference, among the Bataks of Sumatra, the Bagobos of the Philippines, the Polynesians and Melanesians of the Pacific, the Bedouins of the Sahara, the Indians of both South and North America.

And so universal and uniform is this primitive religion that in an ethnological conference a missionary from Greenland who had listened to a talk on the animism of the East Indies exclaimed, "Now I understand animism in Greenland!"

This religion, if it is a religion, is usually not dignified by a name. It went nameless in Japan until Chinese Buddhist priests entered the country. They denominated the primitive belief *Shinto*, the way of the spirits or gods, to distinguish it from *Butsudo*, the way of Buddha.

Even India and China had passed through the animistic stage but had largely outgrown it.

But in Japan the notion of rocks and trees that can speak if they wish to and of evil spirits "that swarm and buzz like flies" prevails among the common people to this day. Civilization usually snuffs out animism. They can hardly exist together. In Japan they do.

It must be said in fairness to the Japanese that their present animism is more refined, as we would expect it to be, than that found among savage tribes. Animism at its worst amounts to abject fear of the unseen. Its gods are all evil. Japan has its full quota of evil spirits, but there are also many kindly ones.

The Japanese love of nature is such that they can hardly conceive of a lovely hill or waterfall being inhabited by a devil. So we hear of such pleasant deities as Princess Blossoming-like-the-Flowers-of-the-Trees and neutral deities who may at times be benign and then again malevolent, such as the gods of luck, of fire, of water, of needles, of electricity— yes, Japanese of this day have designated a god of electricity, and many a machine from the typewriter to the automobile has its god. So the people bow to progress!

But there is also a large gallery of distinctly vicious gods. Alms boxes in certain shrines bear the inscription, "For Feeding Hungry Demons." Certain animals, particularly the fox, are feared and prayers of propitiation are made to them. There is no love for the gods of volcanoes, earthquakes, typhoons, and plagues.

•

Strangely enough, the most troublesome demons with which the devotee must reckon may be the deceased members of his own family.

This also is of a pattern with primitive belief the world over. It is commonly believed that the dead need to have offerings of food, prayers, and ceremonies to keep them happy in the other world—and if they do not get them, they revenge themselves upon the living. Since no man has either the time or the means to satisfy all the demands of the priests, he is bound to be oppressed by the guilty feeling that he is neglecting the dead. And a neglected spirit is automatically a bad spirit.

Sexual love has always played a large part in Shinto, in which higher love has had no place.

The original pair, The-Male-Who-Invites and The-Female-Who-Invites, united to propagate the Japanese islands and people. The early religion seems to have been mainly a cult of fertility—the fertility of both fields and women. Under ancestor-worship the dead require descendants. A spirit without a descendant to care for it spends an eternity in misery. Therefore, until contact with the West made the custom seem vulgar, the symbol of Shinto was the phallus.

The worship of the phallus was practiced without concealment until 1860 and, with concealment, into the present. In back-country villages I have seen the symbol in undisguised form.

Every traveler in India is familiar with this object of worship. In Mongolia too, it may be found. It may have been brought to Japan by immigrants from northern Asia, or by

Pacific islanders originating in or near India.

Interesting in this connection is the theory of archaeologist Wales that Shinto is a survival of a religion once widespread in the Pacific region and practiced alike by the people of Cambodia and Java and the Mayas of Central America. He is inclined to see more than a chance resemblance between the names of the Mayan god Itasamna and the Japanese Izanami. This adds to the evidence that at least some of the Japanese came from southern Pacific lands influenced by India.

Japan got many customs from China, but this is not one of them. No trace of phallic belief has been discovered in China, and Chinese literature is devoid of sex myths.

If you visit the remoter districts of Japan you will find erect stones of phallic shape set up on the edge of rice fields and bearing such inscriptions as "For Fertility." They are supposed to insure a good crop. Sometimes they are cut in wood. Usually the symbol stands alone but is occasionally combined with a representation of the female sex organ. The whole is called *in-yo-seki*, female-male-stone.

Barren women worship it and set before it offerings of food and drink. Also they may place before it votive offerings in the same shape. This custom led to the manufacture of thousands of small phallic images made of stone, wood, iron, clay, porcelain, or ivory and these were sold in city shops and carried through the countryside by itinerant venders.

The *awabi* shell, because of its fancied resemblance to the female organ, may be offered to a phallic image by an infertile woman. The peach or the bean may be similarly used. The mushroom and the snout of a hog are accepted as phallic emblems.

Phallic festivals used to be held at which promiscuous liberties between the men and women present were allowed and expected. Shinto liturgies were written to fit such occasions.

Certain of these festivals celebrated the begetting of the islands of Japan, each of which was supposed to have been born as small as any babe but grew larger as more space was needed by the increasing numbers of inhabitants. The process is said to be still continuing. If this is true, then Japan's population problem is on the way to solution, after all.

Other festivals were held in the planting season and prayers for rain were offered. The use of the phallus in such festivals was due to the myth that rain is the fertilizing fluid coming from the god of the sky to the recumbent goddess of earth.

The Japanese "god of the crossroads" was a phallus set at any intersection frequented by many people and the scene of indiscriminate intercourse at festival time.

The phallus is also the patron god of harlots and may be found on the *kamidana*, or god-shelf, in houses of prostitution.

Couples who desire many children may journey to do homage at the islet of Onogoro, the entire islet being a gigantic phallus-shaped rock. According to one legend, it is the "heavenly pillar" around which the heavenly pair ran to meet each other and beget the Japanese islands and people.

Shinto, from the beginning, inspired the Japanese to think of themselves as the chosen people. It flagged for some centuries, then was deliberately revived by the Japanese military who saw that it could be used to stimulate the Japanese to conquer Asia and perhaps the world.

It was not a Japanese, but a German, who sparked this revival. Bismarck told his Japanese visitor, Count Ito, how he had prepared Germany for war. He made a semigod of the emperor. He taught the Germans to obey the emperor as they would the Deity. Then Bismarck told the emperor what to demand of the people. The result was the unification of all the previously quarreling German kingdoms into one united nation controlled by the emperor (who, in turn, was controlled by Bismarck).

His advice to Ito was this: "Revive those parts of Shinto that exalt the authority and divinity of the emperor."

Bismarck himself had made it work. He stirred Germany to undertake three unprovoked wars, one with Denmark, one with Austria, one with France. Germany flourished temporarily on its diet of blood and iron. When Ito visited it, the evidence was overwhelming that aggression pays.

•

All this was easier in Japan. Bismarck had to *create* his divine emperor. In Japan the tradition that the Japanese emperor was divine was already two thousand years old and only needed to be reawakened.

Professor Basil Hall Chamberlain, who lived in Japan during those years of change, wrote:

> Shinto, a primitive nature cult, which had fallen into discredit, was taken out of its cupboard and dusted. . . .
>
> The governing class insisted on the Shinto doctrine that the mikado descends in direct succession from the native Goddess of the Sun. . . .
>
> The important right of burial, never before possessed by it [Shinto] was granted to its priests. Later on, the right of marriage was granted likewise—an entirely novel departure in a land where marriage had never been more than a civil contract. Thus the Shinto priesthood was encouraged to penetrate into the intimacy of family life, while in another direction it encroached on the field of ethics by borrowing bits here and there from Confucian and even from Christian sources.
>
> Under a regime of ostensible religious toleration, the attendance of officials at certain Shinto services was required, and the practice was established in all schools of bowing down several times yearly before the emperor's picture. . . .
>
> History is so taught to the young as to focus everything upon imperialism. . . .
>
> Such is the fabric of ideas which the official class is busy building up by every means in its power, including the punishment of those who presume to stickle for historic truth.

A distinction was drawn between sectarian Shinto and State Shinto. The former was the old faith, the latter the new. Belief in the old was voluntary, belief in the new, compulsory. Shrines of the old were called *kyokai*, or "churches," and had the same standing as Buddhist and Christian institutions. Shrines of State Shinto were named *jinja*, meaning "god-house" or "home of the deities," the deities being the emperors past and present. If the state cult could have the emperors, it was content to leave the eight million gods of wind, wave, and what-not to old Shinto.

The framers of State Shinto undertook to pick and choose from the old beliefs only those that would serve their purpose. As Reinsch says, "The attitude of mind of the leaders in this great transformation was purely secular. They judged all religions by their fruits."

They had little use for the god-myths except those relating to Amaterasu, supposed to be the ancestress of the emperors. She had been only one among many, her very name unknown to multitudes. Now she was singled out for special attention and *jinja* built in her honor.

Her naughty brother, Susanoo, might have been allowed to lapse into oblivion had he not plucked the sword from the tail of the dragon. As "god of the sword" he could be used to exalt war. So the most vicious of the gods became (along with Hachiman) a deity of martial "virtues." Ritualistically purified carpenters built shrines for him.

Phallicism—that was a difficult one in view of the possible publicity in civilized lands. The phallic symbols had better be officially suppressed—but the cult might well be encouraged under the surface as a cult of fertility. Sex-mindedness would provoke population increase, which in turn would mean national power and expansion.

The Japanese, with their eyes turned abroad during the "foreign fever," had forgotten that their own land was divine. This was a useful notion and must be resurrected.

So the legend of the divine birth of the Japanese islands which came into the world as eight-pound infants and grew large was soberly propagandized through press, literature, drama, and school. Stress was laid on the point that "foreign countries were not begotten by the sun, which is the cause of their inferiority."

Japan was the very flesh of the gods, other lands were the scum tossed up by the sea. The name *Shinsu*, Divine Land, was popularized. Professors in the universities could explain with a straight face that geology, biology, botany, and all else would be nonexistent were it not for Japan, where all things had their beginning.

"Thus all nations should be grateful to Japan, for in the creation of this country, the rest of the world likewise was formed."

Historians knitted their brows over the fables of the *Kojiki*. Archaeologists and anthropologists found the origin of the human race in Nippon, or resigned. Astronomers developed theories to glorify Japan.

"Some celebrated ones of this class came to me the other day," reported the American missionary Verbeck, "saying that Japan was created in perfect harmony with the heavenly bodies, for as there were sixteen planets, so Japan had originally been created in sixteen distinct parts. When I told them that there never were exactly sixteen planets and gave them a correct list, their faces grew rather longer than before....

"Of course, such things are transacted in a spirit of gentleness and kindness; but in reconsidering that men capable of better things should spend their precious powers and time (to say the least) in trying to harmonize the distinct parts of their country (which never had sixteen such distinct parts) with the sixteen planets of our solar system (which never had just sixteen planets), one cannot help being provoked at the waste and stupidity."

The Japanese love of their natural surroundings was easily elevated into the doctrine of the "union of man and land." The theory made use of the old animistic notion that every tree, rock, and blade of grass was spiritually alive. Humanity and nature were born from the same womb. Making every man feel that he was part and parcel with the soil under his feet encouraged patriotism.

•

Next, the divine-race concept. Ito and his companions under the spell of Bismarck had turned their backs on friendly co-operation among nations as naive and unrealistic. The "master race" idea was developing in Germany; it must be fostered in Japan. The people who would rule the world must hold all other people in contempt.

Could such a fantastic program succeed? During thirty years of occasional visits to Japan and five years' continuous residence, I saw it succeeding far better than its founders would have believed possible.

When Prince Akihito was born, a Japanese newspaper had this to say:

"We, the subjects of His Imperial Majesty, express our heartiest felicitation. We take pride in coherency of national genealogy, that we have all descended from the very ancestor to which our most distinguished line of August Rulers owes its beginning."

It was a hard-boiled newspaperman who wrote that.

The *History for Middle Schools* taught that Japan's inhabitants were the offspring of the gods who came down to live in the land. "Such a national character is without a parallel throughout the world."

"From the fact of the divine descent of the Japanese people," according to "historian" Hirata, "proceeds their immeasurable superiority to the natives of other countries in courage and intelligence."

"Land and man . . . are blood-brethren, born of the same divine parents," declared Professor Chikao Fujisawa.

And Matsuoka, educated in America, could say to his own people, "It is my conviction that the mission of the Yamato race is to prevent the human race from becoming devilish, to rescue it from destruction and lead it to the world of light."

Irishman Taid O'Conroy, who spent fifteen years in Japan, became a Shintoist, took a Japanese wife, taught in Keio University and later in the Imperial Naval Staff College, came away with this conclusion:

"The Japanese are convinced, they are even more than convinced, they *know*, that they are descended from the gods; and, further, they know that they are the only race on earth that can make this claim."

"Because they are taught that they descend from the gods," said Joseph Grew in *Report from Tokyo*, "the Japanese are not allowed to know the scientific and historical truth of their racial origins. They are led to believe—and many do believe it—that they are different from all the rest of the world. Just the other day a broadcast from Japan intended for Japanese ears announced: 'Japan is a nation made by gods. Japan is a mother-nation, and those who are born in Japan are born of God. We are the greatest people in the world.' "

There is no end to such evidence. Many a GI in the Pacific heard it straight from the lips of a captured son of heaven: "We know we will win because we are gods."

Count Ito struck the keynote in his famous *Commentary on the Constitution* in 1889:

> The Sacred Throne was established at the time when the heavens and the earth became separated. The Emperor is Heaven descended, divine and sacred; He is pre-eminent above all his subjects. He must be reverenced and is inviolable. He has indeed

to pay due respect to the law, but the law has no power to hold him accountable to it. Not only shall there be no irreverence for the Emperor's person, but also He shall not be made a topic of derogatory comment nor one of discussion.

Ito himself framed the constitution, using the Prussian model. His Commentary upon it was regarded with as much respect as the constitution itself. Therefore, if any Japanese wished to settle an argument as to whether the mikado was divine and always had been, he had only to refer to the Commentary which dates the sacred rule from the time when the heavens and earth were separated.

Note too that the emperor could not be held accountable to the law. He was above law. In this respect he was an improvement on the Christian God who was a God of law.

Ito struck his most telling blow in laying down the rule that the emperor must not be made a subject of discussion. Here was a topic without pros and cons. It was doubtless realized that the subject would not bear intelligent discussion.

Thousands of State Shinto shrines were built, a priesthood organized and indoctrinated, and a high-powered publicity campaign launched that would have done credit to a more modern age. Particularly the scholars and historians were enlisted to put over the pretended antiquity of the new faith. University classrooms, lecture halls, textbooks on "political science," histories, theological tomes, all took up the cry.

Such phrases as these were dinned into the public ear and mind until they were believed: "the unbroken line of his descent from the Immortals," "the splendid traditions that no other nation in the world has ever enjoyed," "the aura of beauty and reverence which has always surrounded the throne," "gods have been our monarchs and our monarchs gods," "the flawless perfection of our rulers from time immemorial," "every child of the Yamato race should model his conduct according to the example of those paragons of purity and virtue sent to us from heaven."

The defeat of Japan in World War II served only to unite the people more completely and spur them to greater effort. The results of this unquenchable faith in their own destiny we see today in Japan's preeminence or near preeminence over competing nations.

The Japanese are a strangely contradictory people. Along with their towering self-confidence, they have a becoming humility in their willingness and eagerness to learn from others. Actually, their conceit and humility have the same motivation. Humbly they copy from others—but with the inner conviction that they can improve what they copy. What others can do, they feel they can do better. They are proving their case.

Having sketched the course of Japan's conceit, let us drop back to the early days to trace the course of her humility.

3

HUMILITY

Japan, ignorant, benighted, illiterate, studied at the knees of China.

History does not know a more striking contrast than that between the two Japans before and after the coming of Chinese civilization in the seventh century.

The Japanese were a composite people, not meriting the word "race." They were made up of widely diverse elements which had just one feature in common—their primitive, barbarian character.

One of the ingredients was the aboriginal caveman population, the Koro-pok-guru, whose pit-dwellings and shell mounds may still be found. They merged with another ingredient, the Ainu people, who, while Egypt was in her glory, lived in burrows in the ground, used stone implements and practiced cannibalism.

Civilization was far advanced in China, India, Siam, Persia, and parts of Europe when the next ingredients were added, but they were equally savage. One was the Mongol from

Asia, the other, the Malay from the South Pacific.

The latter brought his house with him and since it was better than anything the cave-dwelling and tent-dwelling people of the Japanese islands had previously known it was largely adopted.

Japanese propagandists love to dilate upon the imaginary glories of their ancient civilization. But if the marble homes of the Greeks of this period could be set down beside the typical Japanese residence the latter would suffer severely by comparison.

It was an oblong hut made of poles with the bark still on and tied together with vines—although the world had long known both the rope and the peg. Matted grass made the walls. Where the wind blew holes, boughs were thrust in. The roof was grass thatch. Since it was easily scattered by the wind, heavy logs were laid on it to keep it in place. Large stones were used for the same purpose—and are in some parts of the country still used today.

The windows and doors were holes which could be plugged shut with brush. The floor was dirt. The fire was built in the center of the floor and the smoke was absorbed by the grass walls and roof and the eyes and lungs of the occupants.

Frequently the hut was semisubterranean, being partly sunk into the ground or in a hillside for protection against the elements.

The Japanese wore little but loincloth and sandals, adding occasionally a mantle made of animal skin, straw, grass, or asbestos! Silk and cotton were unknown. The Roman toga would have been viewed with as much wonder as was the European button many centuries later.

The food was roots, seaweed, fish, venison, and bear meat. A few vegetables were grown, but agriculture as it had already existed for a thousand years in the valley of the Nile was undreamed of. Japanese society was still in the most primitive economic stage, that of hunter and hunted.

For more than a millennium the world had possessed the power to read and write. But in Japan anything a man could not remember was lost. What is the more astonishing is that not even the beginnings had been made. Not only had no alphabet been devised, but the primitive picture-writing practiced by many of the world's savage tribes was unknown.

There was no central government. The people were divided into scores of warring tribes. Each tribe had its own tribal god. The chief of the clan claimed a certain measure of divinity and was supposed to be able to interpret the wishes of the god. All natural phenomena were ascribed to spirits. This primitive animism had not yet even acquired a moral code—although the great religious philosophies of the world were already centuries old.

When Buddhists and Confucianists entered the country they were unable to find in the Japanese spoken language any words for such concepts as benevolence, justice, propriety, sagacity, and truth.

Then, like the dazzling white explosion of an atomic bomb, came Chinese civilization.

It was brought in by Buddhist priests. Some of them were direct from China, some from nearby Korea which had long since learned from China.

The priests brought not only a highly sophisticated religion, but secular knowledge of all sorts. Encouraged by the Japanese court, which was avid for the new learning, they taught the art of reading and writing along with the clumsy Chinese ideographs that still make up the bulk of the Japanese language to this day.

They introduced the great classic works of China on astronomy, geography, music, and medicine. They brought in great painters, carvers, and architects.

They taught the half-nomadic Japanese, who had always followed random trails through the jungle, how to make permanent roads.

Natives who had depended for their water upon erratic

rainfall or streams that dried up in months of drought were shown how to dig wells that would supply good water every day in the year.

Practical priests of the soil taught the miracles of agriculture. They imported horses to help in agriculture and transportation. They introduced millstones for grinding grain. They planted at one time 462 mulberry trees and taught the Japanese the intricate processes of the care of the silkworm and the spinning and weaving of silk. In all cases, the Japanese were humbly eager to learn.

Gold was discovered in eastern Japan and the court spent lavishly to bring in still more of the arts and artists of the continent. One incoming ship was loaded to the gunwales with tailors. And the Japanese, always quick to learn, entered the garment trade with gusto to become in time one of the world's most expert peoples in the manufacture of textiles.

Lacquer, another art in which the Japanese excel, came from China. Gunpowder was another of China's contributions, later to be turned against China and the world to the ruin of Japan itself.

Flowers were unappreciated until the Chinese taught their cultivation and arrangement—an art in which the Japanese now surpass their teachers. The fine art of garden landscaping was of Chinese origin.

We are so used to the pot, the bowl, and the kettle, that we fail to do them full honor. But they were a vast improvement upon the primitive basket. True, it had always been possible to suspend a cut of venison over a fire, but waterproof and fireproof receptacles for cooking, serving, and preserving foods opened the way to gustatory delights never known before by the Japanese. They were fortunate to have as their teachers the best cooks in Asia.

The Chinese showed their ignorant but eager pupils how to shut out the weather with oiled paper windows, how to cut, square, and join timber, how to make plaster and brick, how to roof houses with tile instead of soggy and vermin-infested thatch, how to divert smoke through chimneys, how to dispel darkness by means of a long-burning lamp instead of a quickly burned-out torch.

In these and a thousand other ways the daily life of Japan was transformed by the priests, scholars, and artisans of China. But the influence went much higher and pervaded the entire governmental and philosophical structure.

The clans made the chief of the principal clan their emperor, attached to him the Chinese title of *Tenshi*, Son of Heaven, organized an aristocracy of hereditary nobles, and enforced a system of taxation after the Chinese model. Copper coinage of the Chinese style was introduced and people learned to count above a hundred—although many of the nobles still refused to touch money and scorned mathematics as an art of tradesmen. Nevertheless trade and industry profited enormously by the change.

New words bring new ideas, and the imported vocabulary of China opened up new worlds of thought to the Japanese. The teachings of Buddha, Confucius, and Mencius were too deep for the unphilosophical Japanese to penetrate completely, yet they derived much from them. Beliefs and traits which we think of as distinctly Nipponese came from China, among them ancestor worship and filial piety.

The Japanese rulers who were responsible for bringing in Chinese civilization took good care that it should not endanger their own position. While they adopted the pomp and prerogatives of the Chinese imperial system, they barred its democratic features. For seventh-century China, while far from being a democracy in the modern sense, had more of the characteristics of democracy than any other nation at that time. Men attained public office not through rank or birth, but through competitive examinations. The aristocratic and wealthy classes had no more and no less chance than the most humble. Anyone, high or low, with sufficient talent to pass the tests might share in the government. The Japanese took over the examination system but limited it strictly to the nobility.

The Chinese emperor was regarded by his subjects as holding the mandate of heaven only so long as his rule was heavenly, that is, beneficent. When it was not, he might be deposed by his people. No one was held guilty of lese majesty for freely criticizing the emperor. Imperial proclamations were conciliatory and even humble in tone. The people were at least in theory and often in practice the final arbiters of Chinese government. The Right of Revolution, taught by both Confucius and Mencius, was held by the people to be their most sacred right.

In Japan revolution was treason. The emperor was made answerable only to the sun goddess; which meant, in effect, answerable only to the group in control of the throne. Rites and ceremonies were taken over complete, humanity was left behind. The form was copied, the essence lost.

Buddhism suffered in the same way. The profound conceptions born in India and later charged with practical idealism by the Chinese were little understood in Japan. The Japanese acquired through Buddhism the well, the millstone, the brick, the painting, the ideograph, and the thousand benefits of material civilization; also an assortment of ceremonies, the tinkling of bells, the tonguing of prayers, the burning of incense, and the notion that it was sinful to eat meat.

But the great tolerant humanitarianism of Buddhism and its concept of man in relation to the universe were not for the Japanese.

Nothing else could have been expected—for the Japanese were just emerging from simple savagery. They could appreciate anything that could be seen, felt, tasted, or worn like a mantle. But underneath was still the primitive fighter whose hand was against every man.

•

The Japanese had another teacher—Korea.

Because Korea was the closest foreign nation to Japan, her

influence was felt even before that of China. Korea had learned much from China. She passed this learning on to Japan. She had a long head start on Japan. While Japanese history fades into legend when we try to go back more than fifteen hundred years, Korean civilization is at least three thousand years old and some scholars trace it back a thousand years farther.

Korean knowledge flourished for more than two millenniums before Japan learned to read and write.

Early Japan scorned intellectual pursuits. The man of letters was at a discount. The soldier ranked first.

Even after the importation of the art of writing from Korea, the samurai was ashamed to be caught with a writing brush in his hand. It was unmanly.

History records that in the twelfth century when an Imperial Mandate was sent to a certain troop of five thousand soldiers only one man in the five thousand could read it. His ability, far from distinguishing him, disgraced him in the eyes of his fellows. The only arts and sciences honored were those of war.

In Korea war was considered an evil, if sometimes a necessary one. It interfered with the true purpose of man, the advance of civilization. Learning, far from being scorned, was the badge of honor. To win a government post it was necessary to pass a literary examination.

So greatly was education respected that the title of address such as our "Mr." was *So-bang*, meaning "Schoolroom" or "Schoolman." Even Kim who dug ditches and never saw the inside of a school must be addressed as "Schoolman Kim."

One of the great intellectual inventions of the Koreans was movable type. This invention is the very foundation of modern printing. Imagine the labor if every word in this book had to be carved out by hand on blocks of wood, one block for each page. That was the ancient system, in Europe as well as in Asia. Once the page was printed, the block was of no further use since the letters were not movable.

A Korean genius conceived the idea of making a separate block for each letter. Then, after a page had been printed, the letters could be taken up, reassembled to form new sentences, and used to print another page. Without movable types the rapid production of books and periodicals at low prices would have been impossible.

Specimens of early Korean types may be seen in the Natural History Museum in New York. The invention dates back to 1232, and was in general use by 1406. It was not until a half century later that Gutenberg perfected a similar system for use in Europe.

Korea had many other "firsts" to her credit.

A Korean engineer built what is believed to have been the world's first suspension bridge only a hundred years after Columbus discovered America. With the first ironclad ships Korea defeated Japan nearly three centuries before the *Monitor* and *Merrimac.*

In the little village of Kyung-ju you may still see an astronomical observatory built by a Korean queen some fifteen hundred years ago. It is the oldest existing observatory in the Far East. But it was preceded by another from whose tower astronomers studied the stars and kept records of comets, sunspots, meteors, and the movement of the planets during the first century before Christ. They even calculated in advance eclipses of the sun and moon.

Korea helped to lead Japan out of the Dark Ages. Much of the culture which Korea gave Nippon was Chinese; but to go back further still, it was the hand of India that reached through China and Korea and lifted Japan. Indian Buddhism, enriched in China and Korea, carried civilization with it.

Some of the Japanese resented the fact that they must learn from others and instinctively plotted revenge. They ached to show the superior Koreans and Chinese that they, the Japanese, were, after all, better men—just as in a later century they could not rest until they had flung down the gauntlet to their teacher, the West.

The swashbuckling General Hideyoshi in 1592 resolved to punish Asia for her superiority. Hideyoshi set out to conquer Japan's benefactors, Korea, China, and India.

"I shall do it," he bragged, "as easily as a man rolls up a mat and puts it under his arm." He believed that destiny was his, for a soothsayer had told him, "Wherever the sun shines, all places shall be subject to you."

When warned that he should take along a Chinese interpreter he retorted, "We shall teach these Chinese to use *our* literature."

He announced that he would fill the sky of Asia with the hoarfrost from his sword.

He would clean up Korea first. In 1592 he dispatched an army of nearly 300,000 men to Korea, and later another 150,000, "the largest armies," Upton Close reminds us in his *Behind the Face of Japan*, "transported overseas between the fall of Rome and the Boer War."

For six years Japanese armies ravaged Korea. In the end they were beaten. Korea thus stands out as the only nation in the world that has, until 1945, ever whipped Japan. She had the help of friendly Chinese. But the chief genius was her own in devising weapons that broke the morale of the Japanese.

•

One of these weapons was the world's first bomb. One day a great iron ball came hurtling into the courtyard of a castle held by the Japanese. The samurai gathered to look at it. Suddenly it exploded, killing thirty men.

Gunpowder had of course long been known and used. But the exploding shell was new. Its inventor was a Korean by the name of Yi Jang-son and he appropriately named it The Flying Thunderbolt.

It came into general use on the part of the Koreans and their Chinese allies. Japanese soldiers were inclined to regard it as supernatural and it had a great effect in disorganizing and demoralizing Nippon's armies.

When a large Japanese fleet attempted to go to the relief of the Japanese troops it encountered a new horror—nothing less than a gigantic tortoise, as large as a ship, which came swiftly toward them over the water.

It had a dragon's head fitted with horns and from the mouth came blasts of flame. The terrified sailors could not know that the flame came from a bronze rocket gun—prototype of the modern flamethrower.

Long oars projected through ports and propelled the craft swiftly over the surface. Above the oar ports were other ports from which cannon were fired. The top of the ship was curved like a turtle's back and covered with metal plates, as were the sides—for this was history's first ironclad. Japanese balls bounced harmlessly from the copper and iron shell.

This *Kwi-sun* or "Tortoise-boat" had been invented by the Korean Admiral Yi Sun-sin. Numbers of them appeared before the war was over.

Humility finally overtook Hideyoshi on his deathbed in 1598.

"Alas!" he murmured. "Like the falling and vanishing dew am I."

He recalled the warning of the Korean king that an attempt to conquer Asia was like trying to bail out the ocean with a cockle shell. He had stubbornly forced his discouraged troops to fight on in Korea. Now he turned to his aide.

"Let them come home," he said, and died.

The troops gladly came home. They brought with them the ears of forty thousand of their victims. These were placed in a mound near the statue of Buddha at Kyoto. The "Ear Mound" still stands and teachers bring their children to it that they may have clear evidence that Japan was really victorious over Korea. For it was a jealously guarded tradition of Japan that she had never been and would never be defeated. Japan now lost no time in making her own bomb, her own rocket gun, her own "Tortoise-boat."

•

Early in 1542 some Portuguese adventurers were wrecked upon the shores of Japan. The Japanese confined them to a small area in the island of Kyushu, then—still humbly thirsty for knowledge—proceeded to milk them for information about the outside world. Through them they acquired glassware, woolen cloth, velvet, cotton, sugar, medicine, ceramics, gold, silver, and copper.

Firearms and Christianity arrived in the same year. The Jesuit missionary, Francis Xavier, fearlessly ventured to invade the main island. He was tolerated, because he was a fountain of knowledge. He informed the Japanese that the world was round and explained comets, thunderbolts, and rain. Since he was so wise in matters of science, his religion was also respected. Many became Christians. By 1582 there were 150,000 Christians in Japan—a far greater number in proportion to population than there are today.

But the fortunes of Xavier and the Jesuits who followed him waned when they began to take a hand in politics. Japanese authorities grew suspicious. A shipwrecked Spanish captain, hoping to undermine the Portuguese, warned the Japanese authorities:

"The Portuguese begin by sending missionaries into lands they wish to conquer. Later, troops follow, and these countries become vassals of the Portuguese."

Promptly, all missionaries were condemned to death. Twenty-three Franciscan priests and three Jesuits were crucified. Thirty-three thousand Christians were massacred.

Dutch traders had somewhat better luck. They were

confined to the island of Deshima off Nagasaki. So long as they stayed put, they were respected.

The Dutch carefully avoided religious controversy. They did not dispute the legend that the emperor was the direct descendant of Amaterasu, the sun goddess. This meant nothing to them, so long as they could sell their wares and be let alone.

The Japanese learned much from the Dutch—concerning anatomy, medicine, botany, natural history, horsebreeding, astronomy, and that newly discovered wonder, electricity.

But when the Japanese began to duplicate their inventions, the Dutch were no longer teachers, but competitors.

•

The Hollanders came under increasing suspicion as it became known that they had penetrated the East Indies just as they had Japan, and the objective of that penetration was quite evidently the control of that vast archipelago.

The Portuguese had traded in China's Macao, only to take it over as a colony of Portugal.

Britain was worming her way into India through the East India Company.

Russia had thrown a long arm over Europe and Asia to the Bering Strait.

Spain had first explored, then swallowed, the seven thousand islands of the Philippines and had already begun to absorb the two thousand of Micronesia, thus bringing Spanish power close to the back door of Japan.

Japan was completely surrounded, west, north, east, south, by avaricious colonial powers now in control of much of Asia and the Pacific. Would the same thing happen to Japan that had happened to Japan's neighbors?

The shogun (who ruled in the name of the emperor) and the *daimyo* (nobles) resolved that it must not happen. Henceforth no alien ships would be allowed to enter Japanese ports. No Japanese citizens would be allowed to leave Japan. No foreigners could enter. Shipwrecked strangers cast up on Japanese shores would be executed. In 1624 the shogun promulgated his great *Edict of Isolation.*

Japan remained hermetically closed for two centuries.

4

250 GUNS OPENED JAPAN

The long-feared foreign invasion of Japan came on the morning of July 8, 1853.

The commotion in Yedo (Tokyo) was beyond all description. A Japanese citizen tried:

"The whole city is in an uproar. In all directions are seen mothers flying with children in their arms, and men with mothers on their backs. Rumors of immediate disaster, communicated from mouth to mouth, add horror to the horror-stricken. Many commit suicide rather than fall into the hands of the hairy barbarians."

•

The hairy barbarians had been dispatched by William Seward, powerful secretary of state under President Fillmore.

America was feeling her oats. "The Pacific Ocean," declared Seward, "its shores, its islands, and the vast regions beyond will become the chief theater of events in the world's great hereafter. This nation must command the empire of the seas, which alone is real empire."

Equally expansive was the chief of the expedition, Commodore Matthew Perry. He too thought in terms of empire. It would begin as elsewhere, with trade. Where it would end, who could say? Much of Asia had already been subjugated by great powers. America must not be left behind.

•

There was a hush of excitement on the four ships of the American squadron as they drew within sight of the Japanese coast. The decks were cleared for action. Gun ports were opened. Guns were run out and shotted. Ammunition was stacked. Pistols, cutlasses, pikes were put within easy reach of every sailor. Obstructions were removed so that bow and stern cannon could operate. The white man was ready to extend the hand of friendship to the yellow.

The *Susquehanna* led, as a flagship should. It was a weird sight, neither fish nor fowl. It carried the conventional masts and sails, but it was also equipped with an extraordinary contraption of recent invention, the steam engine, operating two great paddle wheels on either side of the ship. The *Mississippi*, nearly alongside, was similarly equipped. Great volumes of black smoke belched from their stacks.

The sailors, accustomed to sailing ships, were still a bit awkward in handling the double duties of a steam frigate. Those who could not make the grade were passed back to the *Saratoga* or the *Plymouth*, sloops-of-war that gave assurance by their unsullied snowy expanses that the world had not gone completely mad. They depended solely upon the wind, as God meant them to do.

This morning, however, since the wind was contrary, the two sloops were being towed by the two steamers, and all sails were furled. Now the bleak cliffs of Izu were rounded, and just ahead lay a fleet of Japanese junks and fishing boats. The junks changed their course to avoid the apparition; the fishing boats ran up their sails and fled. The crew of one, exactly in the path of the *Susquehanna*, too terrified to manage raising the sails, took to their oars.

On land, a large village of thatched houses disgorged its occupants, and the shore was suddenly black with people. The first steamers ever seen in Japanese waters, plowing along at eight knots without the help of a sail, splashing, thundering, pouring black volcanic smoke from their black craters, were creating a profound impression.

The commodore was gratified.

"He looks as if he had just swallowed the canary," said Wells Williams to a midshipman. Williams was the interpreter, the only man in the fleet who could speak Japanese. Williams added, "He thinks he's the whole United States of America."

Commodore Matthew Perry, never insignificant, seemed to loom to gigantic size in the morning haze. Standing at the weather rail of the quarter-deck, he scanned the shore through a Dolland telescope. His raised elbows and large projecting epaulettes made him look like a great bird about to swoop. He was tall and impressively heavy in proportion, every cubic inch a commodore. The white collar that stood up abruptly on either side of his bull neck accented his height and dignity. His face had extraordinary breadth and power. His mouth curved slightly down at the corners, but the lower edge of his large nose slanted upward in a way suggesting self-assurance, if not obstinacy. It was the nose of a man who believes that he and his country are right.

Under his gold-emblazoned cap his hair rolled out around his ears like a lion's mane. But it was a question whether it was the great leonine head that first attracted one's attention, or the paunch. Certainly the latter was well to the fore. It was not of the soft-balloon variety, but like the bole of an oak. There was a slow steady rise beginning at the chin and reaching a crescendo just below the waist, and this rise was accented by the two rows of gold buttons which made a processional highway down his coat, gradually narrowing, as a road narrows in perspective on its way up a mountain. Where the golden highway ended, at the abdominal summit, one had a feeling there must be something of great importance.

The commodore himself seemed to share this feeling, for, when he was not occupied with his telescope or otherwise, he habitually stood with his right palm across his summit, the thumb tucked under his coat, the four fingers lying flat on top. It was a pose as effective as the Napoleonic, and perhaps more appropriate to the commodore's present oriental environment since the Orientals have it that the abdomen is the seat of all wisdom.

•

Perry had been brilliantly right so much of his life that he was now used to it. He had begun his career precociously; at fourteen he was the youngest midshipman ever to be commissioned in the American navy. Brother of Oliver Hazard Perry, he also fought successfully in the War of 1812. Successfully he established the American Negro settlement in Liberia; successfully he commanded in the Mexican War the largest American fleet ever assembled up to that time.

But his most memorable exploit was in the new medium of steam. He superintended the building of the American navy's first steamer and sailed the four-stacked, paddle-wheeled monster across Long Island Sound at the rate of fourteen miles an hour. The unwieldy craft did not attempt the open sea. He then looked after the building of the *Mississippi* and the *Missouri*, the navy's first oceangoing steam warships. Critics prophesied that they would sink in the first storm, but he sailed the *Mississippi* round the globe.

"Perry's luck" became proverbial.

But he felt himself capable of greater things. He had made his mark as a naval officer; he had earned well the sobriquet, "father of the American steam navy." He now had the ambition to crown his life by a far more tremendous success. He would plant American power in the Orient.

The idea was a popular one in the United States. Such imperialistic fervor had never before shaken the American people, and perhaps never would again. Perry's proposal that he should establish coaling stations and naval bases in the Far East and open the way for American trade had been hailed as an inspiration.

The hardest nut to crack was Japan. American trade and American influence were alike impossible so long as Japan maintained her policy of absolute seclusion.

Now Japan was to be opened to the blessings of American civilization and commerce, by persuasion if possible, by force if necessary. On his way, Perry had already hoisted the American flag on Japan's island of Great Luchu as a "material guarantee" for the concession of American demands. He had also made the beginnings of a base on Japan's Peel Island. Upon arrival at Japan proper, he must step more cautiously, for he had only five hundred and sixty men, and Japan had thirty million. But it is a commentary upon his courage and his faith in "Perry's luck" that, even in the face of such odds, he was fully prepared to fight.

•

Uraga appeared, a populous city at the head of a narrow bay swarming with boats and commanded by headlands where could be seen line upon line of forts. It seemed a trap to be avoided at all costs.

The commodore summoned a midshipman.

"Message to Captain Buchanan: Enter Uraga Bay. Anchor broadside to the shore batteries."

As the flagship led the squadron into Uraga Bay, a ball of smoke over a headland showed that a rocket had been fired. It was quite evidently a signal demanding that the fleet should halt. The fleet sailed on. Then the shore batteries opened fire. When no response was forthcoming from the squadron, they fell silent. The commodore, being a diplomat as well as a naval officer, knew the terrifying effect of contempt. The monstrous floating volcanoes continued without concerning themselves with the peppering fire of the Lilliputians.

Swift, beautiful craft, each manned by thirty men and bearing banners indicating that they were police boats, put out. The fleet, moving up the bay without a sail or an oar, outstripped them, left them wallowing in the wake, and they returned to shore.

Far up the bay, in a position to command all forts within range, the ships dropped anchor. The *Plymouth*, maneuvering for position, let off a blast of her whistle. The startled crew of a nearby fishing boat dived overboard to a man.

Now police boats swarmed around the intruders, and officials attempted to board. This is the natural privilege of harbor police in any port in the world, but the commodore had his own reasons for refusing to allow any such familiarity. The officials were pertinacious. They were used to having their own way in official-ridden Japan. But when they attempted to climb up by the chains, they received smart raps over the knuckles from pikes in the brawny hands of oversized sailors. They saw other sailors armed with pistols and cutlasses and apparently very ready to use them. They withdrew angrily.

Wells Williams was talking to the commodore.

"I know something of these people," he was saying in his usual rather rhetorical manner. "We shall not do well to deal with them in so high-handed a manner."

"Thank you," replied the commodore. The hairs in his bushy eyebrows seemed to stand out individually, and his face purpled.

No other man in the expedition would talk so to the commodore. But Williams was not a member of the crew. He had consented only very haughtily to serve as interpreter, reluctant to leave his mission church in Canton. The beak-nosed, mutton-chop-whiskered missionary was oddly out of place on a man-of-war. He scorned the discipline of captains and commodore, for was he not commissioned by a far mightier Master, the Lord of All?

"If you decline to think of their rights as human beings," went on Williams, "consider your own danger. Everything you do is increasing the resentment of this kindly but resolute people, and they may soon turn upon you, hundreds of thousands strong. Even your guns would be of no use then."

"I am not so sure of that," retorted the commodore. His voice was the more calm because he was making an effort to control his choler.

"By entering this fortified harbor you are bearding the lion in his den."

The commodore turned upon him. "Exactly. And where else should you beard a lion? I entered this harbor just because it was the best fortified on the coast. If your lion trainer wants the lion to behave, he walks up to it and uses his whip. If he shows any fear or indecision, he is lost. You say you know the Orientals. But you seem to know nothing of human nature. The Dutch and the Russians have licked the hands of these people, and how far has it got them? No, there are only two ways to open Japan: by show of force, or by force. I shall use the first way if possible, the second if necessary."

He turned on his heel. Williams, his side-whiskers vibrating with righteous indignation, left the quarterdeck.

•

Going amidships he found a boat alongside. In it were several lacquer-hatted, long-gowned officials. One of them bore a great scroll. They made signs for the gangway ladder to be dropped, but the sentinels ignored them. Here was a job for an interpreter, and Williams approached the rail.

"What do you wish?" he called in Japanese.

They looked up at him with startled interest. A barbarian who spoke Japanese! True it was a sort of barbarian Japanese, for Williams had learned it from ignorant Japanese sailors.

"We wish to confer with your lord," replied one.

"That is impossible," answered Williams. "The Lord of the Forbidden Interior is of the highest rank in our country and can confer only with a functionary of equal rank."

This was all poppycock, but he was following the commodore's instructions. "These people are worshipers of rank and form," the commodore had said. "We must be equally precise, or we shall get nowhere with them."

The Japanese bowed gravely. They held a whispered conference. Then their spokesman said:

"The Vice-Governor of Uraga is in this boat. He is of the highest rank, and the proper person to be received."

It was a lie, for the boat contained none but petty police officers.

Japanese–American relations had begun with a lie on each side.

Williams was vaguely suspicious. But he reflected that if the commodore chose to put on an act, the Japanese could hardly be censured for putting on another.

He sent a messenger to inquire the will of the Lord of the Forbidden Interior. The commodore's answer was that the vice-governor might confer with Lieutenant Contee in the captain's cabin.

•

The conference was an odd experience for all concerned. The "vice-governor" and his aide sat with supreme discomfort on the edges of chairs. The supposed aide seemed to be of a distinctly higher cut than the "vice-governor" himself. He showed a scholarly courtesy. He spoke Dutch fluently but only enough English to be able to say, "I speak no English."

Williams was on hand, but his sailor Japanese was not only scanty, but sadly inappropriate to the occasion, and brought the ghost of a smile now and then to the face of the scholar. The expedition's Dutch interpreter, Mr. Portman, proved rather more useful.

Conversation was a cumbersome process. The "vice-governor" spoke in Japanese, his interpreter put the words into Dutch, Mr. Portman translated into English. Lieutenant Contee nodded and dispatched his messenger to the commodore's cabin—for the commodore, although he remained in seclusion, insisted upon personally controlling the interview. The commodore would give his reply to the messenger, who would carry it to Lieutenant Contee, who would pronounce it to Mr. Portman, who would repeat it in Dutch to the scholar, who would put it into Japanese for the policeman-become-plenipotentiary, who would receive it with bows and indrawn hisses. By this time no one was quite clear as to what the original question had been.

Over such hurdles toiled the following questions and answers.

"Why have you come to Japan?"

"To deliver a letter from the President of the United States to the Emperor of Japan."

"Why was it necessary to send four armed ships to carry a letter?"

"To show respect to your emperor."

"Communications can be received only at Nagasaki. You must go there."

"The commodore will remain here until the letter is delivered. He desires only the friendship of Japan but will suffer no indignity. If a proper functionary is not appointed to receive the letter, the commodore will land with a sufficient force and deliver it in person."

At this stunning insolence the Japanese laughed politely as if they wished to relieve the embarrassment the Americans must feel for their own rudeness. And the "vice-governor," in an attempt to divert the conversation into more pleasant channels, asked:

"Are the women of your country white?"

Duly the commodore's answer came back.

"They are. The interview is at an end."

•

That night beacon fires telegraphed the message from hilltop to hilltop: "Arm to expel barbarians."

In every village the fire gongs rang. Men who had nothing but fire uniforms put them on. Samurai donned their armor, sashed on their two swords, took up their great bows, and marched toward Uraga.

Stories ran like wildfire. Perry's four ships became one hundred, his half thousand men, one hundred thousand. His ships were propelled by imprisoned volcanoes as great as Asama. His men were half animal and as full of sinister magic as foxes.

Perry was helped that night by the appearance of a remarkable meteor whose luminous blue sphere and red tail cast an unearthly glow over Japan from midnight until dawn. It was taken as proof of the foreigners' league with the devil.

Women streamed to the temples. Children wept in their dreams as the claws of the hairy barbarians closed around their throats.

The mikado commanded the Shinto priests to pray for a god-wind to sweep away these invaders as it had the Tartar fleet six centuries before.

On shipboard every precaution was taken. Four stands of grape and one of round shot were piled at each gun. Muskets were stacked on the quarterdeck. Sentinels were posted fore and aft and at all gangways and chains.

Williams, shaking his long beak forebodingly over his diary, wrote, "I pray God to order these combustible forces now brought together so that they shall warm each other rather than mutually consume one another."

The tension continued for six days.

When Perry impatiently sailed his ships closer to the shogun's palace at Yedo, the resistance cracked. He was notified that if he would only go back to Uraga, two princes of the imperial blood would receive the President's letter. He condescended to return.

•

On July fourteenth, Perry walked on eggs. Never before and never after was he so near death.

With three hundred men he landed on Kurihama beach among ten thousand armed Japanese, with a hundred thousand more Japanese troops in the near background. A brilliantly colored royal pavilion had been erected on the beach. Here the princes awaited the President's letter. The thirteen guns of the *Susquehanna* boomed as the "Lord of the Forbidden Interior" appeared at the gangway and entered his barge. On the way to shore, the combined bands of the ships struck up a lively air.

"Ought to play the 'Death March,'" Williams mumbled into his beard. He knew what oriental treachery could be.

Stepping ashore, the American sailors formed two lines from the beach to the pavilion. Two thin lines they were, between massed thousands armed with muskets, swords, bows, spears, and lances and trained from childhood to be indifferent to death.

Up this path the commodore led the way to the pavilion. But he was not quite first. Before him went the President's letter, written on vellum, bound in blue velvet, enclosed in a rosewood and gold box, the whole enclosed again in a magnificent envelope of scarlet cloth. This was borne by two midshipmen. They were possibly the two most proud and palpitating young men on earth—or floating just above it—at that particular moment. The commodore had impressed upon them the importance of their mission:

"You will bear the President's letter into Japan. You will carry the key that will open Japan."

Flanking them were two sailors, one carrying the American flag, the other the broad pennant.

Behind them was the commodore, flanked on either side by a gigantic Negro armed to the teeth. The two glistening blacks were the first Negroes ever seen in Japan, and quite enough to strike terror in the hearts of the superstitious.

Then came the commodore's officers and the bands, lustily playing. It was a brave scene. But the mice of fear scurried up more than one American backbone.

•

The Japanese scholar-interpreter, silkenly clad, stood at the entrance of the gorgeously bannered pavilion. He bowed as the procession approached, then led the way into the pavilion. Two richly brocaded figures, as cold as graven images, rose from their chairs and bowed. The scholar announced that they were Toda, Prince of Izu, and Ido, Prince of Iwami.

The commodore bowed—as well as a commodore could bow—from the neck. The two resumed their seats and pursed themselves up into a dignity befitting royal blood. The scholar led the commodore and his officers over the red carpet to chairs at the opposite side of the room.

All this business the scholar handled with admirable respect and tact. He would reserve for a geisha party in the evening his mirth over the joke played upon the fools from another hemisphere. The chairs upon which they sat had been brought from a nearby temple and were used by Buddhist priests in conducting funeral rites. The two "princes" were the governor and his assistant of the small town of Uraga and of no more consequence than the pettiest officers on Perry's ships.

The two boys remained standing in the middle of the room with their precious burden. The scholar went on his knees before "Prince Toda" and pressed his forehead to the carpet. He then inquired whether the letter from the President of the United States might now be received. The "prince," without unpursing his lips or relaxing the rigid muscles of his neck, responded with the slightest of bows. The scholar backed away, never rising from his knees, to the other side of the room. There he addressed the commodore through Portman:

"You may now advance and deliver the letter. You will kneel before the envoys."

"I'll be hanged if I do!" said the commodore.

But Portman translated his response more diplomatically: "The commodore replies that in his country respect is shown by standing, not kneeling. Therefore he will stand to deliver the letter."

And the commodore stood, a solid, dominating figure in the frail room. He took the scarlet case from the hands of the boys, carried it to the edge of the dais upon which sat the two mighty ones, and laid it in a crimson box which had been placed there to receive it. He repeated his commodore's bow, then turned his broad shoulders squarely upon the imperial envoys and strode back to his seat. It squeaked funereally as his unaccustomed weight settled upon it.

•

There was silence. The President's letter had been delivered. It seemed to lie quietly there in the crimson box. But in reality it had already produced the most violent commotion in Japan and was to bring destruction, construction, bloodshed, revolution, glory, and disgust. Yet its words were calm enough:

> I have directed Commodore Perry to assure your imperial majesty that I entertain the kindest feelings toward your majesty's person and government, and that I have no other object in sending him to Japan but to propose to your imperial majesty that the United States and Japan should live in friendship and have commercial intercourse with each other.
> The United States of America reaches from ocean to ocean, and our Territory of Oregon and State of California lie directly opposite to the dominions of your imperial majesty. Our steamships can go from California to Japan in eighteen days. . . . I am desirous that our two countries should trade with each other, for the benefit both of Japan and the United States.

Haven for shipwrecked American whalers was requested, and coaling privileges for American ships.

"State to the imperial envoys," said the commodore, "that I shall return in the spring for the emperor's answer."

"Shall you bring all these ships?" inquired the interpreter.

"These, and more."

This information, which was to produce consternation and panic throughout Japan, brought not the faintest glimmer to the faces of the two graven images.

The commodore gazed at them curiously for a moment. Then he rose impatiently and passed out of the chamber, followed by his retinue. The band struck up, the flags waved, and through the Red Sea of muskets, bows, and spears stretching away on both sides to the hills, the slender column of nihilists, having left behind them the bomb that was to disrupt a nation, passed to their boats.

•

The black ships returned the following February. But now the four had grown to seven. And these were shortly joined by three others. And the commodore talked of sending to America for still more.

The Japanese had been preparing for war. They had fully resolved to resist the intruder this time with force. In the five months of Perry's absence, they had accomplished the amazing feat of building five artificial islands in the bay before the cherished city of Yedo. On them they had constructed forts and mounted cannon. Temple bells had been melted to make the cannon.

Samurai had been drilled in the use of European muskets and artillery. Battleships of a sort had been hastily constructed.

But when the doughty commodore sailed into Yedo Bay, all these warlike preparations melted away like a flock of sheep before a charging buffalo. The shogun and his advisers decided that Japan was not yet ready. It would be better to put the commodore off with a sort of promise, then spend the next few years acquiring western military arts so that the foreigner might be driven away for good and all.

So a gracious and favorable reply was made to the letter of President Fillmore. A treaty of amity was signed on the beach before a dirty little fishing village called Yokohama.

Perry, triumphant, sealed the bargain with gifts—gifts reflecting the glory of American civilization. A barrel of whiskey for the emperor. Also, for the emperor, large stores of champagne, wine, and cherry brandy, eight baskets of Irish potatoes, a telegraph, a miniature locomotive, a daguerreotype outfit, a telescope, two cannon, five Hall's rifles, three Maynard's muskets, twelve cavalry swords, six artillery swords, one carbine, twenty army pistols.

For other officials there were pistols, carbines, cartridges, and a bewildering collection of assorted weapons, agricultural implements, three volumes of Audubon's *Quadrupeds*, three stoves, cases of champagne and maraschino, and ten ship's beakers containing one hundred gallons of whiskey.

The empress was not forgotten. There were perfumes, boxes of tea, and many other dainties for her. The empress was the only one who received no whiskey.

Backward Japan could offer no such charming gifts as guns, powder, and strong liquor. The Japanese gifts to the commodore and his President were specimens of gold lacquer, bronze urns, porcelain vases, silver censers, carvings in wood and ivory, examples of Satsuma ware, damascene, cloisonné, rolls of brocade, large water-color paintings, and one hundred and thirty-two pieces of flowered silk.

At a party on board, a guest, warmed through to his cockles by American champagne, clasped the commodore to his bosom and cried:

"Nippon and America, all the same heart."

Another guest remained carefully sober, saw to it that his swords would slip easily from their scabbards, for he had been appointed by his clan to end the commodore's life. The long sword was for the barbarian, the short one for himself. He saw his opportunity as the commodore was saying farewell to his guests at the gangway. But just as the sword was loosened, it chanced that a common sailor lost his balance and would have fallen overboard if the commodore had not reached and caught him.

That night the *ronin* reported to his fellows:

"A mighty lord who would thus deign to save the life of one of his humblest servants is no enemy of Japan."

Since his companions who had not seen the act were unconvinced, he quietly dispatched himself with the short sword.

Perry's visits have been romanticized until many school children picture him as a Galahad or a Good Samaritan who responded to the appeal of a benighted nation that longed for nothing so much as to throw off its age-old chains and embrace the benefits of American civilization.

Contemporary Japanese accounts give a different picture.

The newcomers were referred to as *shu-i*, hideous aliens, *banzoku*, barbarian bandits, and *kaikwai*, sea monsters. There was no thirst for western customs. On the contrary, there was much proud talk of *kwofu*, imperial customs, *shin-i*, divine dignity, and *shin-shu*, the land of the gods. The official slogan rang through Japan, *Son no jo-i*, Revere the sovereign, expel the alien.

For more than two centuries, that had been the official doctrine. But the Japanese desire to learn had never really died. Now it reappeared in full force. America's gifts were examined almost with reverence. The pistols and other weapons were at once copied, though clumsily, by native craftsmen. The strong liquors were sampled liberally, with dire results. Scholars struggled to translate Audubon's *Quadrupeds*. A shipbuilder undertook to build a steam engine. The boiler burst and destroyed the shipyard. That was a poor start for a nation that was some day to lead the world in shipping.

5

ROMANCE OF THE FIRST CONSUL

While Japan wanted foreign goods and foreign know-how she did not want foreigners.

So when an American frigate brought Townsend Harris in 1856 and dropped him and his assistant Heusken on the Shimoda shore like abandoned kittens, there was no reception committee waiting to greet them. The Perry treaty had stipulated that an American consul might live at Shimoda. Now the Japanese sought to evade the treaty. There was no place for him to live, they said. He must go home.

But since his ship had already sailed away, he and Henry Heusken were stuffed into a romantic old temple with very unromantic lack of plumbing and other facilities.

The Japanese went about forgetting him, as his country had already forgotten him. The commodore of the frigate had promised to return in six months. Harris wrote in his journal on May 5, 1857:

"It is now eight months and three days since the *San Jacinto* left here.... I am a prey to increasing anxiety. I have not heard from Washington since I left the United States, October, 1855."

But it was another four months before a ship called, and then only by accident. There was no mail from the State Department.

Under such discouraging conditions, he faithfully carried on his negotiations with Japanese officials. He was desperately lonely. Officials offered to provide him with "female companionship" but he refused. Japanese and Chinese men were employed about the consulate. Finally two maids were added, Okichi and Ofuku.

Heusken took a fancy to Ofuku. Okichi, a lovely seventeen-year-old geisha, tried to break down the apparent indifference of the consul. She appears to have won his regard when he became ill and she ministered to him day and night.

Harris's journal, faithfully kept day to day, tells his story in detail. Heusken also kept a journal. Okichi put down random notes on her personal experiences. Ofuku perhaps could not write, but she talked, and since there was great public curiosity as to the daily life of the first foreign consul, what she said was written by others. With all these sources available, it is possible to reconstruct the tale of the consul and Okichi. The reader must be warned that the story as told here is not history alone, but history tinged by legend. The Japanese treasure it as one of the loveliest tales of old Japan. The incidents are authentic; the conversation is not. What the lovers said to each other behind closed doors was, of course, not recorded. It had to be imagined, and Japanese chroniclers, knowing the characters of the participants and the situations involved, made a skillful attempt to reproduce what two persons of such character and in such situations would have said. In spite of this fictional element, or perhaps because of it, the story as the Japanese tell it is well worth retelling since it reveals, as no bald historical account could, Townsend Harris, the man, his bitter loneliness when neglected by his own country, his life in the prisonlike temple of Shimoda relieved at last by the presence of Okichi, his final victory over almost insurmountable obstacles in reaching the shogun and opening wide the door that Commodore Perry had set ajar. No event before or since has more greatly contributed to the astounding success of today's Japan.

•

Cholera morbus. The griping abdominal pain, the violent cramps in legs and arms, the retching and vomiting, the extreme prostration. Deathlike chill of the sweat-soaked body. Apprehension that the clammy fingers of the dark graveyard outside were reaching in through holes in the paper windows and closing upon him.

No white physician in all Japan. No other white man there but Henry. Henry was willing enough, but there was nothing he could do. "Better go to bed, Henry." So Henry slept beside Ofuku.

Harris had told Okichi the same thing in the halting Japanese he had learned. "I'll be all right, Okichi. You'd better get some sleep."

But Okichi sat on her heels beside the bed, and watched. Now and then she rose in a single motion, like a bird taking flight, to fetch a cold towel for the forehead, or a hot one for the chill body.

For an hour he would rave in a delirium of agony. Then he would come to himself and gaze in surprise at the small figure crouched beside his bed.

He stretched out his hand to her. "You are very good, Okichi. I could never do without you."

"You never will, Consuru-san." She pronounced the name as tenderly as if it had been something very intimate, not merely "Mr. Consul."

"You will always stay with me?"

"Of course, Consuru-san."

"But it took all the king's horses and all the king's men to make you come here in the first place."

"I had foolish ideas about foreigners."

"And you came only when the officials insisted that you must for your country's sake. Is that why you stay now—for your country's sake?"

"Consuru-san is raving again. He needs another towel."

He heard her in the bath, putting more charcoal in the stove, heating water, singing a little. Comforting sounds.

Yes, this gloomy old barn of a temple had needed the brightness of Okichi and Ofuku. What the authorities in Washington would think of such an arrangement he could only guess. Fortunately they need not know.

They did not deserve to know. They had abandoned him. He had not received one word from the United States in more than a year. He was the most isolated American official in the world. His government had sent him as the first consul general to Japan with the difficult task of concluding a commercial treaty with the Japanese, and then proceeded to withdraw all support, all communication. The frigate which had landed him had promptly sailed away, Commodore Armstrong promising to return in six months. Six months were a lifetime. But it was now twice six months, and no frigate. Every day a servant was posted all day long on the hill behind the temple, with no other duty than to watch for a ship.

There would be a doctor on the frigate.

Two books lay on the bed—Harris's Bible and his journal. He picked up the journal and thumbed its pages. With what high hopes he had approached the shores of Japan a year ago:

"I shall be the first recognized agent from a civilized power to reside in Japan. This forms an epoch in my life and may be the beginning of a new order of things in Japan. I hope I may so conduct myself that I may have honorable mention in the histories which will be written on Japan and its future destiny."

Then the landing at the fishing village of Shimoda, after

many protests by Japanese officials. And on September 6, 1856, a flagstaff was erected before the rickety old temple which must serve as a consulate.

"I hoist the first consular flag ever seen in this empire. Grim reflections—ominous of change—undoubted beginning of the end. Query, if for the real good of Japan?"

Then days, weeks, months of futile argument with stiff-necked local officials. They had no power to negotiate a commercial treaty and would not permit him to reach those who had power. Shimoda became his prison. It was barred on one side by sea—without ships—and on the other by high mountains. It was shut away even from Japan. He must get to Yedo, to the palace of the shogun. Petty officials blocked his way, forbade him to go more than seventeen miles from his temple home, created endless personal annoyances and prohibitions—even refused him milk.

That was a small matter, perhaps, yet the most irritating of all. The privilege of drinking milk—it was so little to ask. Infected Japanese food had destroyed his health. He knew from past experience that his constitution could be trusted to right itself on a diet of cow's milk.

The magistrates objected, "But it is against the law to drink milk."

"Why?"

They were astonished that anyone should question the law.

"How should we know? Perhaps because the very idea of it is obscene. And because milk is for calves. And because extracting milk from the cow by unnatural means will surely kill the cow."

For a year he pled, reasoned, threatened. He wrote unsteadily in his journal:

"My health is miserable, my appetite is gone, and I am so shrunk away that I look as though a vice-consul had been cut out of me."

He had recourse to his Bible and Okichi. In both he found comfort. He knew how scandalized the good folk at home, particularly his sister, Bessie, would be at the blasphemy of classing together the Holy Word and a geisha.

His own conscience was at last satisfied. It had taken some doing. But as a good Bible student and past Sunday school teacher, he had some talent in exegesis, and he found many passages in the Scriptures which could be interpreted as a blessing upon his association with Okichi.

Not that Townsend Harris was a hypocrite. He was intensely sincere. But sincere convictions are often the fruit of sincere desires. We come to believe in what we want. He wanted Okichi. He had seen her in the streets of Shimoda, returning from the public bath. He had stood outside the village inn and listened to her singing to the accompaniment of her samisen at a party of roisterers in an upper room. It outraged him that many men should enjoy her company. It was not good for her. She would be better off in the consulate. Her lovely voice, her fresh beauty, and her gentle spirit would be protected from the contamination that sooner or later destroyed the average geisha. If she were already a sinner, all the more need for rescue. One greater than he had been a friend of publicans and sinners—"I came not to call the righteous, but sinners."

Harris thought of himself not merely as a herald of civilization to Japan, but a herald of Christianity. He spoke once to the magistrates in this vein, but was firmly rebuffed:

"Do not press us on that point. On the article of the Christian religion, our hearts are not of stone, they are of iron. Let time have its course."

Christianity was still proscribed by law. The statute, quaint but grim, spoke from weathered old signboards throughout the empire:

"So long as the sun warms the earth, let no Christian be so bold as to come to Japan, and let all know that if King Philip himself, or even the very God of the Christians, contravene this prohibition, he shall pay for it with his head."

To teach the faith or to listen to the teaching was to risk

death. This risk would only spur on the true believer, particularly if he were obstinate as well. And Harris was obstinate. He envisaged long evenings behind closed shutters, reading the Bible to Okichi, explaining its precepts. She had a ready mind, and it pleased him to think that her eyes were like those of Joan of Arc. She might become the evangel of new life in Japan.

The magistrates were quite willing to send Okichi. In fact they had long since offered to provide the consul with a concubine. They considered that it might improve his disposition. His pent-up passions would have some other outlet than in vituperations thrown at their heads, along with an occasional firepot, when he became infuriated by their constant evasion and deceit.

Their price of two hundred and twenty *ryo* for her annual services was accepted. The deal was closed.

But not quite. For when Okichi was consulted, she flatly refused. She was betrothed to a young carpenter and would not trade him for a hairy ape from beyond the seas.

The magistrates invited Harris to choose someone else. He angrily refused, considering this but one more trick in their campaign of obstruction. The matter began to take on the proportions of an international incident.

They went again to Okichi. Threats of imprisonment and execution failed to move her. But an appeal to her patriotism was effective. She must make this detestable sacrifice for the sake of protecting her country against the wrath and guns of the outside world.

6

OKICHI

Okichi had come; beautifully gowned in silk kimono and black brocade obi, hair high, face alight with a smile in which she allowed not one trace of martyrdom or disgust.

With her was sent Ofuku, to be the sacrificial heifer on the altar of Henry Heusken. She was a willing heifer. Henry had made himself popular in Shimoda. He had distributed his favors widely. Considerable competition had been awakened, and Ofuku came to the consulate in the role of a prize winner. She had not been there five minutes before Henry drew her gently into his room and slid shut the doors.

Harris, seated at his desk before the disused altar of Buddha, with Okichi sitting uncomfortably at the other side of the desk like an applicant for an office job, looked disapprovingly at the closed doors. Suppressed sounds came from behind them. He could excuse all this only on the basis that it was better for Henry to do his lovemaking at home than to be forever tom-catting around the countryside. There was not only the danger to health and morals but the imminent peril to life at the hands of jealous samurai.

Okichi waited. On the opposite side of the large altar space from Henry's room was Harris's. The doors were open. The outside doors were also ajar, and a few feet beyond rose a moist bank crowned by graves. The melancholy, unearthly-sweet notes of the *uguisu*, Japanese nightingale, came from the hill behind.

Through the open front of the temple, one could look past the ancient cedar and gate, down stone steps to the shore of the dreamy bay, dotted with fantastic islets. The bay was surrounded by an unbelievable old-print panorama of pointed mountains, on one of which perched a castle.

It was a perfect setting for an idyl. But Harris continued to smoke his long chinaware pipe.

Conversation was impossible. Neither had as yet learned the other's language. Harris fingered a paper upon which he had written various injunctions, but he was not able to deliver them without Henry to interpret. And he could not disturb Henry just now.

Okichi was smiling at him. He felt himself blushing and hoped that his beard masked his discomposure.

He clapped his hands so violently that the girl jumped. The Chinese butler appeared.

"Show Okichi-san to her room. Do whatever you can to make her comfortable."

Ah Lo beckoned to Okichi. She looked from one man to the other, then, a little disconcerted, gathered up her samisen and the *furoshiki* full of personal belongings, and followed Ah Lo to the servants' quarters.

•

She was not summoned until late evening. She hastily renewed the scarlet thistle-dye on her lips, the safflower rouge on her cheeks, made herself ready for the night's loathsome ordeal.

She found Mr. Harris, Mr. Heusken, and Ofuku seated solemnly around the desk. A book lay open before Mr. Harris. He signaled her to a chair, and she sat down.

"First I shall explain," said the consul, Henry rapidly interpreting, "your duties. You will understand, please, that you have been engaged as servants. The other servants are ten: the Chinese butler, Chinese cook, and his assistant, Chinese washman, and the rest Japanese—two house boys, water carrier, sweeper, gardener, and groom. While you are not expected to duplicate the duties of any of these servants, you will supplement them. More particularly, you will keep these rooms in comfortable order."

He paused and cleared his throat.

"I must ask that you observe discretion in speaking to any outsiders concerning private matters of this consulate. Any infraction of this rule will lead to your immediate dismissal. I . . . " he struggled to say something more agreeable, "I trust your stay with us will be pleasant."

A stilted speech, but the consul in the presence of these two painted, perfumed, and altogether lovely butterflies made so obviously to be sweethearts, not chambermaids, was suffering acute embarrassment. As he himself might have observed, it was not easy to keep all the values in proper perspective.

He turned to his book.

"Every evening we shall endeavor to read a little of the world's greatest story."

He read from the second chapter of Matthew of the birth in the manger. The girls listened in wonder. It was a pretty tale, rather like some of the legends in their own folklore.

Mr. Harris closed the book. He looked uncertainly at Okichi, sitting demurely erect on the edge of her chair.

Henry took Ofuku by the hand and led her out to the great terrace in front of the temple. The moon was shining upon the bay and its cocky little islets. The night was quiet and sweet.

Townsend Harris, diplomatist, master of difficult situations, did not know what to do. Take Okichi to the terrace? Ask her to play her samisen and sing?

Instinctively he drew some papers from his desk and pretended to study them. He grew very warm, then a little irritated.

He glanced up abruptly, as if surprised to find her still there.

"You may go," he said curtly.

She understood the gesture of his head rather than the words and slipped out, her small white *tabi* rustling over the matted floor.

When she was gone, the consul pushed the papers aside and rested his head on his hands. He was bitterly lonely.

Okichi, in her room, drew the padded *futon* from the cupboard and spread them on the floor. She undressed and went to bed, adjusting her neck to the guillotine of the curved wooden pillow so that her coiffure projected into space, touching nothing that would disarrange it.

She was vastly relieved, yet disturbed. What had she done wrong? Had the foreigner found her unattractive? Or had he sensed her disgust, in spite of her efforts to cover it up? If so, he was very kind.

Or was he embarrassed? He did act a little like a small boy. Though Okichi was only seventeen, she had already learned something of male psychology.

The great hairy consul was a small boy. It made him seem less repulsive.

She smiled gently, and slept.

•

That had been the beginning of the geisha's love for Townsend Harris. It was a timid love, at first, that fled from its own shadow. Months went by before it could face itself without revulsion. She loved a barbarian. Impossible, but there it was.

He was unfailingly kind, gentle, aloof. He taught her English. He listened, his eyes glowing through the smoke from his chinaware pipe, as she played and sang. He became so bold that he could sit and look at her for long periods, gathering her to him through the senses of sight, smell, hearing—but never touch.

What Henry did was Henry's business—but Townsend Harris never lost for a moment the dignity of his own convictions, the strictures of his upbringing. He never once left his moral orbit.

"Immoral, I call it," Henry once ventured to say to him. "Stifling your natural instincts. Didn't God give them to you?"

"Specious reasoning, Henry. There is something higher than instinct. Law."

To make this a world of law, between individuals, between nations, that was his instinct. The lover of law does not mind being tightly embraced by it. He may take an almost sadistic pleasure in subjecting himself to discipline. Like Amiel he may say, "I am capable of all the passions, for I bear them all within me. Like a tamer of wild beasts, I keep them caged and lassoed, but I sometimes hear them growling."

Harris liked to hear them growl. He was pleased when they showed themselves to be strong beasts, because that was proof that the cage and lasso of his will must be very strong indeed. Like a cat teasing a mouse, he would let his passion run a bit only to have the satisfaction of snatching it back before it had gone too far.

He enjoyed temptation because he knew how to deal with it. Victory over it gratified him. He felt the strength of ten men every time he discovered anew how pure his heart was. And this was often, for Okichi deliberately tempted him. She still put down his diffidence to embarrassment, though she was less sure of that now. Never understanding his reserve, she used all the means at a woman's command to break it down. She tried the magic of colors, scents, sounds, nearness, smiles, even tears.

One night when he had been especially kind and she believed him to be unusually susceptible, she tried to fell him with one *coup de grâce.*

She contrived to be in the bath when he entered. It was not her hour for bathing, and he could not expect to find her there. She lay at full length in the barbarian tub of white enamel which the consul had requisitioned from the American frigate, for he had refused to learn the delights of the Japanese bath. Her head rested on the slanted end, and she pretended to have dropped asleep. The water softly laved her body, and her breasts stood up from it like islands. Harris stood for a long moment. Then he called,

"Okichi. Okichi."

She sighed and opened her eyes. "Oh," she said. "I am sorry. You wish to take your bath."

She stepped at once from the tub, crystal drops falling from her in the candlelight. Without stopping to dry herself, she pulled the plug, drained and rinsed the tub, filled it from the hot reservoir in the corner of the room.

She moved casually, and he tried to wait casually. He understood perfectly that it is a tenet of Japanese bathing never to be self-conscious. Since a nude body may be seen but not stared at, he tried to see without staring; and the exquisite thing he saw increased his respect for God's handiwork.

She dried herself briefly, bowed, and left the room. His heart was beating fast. The mouse was running too far.

When he returned to his room he found her in his bed, smiling calmly up at him. At first he was not astonished. It seemed right and natural for her to be there. In a flood there came to him all the gentle things she had done for him. She alone had made life in this gloomy prison possible. He cared more for her than for anyone else in the world. She was all he had.

"You have me," his sister Bessie said at his elbow. He came sharply to himself. Yes, he had Bessie to think about—tall, column-straight, very right, she had always been his mentor. He must consider his position and his duty and his principles. This was not his amiable and loyal true love in his bed, but Satan in ambush.

"Get up, Okichi," he said softly, not to rouse anyone. "Get up and go at once."

She stopped smiling, and a dark flush slowly spread over her face. Even a geisha has her pride. For love she had done a bold, forward thing, and it had failed.

She closed her eyes tightly.

"Okichi, you must go."

She looked up at him. "Consuru-san, please tell me. Why do you have me in this house?"

"Because I . . . I need you."

"You need me but will not take me."

"You don't understand, Okichi."

"I understand the men of my country. Are the men of yours so different?"

"Some are. A woman means more in my country—and less. Less physically—more in every other way."

"Every other way?" She groped.

"Mentally, spiritually. A man needs a woman's companionship, her presence near him, her beauty and wit, her sympathy, her help, her love."

It was strange doctrine. She knitted her brows.

"And you are satisfied with that?"

Since Harris did not know the honest answer to that question, he said brusquely, "You will leave this room at once, Okichi. Tomorrow morning you will go back to your own home."

Her eyes widened.

"No, no. I shall never leave your house, Consuru-san."

"Tomorrow morning," he insisted. "Your service with the consulate is ended."

"But I shall come back?"

"No, Okichi. I'm afraid not. I shall not see you in the morning. So I'll say good-bye now."

She slipped out of bed. At the door she stopped to bow as formally as if she had been fully dressed.

"Goo-da-bai, Consuru-san."

7

THE PROUDEST MOMENT

During the next five days, the barnlike temple had dropped into a sullen mood. It was as dark and hollow as a mausoleum. Even Ofuku was depressed. Harris stormed, "Where is Commodore Armstrong?" But it wasn't Commodore Armstrong he wanted.

He justified himself for what he had done. Okichi had brought the serpent into the Garden. She had debased a happy and beautiful relationship. No respectable person—and he thought automatically of his sister Bessie—could approve of having such a person in the house.

Such a person. He tried to keep thinking of her sternly, but his features would soften as his mind strayed to the sound her feet made on the *tatami*, the glow she brought into any room she entered, the quick, eager way—so unlike the driven, dutiful manner of a servant—she had of running any errand of kindness for anybody, especially for him.

Yes, there was good in her. If it had been developed . . .

He had thought sometimes that she was responding to Bible teaching.

As his loneliness deepened, he began to wonder if it would not have been the part of courage to go on teaching her rather than throw her back into the pit of paganism. Surely now more than ever she needed guidance. Was it not selfish of him, at first sight of the devil in their two hearts, to fly for shelter and leave her to be destroyed? Should he not have kept her beside him and fought with her?

Who was he to condemn her? The grim Old Testament texts with which he had justified himself, "So let the wicked perish," "I will not sit with the wicked," "The wicked shall be turned into hell," now gave place to "He that is without sin among you, let him first cast a stone at her," and "They that are whole have no need of a physician, but they that are sick." And many more.

Texts always flocked to him when needed, and he had often said that every step of his life was guided by the Word. Now, so guided, he sent for Okichi.

Mixed with his satisfaction in doing the right thing was apprehension that she might refuse to come. Or come in petulance and reproach. Or come mistaking his concern over her soul for lust for her body. Or come with love extinguished by his harshness.

But his fears vanished when she came running up the temple steps and back through the gloom to him, samisen in one hand, full *furoshiki* in the other, tall coiffure silhouetted against bay and islands and white clouds, crying, "Oh, *danna-sama*, you sent for me. Thank you. Thank you. *Arigato de gozaimasu.*"

She sank to the floor on the opposite side of the desk from him and touched her forehead to the *tatami*.

Harris choked. He had meant to point out that she was being brought back in the interest of her own moral and spiritual welfare; but all he could get out of a crowded throat was, "I need you, Okichi."

She looked up gratefully. Still kneeling and holding her arms downward beside her, palms forward, in a gesture of complete abnegation, she said, "I will be whatever you need, my Consuru-san."

The consul's erratic nerves had been upset by Okichi's absence. Now they were agitated by her return. They had already been overwrought by worry and ill health and the infuriating deviousness of small officials through whom he sought to win an audience with the shogun and conclude a commercial treaty.

To Harris it seemed that all his nerves were hooked to his stomach. Bad nerves meant indigestion; and indigestion, spurred on by bacterial vegetables, turned into dysentery and that into cholera morbus.

He came to rely completely upon Okichi. She was sun, moon, and stars to the man who lay flat on his back, deserted by his country, shunned by his neighbors, scorned by officials, befriended only by failure.

In delirium he would argue with the beams above him: "I tell you I must deal only with the shogun. I am not here as a private citizen. I represent the President of the United States . . . I must go to Yedo . . . liars . . . don't go, Okichi, don't go . . . you are a good woman. Commodore, for God's sake . . . a glass of milk."

•

Okichi brought hot and cold towels. It was nearly dawn. A few cicadas were tuning their instruments for the day-long program of "Mim, mim, mim—"

"Did I hear you talking about milk again?"

He opened his eyes. "Milk? I don't know."

"*Danna-sama*, do you really want milk?" As one would say, do you really want arsenic?

"It would make me well."

"Then I'll get it for you. Yes, yes, I will, I'll get some for you this morning."

"Don't think of it. You would only get yourself into prison."

"No, no. I can do it. I will bring you milk."

She slipped out, all excitement over this daring adventure. Galahad could not have gone in quest of the Holy Grail with any more zeal. In an hour she was back with a sake bottle full of milk.

"You see? I have it . . . the horrid stuff." She held it well away from her wrinkled-up nose.

"How did you do it?"

"He was a friend of mine—the farmer. I gave him money once so he didn't have to send his girl to the Yoshiwara. He couldn't refuse. I told him I wanted it to make medicine."

He watched hungrily as she poured some of the milk into a glass, making a wry face as she caught its odor.

From that time on, the consul did not lack for milk.

•

Perhaps the proudest moment of Okichi's life was when her Consuru-san, restored to health and finally triumphant over petty officialdom, was setting out for Yedo to visit the shogun.

One would scarcely have recognized the recently neglected and disheartened hermit in this exalted plenipotentiary seated in a double-size palanquin upheld by twelve bearers, preceded by a captain of the guard on horseback, four boys calling "Down! Down!" to the multitudes along the line of march, a phalanx of soldiers guarding the American flag, and a great lacquered tablet bearing the distinguished American's name and title in immense Chinese characters, and followed by a humble attendant bearing the consul's shoes and a dozen others carrying other articles of personal use, then more guards with eagles embroidered on their breasts and backs, then Mr. Heusken's palanquin and retinue, then the Vice-Governor of Shimoda with his train, the Mayor of Kakizaki with his, bearers of gifts to the shogun, cooks, grooms, cane-bearers, fan-bearers, standard-bearers, and coolies—three hundred and fifty proud persons in all. Everything had been arranged by the Japanese authorities. Once the brash foreigner's demand for audience with the shogun had been granted, an astounded officialdom bent itself double to do him honor. Permission to approach the Unapproachable immediately elevated him to a dizzy eminence so that earthlings must crack their necks to look up at him.

Okichi, breathless with pride, stood in the crush of townsfolk as the procession moved off. Consul Harris did not glance in her direction, nor had she expected that he would—he who was to stand before the shogun.

Ofuku plucked her sleeve.

"Doesn't Heuske-san look magnificent?"

"Yes," Okichi said, without sparing Heusken a glance.

The procession gone, the crowd milled about, chattering, dissolving.

Two samurai stopped before Okichi and Ofuku.

"They are the foreigners' women."

"Let us salute them then."

The two spat lustily into the girls' faces and went off, laughing.

If it had been the first time, the second time, the tenth time that the foreigners' women had been insulted, they might have screamed or wept.

They drew soft paper from their sleeves and wiped their faces.

"Come to my house," Okichi said. "I think we need a little sake."

•

The triumphal procession took seven days to reach Yedo. No prince's train could have moved in greater state. Advance heralds warned the people to put on their holiday clothes. Sweepers preceded the procession by several miles and broomed the road clean. Four hundred yards in advance marched four youthful harbingers bearing bamboo wands and musically intoning the commands, "Clear the way! Kneel down!"

When the Great Presence itself arrived, the people were well down on their haunches, absolutely silent and with eyes averted.

"The people were ordered to cast down their eyes as I passed," rather gleefully wrote Mr. Harris in a private letter to a friend in America, "as I was too high even to be looked at, but this order was only partially obeyed, for the dear daughters of Eve would have a peep, regardless of consequences. The authorities of the towns and villages met me at their boundaries and saluted me by kneeling and 'knocking head,' then they led the way through their little jurisdictions and took leave by similar prostrations."

When he tired of the palanquin, he rode horseback. Once, when he tried to mount, his temperamental steed both kicked and bit him, giving him so sore a finger that it was necessary to call a native doctor to apply leeches.

Of the incident, Mr. Harris wrote that evening in his journal:

"The doctor approached with great trepidation, while large drops of perspiration stood on his forehead. I asked what ailed him; he said he had never approached any person of such exalted rank before, and he was terrified at the idea of drawing blood from me. He was told to forget all about rank, and to apply his remedy as quickly as possible."

If the shopkeepers of the China coast to whom T. Harris, drummer, had once sold calicoes and linens could see him now. . . . If Bessie could see him . . .

•

Sunday came while they were yet on the road. He would not travel on Sunday. He lodged at an inn and read aloud the entire service for the day with Mr. Heusken as his congregation, and journaled his emotions over the fact that for the first time in history a Christian service had been read in this place, although the law punishing such an act with death was still in force.

On November 30, 1857, the first American and the first foreign flag passed through the streets of Yedo before an absolutely soundless, kneeling multitude, which Harris estimated to number full three hundred thousand people. He was housed in a palace large enough to accommodate five hundred persons and welcomed by the Prince of Shinano and the Prince of Tamba. The latter prince reinforced his welcome with a box of bon-bons weighing one hundred pounds.

Scores of servants, male and female, attended to his wants. There was little opportunity to think of Okichi. Life was new and exciting. The old chapter was closed, chapter of illness, humiliation, imprisonment in a fishing village. Yedo, the capital, was to be his home. He would conclude his treaty here, open the American Legation here.

Of course he could not have brought Okichi and Ofuku. His life and Heusken's would no longer be private. Their conduct from now on would be public knowledge in America and might easily be misinterpreted. Henry had objected that he cared more for Ofuku than for America's good opinion. But Harris, with his higher sense of responsibility, was firm. The girls showed no evidence of being disturbed by the decision except that they smiled more than usual.

"Some day we shall come to Yedo and see you," Okichi teased.

The consul was plainly flustered. "That might be difficult to arrange . . ."

"Have no fear, Consuru-san. We shall look at you from a proper distance."

Princes swarmed to pay their respects to the first American ever to set foot in Yedo. Some of them volunteered to teach him court etiquette. When he should have audience with the shogun he must kneel and knock his head upon the floor—audibly, so that bystanders could hear his skull crack. They demonstrated how it was done, and the thud of their foreheads filled the great room.

But Mr. Harris politely declined to practice.

He smilingly pointed out that as representative of the President of the United States, he would be in effect, during this audience, the President himself; and one king would not knock head to another.

•

The great day arrived. America was borne in his palanquin across the three moats of the shogun's castle and deposited at the last gate before head-knocking chamberlains.

He was ushered into a great hall where three hundred nobles in court dress knelt, motionless as rows of Buddhas.

Accompanied by the Prince of Shinano, he walked past them and into the audience chamber. There the prince immediately threw himself upon his face. A chamberlain cried, "Bassadoru Merican." Mr. Harris stopped and looked down the room.

It was flanked by two rows of councilors, prostrate on their faces. At the far end was a high dais surmounted by a chair on which sat a figure in yellow silk and black lacquered cap.

He was the shogun, mighty tycoon, actual ruler of Japan, before whose power even the emperor in faraway Kyoto had reason to tremble. For the mikado was but a wraith. For two and a half centuries the real authority had been wielded by the mikado's generalissimo. He had command of the army, therefore he had command of the mikado. It was a situation not quite unknown in some other lands.

But even a generalissimo may become flabby if there are no wars to fight. The shogunate had become effeminate. The present incumbent was a nervous boy, guided by some of the very princes who lay on their faces before him.

Townsend Harris bowed. He advanced down the room, the Prince of Shinano crawling on hands and knees beside him. Mr. Harris stopped ten feet from the dais and bowed again. He addressed the shogun in a firm voice:

"May it please your majesty: In presenting my letters of credence from the President of the United States, I am directed to express to your majesty the sincere wishes of the President for your health and happiness and for the prosperity of your dominions. I consider it a great honor that I have been selected to fill the high and important place of plenipotentiary of the United States at the court of your majesty, and, as my earnest wishes are to unite the two countries in the ties of enduring friendship, my constant exertions shall be directed to the attainment of that happy end."

He bowed again. There was a short silence. The shogun began to fidget, jerking his head backwards over his left shoulder, stamping his right foot. Finally the prepared speech came out.

"Pleased with the letter sent with the ambassador from a far distant country, and likewise pleased with his discourse. Intercourse shall be continued forever."

Mr. Heusken advanced a little gingerly with a silk-covered box containing the letters of credence from the President. The Minister of Foreign Affairs rose long enough to receive it and place it upon a lacquered stand, then again pressed his face to the floor. Harris and his secretary, bowing, backed out of the room.

Tea was served in an antechamber. The shogun's five mightiest councilors were presented to the foreigner and congratulated him upon his "greatness of heart." Harris did not understand them. His friend, the Prince of Shinano, explained:

"They were astounded to see you stand erect, look the awful tycoon in the face, speak plainly to him, and all this with no quivering of the muscles. Your nation and your ruler must be great indeed."

And as if considering that one so great in heart must be great in stomach also, they conducted him to a banquet of sixty tray-tables, prepared for him alone, but quite sufficient to feed one hundred hungry men.

Mr. Harris expressed his appreciation—but his nervous stomach flinched. He requested that the repast be sent to his palace for distribution to his retinue.

And so he departed, the two chamberlains at the great gate knocking their heads loudly on the pavement in honor of him who had "looked upon the king and yet lived."

•

The wheels of diplomacy turned more easily after this liberal greasing with prestige. Harris, with no warships to back him up, with no force except that of an oversize will in a pitifully weak body, had compelled the respect of the shogun, his councilors, and his ministers. The greatest officials were now proud to sit with him, listen to his advice, draft a compact to his liking. And so emerged the commercial treaty of 1858, which provided for American trade and residence beginning July, 1859.

In that month American traders swarmed in, along with British, French, and Dutch diplomats, whose governments had hastily followed the treaty road paved by Harris.

8

BLOOD AND TEARS

The authorities accepted the inevitable. But the people had not lost their prejudice against foreigners. They regarded them with utter distaste, and not without some reason. The commercial adventurers from abroad were not a savory lot. The British minister, Sir Rutherford Alcock, appropriately referred to them as "the scum of the earth." Gambling hells, rum mills and lewd houses flourished in the port of Yokohama. The worst Japanese flocked to the town in order to satisfy the worst appetites of the newcomers. The pioneers found it costly to bring wives from home, while "heathen women" were cheap. Sir Rutherford wrote:

> Nowhere is there a greater influx, unless it be at some gold diggings, of the lawless and dissolute from all countries—and nowhere is the danger and the mischief they are calculated to inflict on whole communities and on national interests greater than in these regions. In Japan more especially, an offense or act of violence that could have no other consequence in their own

country, probably, than some temporary injury or inconvenience to one or more individuals, may here, among a sensitive and vindictive race, involve in massacre and ruin all the foreign residents.

The snatches of dialogue one heard in a Yokohama bar were indications of the character of the invaders:

"Hey, gimme some more o' that hangman's blood . . ."

"Ulloa, old cockywax, bet we'll gouge out more gold here than we ever got out o' the diggins in Austrylia . . ."

"God's nightgown, man, I got my dander up, and I says to that lousy Jap . . ."

"Let's go to the red lights—sure, there's a place . . . Two first things the Japs put up here was the Customs House and the Yoshiwara—can't say they don't know what a civilized man needs . . ."

"Come on, sing the 'Bailiff's Daughter,' but don't expect no help from me—I couldn't carry a tune if I had it in a sack . . ."

"He tried to stop me but I pulled out my little forty-four . . ."

"We'll show these bloody niggers what's what."

Japanese servants in the homes of foreigners were beaten and booted. Some of them were killed, and their murderers defied Japanese justice. Several cargoes of them were shanghaied and shipped to Hawaii and California where they were actually sold, the males as servants, the females as prostitutes. Sailors looted Japanese homes and shops.

An American sailor, riding furiously through the streets, ran over a native woman, killing her instantly. He went free. Seamen from the whaler *Europa* stormed through the Yoshiwara, shooting and killing. Foreigners desecrated Japanese holy places, gambling in the temples, defiling them, carrying away whatever they fancied, acting like madmen. The despoilers insisted upon setting up their own courts where their own people could be tried.

Rapists who had assaulted and then killed Japanese girls were brought to court. It took about three minutes for the foreign jury to bring in a verdict of "not guilty." Children screamed with terror when they saw a foreign face.

•

Naturally there were reactions. Alcock's linguist was murdered. The French Legation was burned. Sir Harry Parkes was confronted by a two-sword samurai and only survived by courageous resistance.

Two men in the uniform of the Russian fleet were found in pools of blood. The skull of one was cleft almost clear through, evidently by a single blow delivered from behind. Like a hinged oyster, it was held together only by the nose and mouth. But the assassin had not been content to stop at this. One arm was severed, the thighs had been hacked into ribbons of flesh, and the entrails protruded.

The other man, too, had been killed five times over. From head to foot he had been slashed, and his lungs lay in the mud.

This was not the work of a mere murderer. It was the work of a zealot, a maniac, a soul driven by desperation. It was a labor of love and fury and patriotism.

The two murdered men, with another who had escaped wounded into a shop, had come on shore to buy supplies. They were from one of the ten Russian warships which had arrived some days before to demand of Japan that Russia be given a part of the island of Saghalien. Count Mouravieff, the Russian envoy, had swaggered through the streets with a guard of three hundred armed men.

This was someone's answer to foreign arrogance.

Eight French sailors were massacred. The French Legation demanded that life must be paid for life. Eight of the killers were brought to justice and condemned to death.

Before being executed, each one wrote a death poem:

"Though I regret not my body which becomes as dew scattered by the wind, my country's fate weighs down my heart with anxiety."

"As I also am of the seed of the country of the gods, I create for myself today a glorious subject for reflection in the next world. The sacrifice of my life for the sake of my country gives me a pure heart in my hour of death."

"Unworthy as I am I have not wandered from the straight path of the duty which a Japanese owes to his prince."

"Though reproaches may be cast upon me, those who can fathom the depths of a warrior's heart will appreciate my motives."

"In this age, when the minds of men are darkened, I would show the way to purity of heart."

"In throwing away this life, so insignificant a possession, I would desire to leave behind me an unsullied name."

"The cherry flowers too have their seasons of blossoming and fading. What is there for the Japanese soul to regret in death?"

"Here I leave my soul and exhibit to the world the intrepidity of a Japanese heart."

Ronin attacked the British Legation. Twenty-three persons were killed or wounded. Minister Alcock wrote to England demanding more warships.

Major Baldwin and Lieutenant Bird of Her Majesty's Twentieth Regiment, newly arrived in Japan, were making an excursion to see the *Daibutsu*, a huge bronze statue of Buddha. The trail was narrow, and Major Baldwin rode ahead. He rounded a blind curve near the Hachiman shrine, crossed a flat stone spanning a rivulet, and passed a gnarled and knotted tree trunk. There was a rustling behind him, a splitting pain swept upward from the right hip, severed his spine, and came out at the left shoulder, and he fell dead without a cry.

Seiji, the *ronin* who had killed him, could feel proud of that stroke for the rest of his life—the whole thirty-seven days of it.

His companion, Mamiya, was not so adept with the sword. He was larger than Seiji, but he was only nineteen years old, and this was his introduction to murder. He was taken by surprise when another horseman rounded the corner, and a revolver bullet grazing his ear did not restore his composure. In a fury of fear he attacked Lieutenant Bird, knocked him from his saddle, hacked and hewed bunglingly until there was no more movement.

He bent over the body. What was that regular rapping sound? The fellow's heart? No, a watch had slipped from the victim's pocket. It was a large, fine watch in a gold hunting case. It ticked calmly on as if to say, "Time cannot be destroyed. Time will undo you in the end." Mamiya put out his hand for the watch. He would take it as a prize.

"No," said Seiji, beside him. "We are patriots—not thieves."

•

Two persons witnessed the murder. One was a boy some twelve years old. The other was the widow who kept the sweetmeat stall at the gate of Hachiman. Seiji did not mind having an audience. The boy gaped at him in jaw-hung wonder. Seiji gave him a fierce smile. The lad would treasure that, coming from a hero.

Mamiya was sweating to be off. "Wait, we must celebrate," Seiji said and chose two delectable *an* cakes from the sweetmeat stall. When he offered to pay, the widow said, "No, you have served your country."

People were beginning to gather around the two bodies. "Who killed the foreigners?" one asked. "We did," said Seiji diffidently and strolled off with the quaking Mamiya.

A police officer who knew that times had changed, and

Japan no longer dared to protect the killers of foreigners, quietly followed.

The execution of Mamiya was a pitiable affair. He was not of samurai mettle. He saw no glory in dying. His warders, seeing his terror, mercifully and contemptuously drugged him. They supported him as he stumbled toward the pit. When he saw the executioner waiting, sword in hand, an imbecile expression passed over his face, and he began to whimper. He made a feeble attempt to break away. He was blindfolded and thrown upon the ground. His whines were cut short by a single downward sweep of the sword.

Far different was the death of Seiji.

True, he had not expected to die. His former assaults upon foreigners were known to the police, and he had never been called to account. In few cases had the murderer of a foreigner been brought to justice. The exterminators of foreign vermin had been sheltered from the white man's vengeance and secretly showered with honors.

Still vaguely expecting the credit due him, he stood before the Japanese judge.

"You are apprehended for the murder of an Englishman, Major Baldwin. Are you guilty?"

"I killed the Englishman, but there is no guilt in that."

"Then you confess?"

Seiji was haughty. "Your language is strange. I confess to nothing. I *claim* that I killed the foreigner."

The judge was a grizzled veteran with gray topknot and winged blouse. He showed no offense at the insolent manner of the prisoner. He sucked in his breath wearily.

"My son, you have not yet awakened. You are living in an old world. That world is dying and, I fear, you must die with it. It is a great pity. Warships gather like hawks. The foreign governments have delivered an ultimatum. To save your country, Shimidzu Seiji, you must give your life."

"It is very little to give," Seiji said. "I ask only to die by my own hand."

"Even that honor must be denied you. The foreigners demand that there be no dignity about your death. You must be exhibited on horseback in the streets, you must be executed as a common felon, and your head must be displayed for three days on the bridge to Yokohama."

A fierce eagerness burned in Seiji's eyes. "Let it be as they ask—and they shall be disappointed. They shall see that not ten thousand indignities can prevent a samurai from dying with dignity."

Seiji made good his boast. He rode, bound and guarded, through the streets of Yokohama, singing in a strident recitative:

"My name is Shimidzu Seiji. I am a *ronin* born in Aomori, and I die because I have cut down foreigners.

"This evening my head shall fall, and tomorrow morning it will be exhibited on the Yoshida bridge. The foreigners then will look upon a face that knew no fear of them even unto death.

"It is a bitter day for Japan when a samurai must die because he cut down a foreigner!

"Men of Yokohama, you who hear me, tell the patriots of Japan that the *ronin*, Shimidzu Seiji, did not tremble in the face of death."

He sat on a high saddle. Every person in the dense crowds could see him plainly. He was neatly dressed and shaved, and his topknot, by which one could always judge a gentleman, was arranged with care. His face was like a face carved from a glacier, thin and pale and cold. It was inexpressibly fierce and proud. Seen against the snowfields of distant Fujiyama now reddening under the low sun it seemed more chill than those icy heights. He looked calmly here and there over the crowd as if it were a show ordered for his benefit. Although his legs and arms were tightly bound, anyone could see that he was a free spirit who could never be bound. The two-sworded samurai who led his horse, the armed soldiers before and after him, the heralds with placards announcing his crime and sentence, all turned into a guard of honor under his haughty gaze.

The procession passed out of the city and through the country to the execution grounds of Tobe prison. Now it was dark. The December wind blew cold. Soldiers of the watch loosed Seiji's bonds and helped him down. He rubbed his arms and legs and moved to an open fire to warm himself.

There was a cry of approaching runners, clearing the way for a great man. A lanterned cavalcade entered the field and stopped at the far end. Voices cried, "The Governor."

A soldier spoke to Seiji. "Prepare yourself."

The flame blazed anew in Seiji. "I am ready," he said loudly so all could hear.

Two guards seized his arms and marched him toward the executioner's pit. He began to sing defiantly. One would swear that his spirits rose as he approached the pit.

A messenger of the governor came running and spoke to the officer in command. The officer halted the guards who held Seiji.

"Take him to the prison."

Seiji stood as if turned to stone. What was this? Commutation? Reprieve?

"The execution is postponed until tomorrow," the officer said. "The British minister wishes the Twentieth Regiment to witness it."

"Tomorrow," Seiji muttered, and drooped like a windless flag. He was led, stumbling a little, across the execution grounds to Tobe prison.

•

Most of the inhabitants of Yokohama repaired to the execution grounds the next morning. People flocked from the surrounding countryside and even from Yedo. Officials from the shogun's court stood on a reviewing platform. A grandstand was crowded to capacity with some thousands of lesser officials and Europeans. At about eight the Twentieth Regiment marched into the grounds and took up position facing the pit.

Shimidzu Seiji appeared from the prison, walking freely, followed by guards. The ordeal had finally worn through his theatricalism and reached the essential courage of the man. That he had plenty of courage was evident. His step, his face, signified a spirit that could not be daunted by a thing so trifling as death. The one heart of ten thousand people, friends and enemies, swelled with pride that a man could carry himself so.

An officer approached with a blindfold. Seiji earnestly entreated that he be allowed to go to his death with his eyes open. The request was referred to the governor, who granted it and glanced smiling at the commanding officers of the regiment, delighted that foreigners should witness the deportment of a samurai.

Seiji, not waiting to be led, walked lightly to the edge of the pit into which his head was to fall, pushed a mat into position with his foot, and kneeled upon it. With a quick movement he shook his kimono down to bare his neck and shoulders. The two attendants whose duty it was to support the doomed man saw that they were not needed and stood aside.

The executioner tied back his sleeves. He raised his arms over his head several times to be sure that his clothing did not bind his shoulders. He took up his sword and squinted down the edge.

Seiji looked up. His face was greenish and his lips a single line, but he was smiling.

"Do it neatly," he suggested.

"I always do."

"I hope you have had some practice lately."

"I finished Gempachi," referring to a recent criminal.

"*Sa!* I don't think the sword that cut off Gempachi's head

will do for me. I have a very thick neck."

They both laughed. The executioner was a pleasant fellow, with an open countenance.

"The sword ought to suit you," he said. "It is a Shimidzu blade." The Shimidzu family were sword makers.

"Ah, I'm glad of that. But whet it well with hot water just the same. I don't want a Shimidzu blade to be disgraced."

"Very well, I shall do that—just before making the stroke. Are you ready now?" He later remarked to friends over the sake cups that it was the first time he had ever consulted the convenience of his victim.

"Not quite. I will give you the word." Seiji relished the situation. The criminal acting as his own master of ceremonies, giving orders to the executioner, dying by one of his own blades—it was almost as good as *harakiri*. "I shall sing a death song. Meanwhile you will whet the blade. Then I shall say 'now' and extend my neck. See that you do not embarrass me before all these people by keeping me waiting."

The crowd was mute and tense. No bull ring just before the final thrust of the matador, no arena as lion approached Christian, could have been more silent.

Seiji took a deep breath. He threw everything there was of him into the last cry of the old Japan against the new.

"Men of Nippon. I, Shimidzu Seiji, die without fear and without regret. I die that Japan may live. Japan will live and spread throughout the earth if you destroy the barbarians. Destroy the barbarians! *Destroy the barbarians!*"

A certain member of the diplomatic corps whispered hotly to another, "What is the governor thinking of—to let a condemned criminal rail at us to our very faces?"

Seiji extended his neck as an eagle about to take flight. Still enjoying his control of the situation, he delayed a moment. The executioner waited with sword upraised, held firmly in his two hands.

"Now!" Seiji called in a ringing voice. The blade swept

down. The head dropped into the pit. The body resolutely held its position for a moment, then slowly collapsed.

A sigh swept through the crowd, as ten thousand pairs of lungs began to breathe again.

"Magnificent!" said the governor.

Couriers took up the head, bathed it, ran off with it. The spectators returning to town found the head already staked on the Yoshida bridge, where it remained for three days.

•

Debonair Henry Heusken rode homeward toward the American Legation through the dark streets, preceded by a mounted police officer and followed by two guards. He was not watching the dark corners. His mind was doubtless in some warm teahouse or perhaps the Legation, where several attractive ladies from Yokohama were houseguests.

Heusken did his work well, but casually. Today he had acted as interpreter for Prussian Count Eulenberg in the conclusion of a treaty between Prussia and Japan, new fuel for *ronin* resentment. He had been borrowed from the American Legation because he was the best interpreter in Yedo.

He liked his work not because he cared a hoot about international politics but because he had a genuine feeling for the Japanese and wanted to master their language so completely that he could enter into their hearts. If the hearts were feminine, so much the better.

He was singularly devoid of race prejudice. His research had led to the discovery that although the skins of American and Japanese girls might differ slightly, their hearts were alike.

And there were no unattached American girls in Yedo...

Not that there weren't some who were willing to forget that they were attached.

The darkness under a shop entrance broke into seven parts, springing out into the street. One disposed of the Japanese police officer by smacking the flank of his horse with the flat of a sword. The official dropped his paper lantern emblazoned with the shogun's arms and allowed his mount to transport him from the scene at a dead run.

The two Japanese guards in the rear did not wait even for the flat of a sword but promptly vanished down a side street.

The seven shadows converged upon Heusken.

He was armed only with a riding whip. He dug his spurs into his horse and dashed through his assailants, laying about him with the whip. They struck at him as he passed.

He felt a little pain—not much. Lucky escape!

He clattered on down the street, and they made no attempt to follow but stood and shouted after him as if thinking they had done their work: "You'll make no more treaties." "No more geisha for you, barbarian."

"Just a scratch," Heusken told himself. But he felt a little dizzy. Why did a galloping Japanese horse always have to go up and down like a hammer on an auction block? He pulled the animal down to a walk. He could still hear the thud of hoofs ahead, and he called to the chief of his bodyguard, "It's all right now—come back." But his diaphragm acted strangely—it did not support the call, and he could only wheeze.

He would get down a moment and rest. Trying to dismount, he fell heavily to the ground. The horse ran homeward, stirrups jangling.

Half an hour later, heads were poked cautiously around corners. Making sure that the seven shadows were gone, the bodyguard came out, picked up all of the body that had not irrevocably spilled away, and bore it to the Legation.

The American Legation was housed in the Temple of Peace and Happiness. Under the benediction of an ancient gingko tree, said to have been planted by Shinran himself, founder of the Shin sect of Buddhists, were the sanctuary and buildings accommodating the staff. In the largest room outside of the temple proper, Townsend Harris was entertaining his guests.

They had just risen from a late and lengthy dinner. The male and female groups were about to seclude themselves from each other for a period when the door burst open and the guard, in the midst of a swarm of excited servants, brought in the body of Henry Heusken and laid it upon a couch.

Some of the ladies screamed and hid their faces. Mr. Harris held a bloody wrist between his fingers.

He turned to the guards. "How did this happen?"

The guards were voluble. They had been attacked by no less than thirty men. Perhaps fifty. In spite of such overwhelming odds they had stood fast, given blow for blow, killed a score, and put the rest to flight. Then they had borne their dead master home.

"Ah," said Mr. Harris softly, "but he is not dead. Perhaps he can tell us the story himself. You, Taki, ride to the British Legation. Bring Dr. Myburgh."

He dismissed with a gesture the guards and servants.

Heusken's eyelids fluttered. With reviving consciousness, pain returned to twist his forehead and tighten his lips. He looked up into the faces of Harris and the others. The fog cleared, and he gradually took in the situation.

"They shouldn't have—brought me in here," he gasped. "Shame to spoil your party."

"Lie still," said Harris.

"I'm all right now." He tried to rise.

"Lie still," sharply. "The doctor's on the way. What happened, Henry?"

The young man's eyes were fogging again. "*Ronin.* Six or seven. The guards ran for their lives. So did I, but I wasn't" —the eyes were closed now and the voice faint—"quick enough."

Dr. Myburgh made a practice of entering a sickroom with

a breezy reassurance that started the patient immediately on the road to recovery. His manner was lost upon the unconscious Henry, but it made the guests feel better. "Well, well," he said, as he advanced upon the couch, "by my word, split open. We'll sew him up, and he'll be as good as new."

He dropped on one knee beside the couch and took Henry's wrist. His expression changed. The professional starch drained away. Before one's very eyes he became small and concave.

He turned up Henry's eyelids and looked inside.

•

The entire diplomatic corps assembled at the American Legation four days later to accompany the funeral cortege to the cemetery.

As they were about to start on the dolorous way, a note was brought to Townsend Harris. He read it soberly. Tall Minister Alcock, who had an unflinching appearance because his face appeared to be clamped firmly between his sideburns, regarded him coldly and waited. Minister Alcock could always scent disagreeable news from afar.

"Gentlemen," said Mr. Harris, "this note is from the shogun's government. It warns us that if we persevere in our intention of following the body to the grave, we are likely to lose our own lives. *Ronin* plan to attack the procession."

The high representatives of England, France, Holland, and Prussia stared at Mr. Harris.

Alcock exploded. "*Ronin* indeed! We have as much to fear from the shogun's own officials as from *ronin*. This is just a part of their campaign of intimidation."

"They seek to terrorize us," said bristling Count Eulenberg.

Harris was scratching the pink skin under his beard. "What is your opinion, Mr. Harris?" inquired the French envoy.

"My opinion doesn't matter at the moment. It is time to go to the cemetery."

"But perhaps it would be the part of wisdom . . ."

"We must go."

The cortege passed through narrow streets, then along a river bank, a mile altogether, to the Buddhist cemetery. It might have been supposed, the government having been apprised of a plot to massacre the representatives of the world's five great powers, that the route would have been flanked on both sides with the shogun's soldiers.

Along the entire route, not a soldier or guard was to be seen.

Alcock's ire rose at every step. "The government is evidently quite willing to see us murdered—or else their warning is a bluff. On either count they stand condemned."

The cemetery was a place of evergreens, birds, and bright sun. Henry's grave stood open to receive him. Beside it was another grave, a year old. Its stone bore the inscription, "Dankirche, linguist to the British Legation, murdered by Japanese assassins on January 21, 1860."

A Roman Catholic priest in white robes stood by the new grave. Europeans and Americans crowded around him. In the background were shaven-pated Buddhist priests of the cemetery. On a terrace above stood a few Japanese dignitaries from the Foreign Affairs Department, coldly aloof and evidently vexed that the demonstration they had tried to prevent had materialized.

9

DEATH OF OKICHI

Incongruous in the funereal scene were two brightly dressed geisha. Hovering on the edge of the crowd, they tried to peer past the tall foreigners, but did not venture to intrude.

Though they looked like two of a kind, their faces were sharply different. The face of one was drawn and tense—not from weeping, but from refusing to weep. The face of the other was bland and irresponsible. She was Okichi. Now she seemed unimpressed, as if she had drunk indifference.

"Come, Ofuku. We've been here long enough. I'm thirsty."

Ofuku craned to see. The cords of her throat were tight. "Wait. You can look at Harris-san. That ought to please you."

"That hairy old monkey!" Okichi spat inelegantly. "I tell you I want a drink."

The band from the Prussian frigate struck up a sad air. The bier, covered by the American flag, sank into the grave. The flags of five nations were lowered. Heads uncovered, the ministers each cast in a handful of earth.

The foreigners left the grave. But, before they quit the cemetery, they turned by common impulse to look back.

Two giddy-hued geisha were beside the grave, one of them kneeling.

Alcock exclaimed: "Scarcely appropriate, that. Better have them sent away."

Harris's eyes misted. His mind went back, and a strange object rose before his vision. A jug of milk. Milk that had saved his life. A jug of milk in the hands of the geisha who now stood beside the grave.

He knew the bitterness in her heart. He knew the pain in the heart of the other. He did not think the grave of Henry Heusken was being dishonored.

"No," he said. "Let them be."

•

Harris was more lonely than ever, now that Henry was gone. Okichi was in the city—perhaps she would come to see him. She did not. Sternly rebuffed, ordered never to follow him, she had obeyed.

He sent a Japanese messenger to search her out. Kan knew his way about. Okichi had been a geisha. So he visited the *machiai*, geisha-meeting houses.

He tried the House of the Moon Maid. The mistress came briskly forward. She had freshly blacked teeth, as one in her position should have, and her hair was piled high.

"You want a geisha?"

"Do you have one called Okichi?"

"Yes. But you wouldn't want her. She is old."

"Will you call her, please."

Madame ushered him into a small private room and closed the door. He sat down on a cushion beside the shin-high table. The place was not very clean. This was a very poor *machiai*.

The paper door ornamented with maple leaves, once brilliant but now faded and smudged, opened. A woman came in and closed the door behind her. She said "Good evening" as if she were making a concession, and did not trouble to smile at her guest as she sat down at the opposite side of the table.

Kan realized that she had been very pretty once. Now her face was rutted, perhaps by sake, perhaps by tears, like a field eroded by storms until it is an uneven, barren waste.

"I didn't bring my samisen," she said. "You want to drink?"

"Yes."

"I have ordered sake. If you drink with me it must be sake, nothing else."

A maid came in and set two china bottles of hot sake and two small handleless cups on the table. The geisha ignored her cup, took up her bottle, and drained it.

"More," she said. The maid, bewildered, hurried out.

"What is your name?" Kan asked.

"Kichi," she said, leaving off the honorific. "Black Ship Kichi." She stared at him, waiting. "Well, don't you understand? I am the foreigner's Kichi. I am not fit for any Japanese gentleman to associate with. If you want to dismiss me and get another geisha . . ."

"You were Townsend Harris's sweetheart."

"Sweetheart, hell!" she exclaimed. "Harrisu-san was too good for the likes of me . . . Well, are you forgetting to drink?"

Kan was forgetting.

"Why did you tell me you were Okichi?"

"Because I am. And it doesn't make a cricket's chirp of difference to me what you or anyone thinks."

But the bitter words revealed how much difference it had made, the years of disgrace and scorn because she had been a barbarian's woman, years that had led her down from silk kimono and palanquin to a dirty third-rate house where a drunken slut could still find a little foothold between life and death. "They soon find it out anyhow," she said. "So I tell 'em. Then they want somebody else. Don't you want somebody else?"

"You're good enough to drink with," Kan said, and drank.

The maid brought more bottles. She also placed a small pasteboard box at Okichi's elbow. "It just came," she said.

Okichi brushed it to the floor. The lid came off, and a yellow powder spilled out.

"I don't want it," she said. She drank again. The liquor lent a fictitious health to her cheeks and loosened her tongue. "I'm sick. The doctor told me I'm drinking myself to death. Two months to live, if I take this powder. But if I don't want to live that long? Two months, and then die? Why wait? I don't like to be kept waiting. Death shan't keep me waiting."

"Now you're joking," said Kan.

She leered tipsily. "Of course I'm joking. I'll be joking when I drop into the mountain pool of the river of Shimoda. They were joking when they made me go to Harrisu-san. I was joking when I fell in love with the hairy monster. Everybody has been joking ever since when they spat on me and broke my samisen and kicked me when I lay drunk. This bottle is hotter." She pushed it to him and he drank.

"Harrisu-san wants to see you."

"Oh, is that why you came? Tell him to go to hell."

She went out, angrily sliding the door shut behind her.

•

Late the next afternoon the little coasting steamer brought Okichi into the harbor of Shimoda with its islands like arched cats, its castle on a peak—and its memories.

She went to the temple that had been the consulate of Townsend Harris. It was open, and she walked through it, feeling strangely like a ghost. There his desk had stood, here his bed.

In a cupboard the priests had assembled a few memorials of the first American to live in Japan. Among them was a sake bottle. When Okichi saw it, a hand gripped her heart. She scarcely heard the explanations of the young priest:

"It was before my time. There was a geisha named Okichi, who many times unlawfully brought him milk in this bottle."

When he had gone, she took the bottle and slipped it into the bosom of her kimono.

The little river which empties into the harbor of Shimoda is broad enough at the mouth for many boats. It narrows as you trace it up through the village and then through country groves. Finally, when you think it cannot become much narrower, it grows wider and opens out into a broad deep pool with a charming path close to it through the trees.

Harris and Heusken had often walked here. Okichi and Ofuku had sometimes been allowed, not to walk with them, but to follow two or three hundred feet behind. Harris had loved this spot, haunted by the Japanese nightingale, the still surface of the water reflecting the Shimoda Fuji whose cone was almost as perfect as that of Mount Fuji the great. Okichi, who had seen him very unhappy, had said,

"You seem happiest there. I shall always remember you as you are there."

By the pool stood rough stone god-images with offerings of one sort or another laid before them. Okichi drew from her dress the symbol of her devotion and placed it before the mossy gods. She kneeled and prayed, then clapped her hands and rose.

A boy going along the path saw a kimono sleeve floating on the surface of the pool and ran home to tell of it. The body was dragged from the water. Old-timers identified it as that of "Tojin Okichi," Barbarian's Okichi. Since she had no relatives, the head man of the village had the remains carried on a house door to the base of Shimoda Fuji and there burned.

The urn of her ashes was taken to the nearest Buddhist temple, but the priest, learning her identity, indignantly refused to perform the ritual. Under a slab of stone where the ashes of the nameless were buried, her urn was abandoned, and there it moldered for many years.

But in time her name became a legend, and poems, novels, and plays began to cluster around her memory. Today, if you go to Shimoda and visit the temple of Harris you will find it converted into a museum. Within, you will see Harris's eight-inch-long chinaware pipe, his horn-handled knife, daguerreotypes, oil paintings of Harris and his predecessor Perry, Okichi's black brocade *obi*, a French tapestry pocketbook said to have been given to Okichi, Ofuku's comb, steel mirror, tortoise shell hairpins, kimono, and bamboo trousseau chest which she used when she married after leaving Heusken. In a lichen-gray cemetery behind the temple, Ofuku is buried.

Then you will go to the once-quiet pool in which Okichi drowned herself. It is quiet no longer. Crowds visit it daily. In the graveyard are two tombs to the memory of Okichi. One, the original, is rough and simple and accompanied by a letter box into which you may drop your calling card as a sign of respect. This is in a dark corner. But the unrequited love of Okichi has become a famous legend in Japan. Hence the town authorities, alive to publicity values, have erected a fine new tomb directly before the temple, and the approaches to it are lined with booths exploiting Okichi in every aspect of her life and death.

You may buy Okichi postcards, Okichi wood carvings, Okichi on metal and Okichi in ivory, and the Song of Okichi inscribed on the inside of an oyster shell. The oyster shell symbolizes to the Japanese one-sided love.

You may drop into the Okichi Café, opposite which there is an Okichi Shooting Gallery; and in the geisha district certain houses of merriment as well as some of their inmates bear the name Okichi.

But all this came later. At the time of her death the incident was worth only a brief item in the Yokohama paper.

10

WAR

The Japanese hate campaign culminated in the murder of the important English merchant, Richardson. He neglected to get out of the way of a princely procession. The Prince of Satsuma, a notoriously antiforeign daimyo, angrily ordered, "Cut him down." And Richardson was not only cut down but cut to shreds.

His three companions, one of them a woman, were wounded but escaped to tell the tale. Richardson, it seemed, had protested that they should not demean themselves by dismounting and showing groveling respect for the pompous noble. The road was free to everyone. He had but recently come from China and to him all Asiatics were alike. "I have lived in China fourteen years, and I know how to manage these people." He held his horse firmly in the road despite the sensible brute's efforts to pull aside.

Then a gigantic guardian of the prince's palanquin slipped the clothing off his shoulders so that he was bare to the waist and grasped his sword with both hands. Other retainers followed suit. The rest was but a matter of seconds.

Richardson was killed and rekilled. The other two men fainted in flight for loss of blood.

The woman reached Yokohama hysterical and swooning, spattered with blood and drenched with salt water, for she had escaped her pursuers only by riding into the sea.

The British government demanded an indemnity of £100,000 from the Japanese government and £25,000 from the Prince of Satsuma. The alternative was war.

•

"War let it be," said the little brown brothers.

Japanese merchants deserted Yokohama. Business stopped. Native servants vanished overnight from white men's homes. Peasants within two miles of Yokohama were ordered to make room in their homes for Japanese troops. Princes residing in Yedo were sent home to their own provinces to make ready for war.

The mikado and shogun declared June 25th as the date for the expulsion of the barbarians.

Admiral Kuper in command of the British squadron became uneasy. He had never seen a gun fired in action. Though he was not a coward, the idea of real war bewildered him. He advised all foreigners to leave Yokohama. They stoutly refused to do so, but some sent away their wives and children.

Admiral Kuper gave warning that even with the help of other foreign ships he could not hold Yokohama against a real Japanese attack.

Civilians organized a volunteer corps. No day passed murderless. Not only foreigners were attacked, but native merchants who had dealt with foreigners were beheaded, and their heads were pilloried on the bridges above the notice:

"These unprincipled persons have been dealing with foreign barbarians for their own gain and have caused all goods to rise in price whereby the majority of the people are suffering."

The fateful day arrived when every barbarian was to be swept into the sea. But Yokohama, ready and tense, was not attacked. Instead, hostilities broke out at the other end of the island. The Prince of Choshu, in obedience to the imperial mandate, fired upon ships passing by his domain. The victims were the American ship, *Pembroke*, the French *Kien-chang*, and the Dutch *Medusa*.

•

"They'll have to be taught a lesson," stormed Captain McDougall, U.S.N., commander of the U.S.S. *Wyoming*. He had been chasing Confederate blockade runners preying upon North Pacific whalers and had put in at Yokohama for supplies. There he had been ordered to punish the Prince of Choshu.

Captain McDougall expected to find one Japanese warship at Shimonoseki. But, as the *Wyoming* rounded the point, he was startled to see not one but three ships anchored close together near the town under the grim protection of the shore guns. One was a steamer, one a barque, the third a brig. All were heavily armed. The three vessels, along with the shore batteries, made the odds against the *Wyoming* about four to one.

It was more than Captain McDougall had counted upon.

"Better swing out," he told the pilot. "Perhaps they'll come after us, out of range of the batteries. Then we may get a chance to pick them off one at a time."

The pilot objected. "Can't go out there, Mac," he said. "Shoals." That was not strictly true. "Reckon we gotta face up to them." He looked to the commander for approval. "Lessen you want me to turn tail and run for it."

"Damn your eyes, no," blazed McDougall. "Let's at 'em." And having established that his was the decision to attack, overriding the pilot's suggestion of retreat, he began shouting stentorian orders.

The pilot steered straight for the shore batteries. A tongue of fire leaped from the nearest wooded hill, and smoke rose. Then came the boom of the gun, and, last, the screech of the missile not twenty yards from the *Wyoming.*

The tarpaulin that had covered the ports to make the ship look like a merchantman was peeled off. The quartermaster hoisted the American flag at the peak. Guns were run out. Firearms and cutlasses were posted on deck.

Three guns spoke at once from the shore. Columns of water spurted up fore and aft. Those fellows were smart. They would soon get the range. But by the time they got it, it would be too late. "Get under them," growled McDougall. That had been the pilot's idea, but he was thankful the captain had made it his own.

The whole shore was thundering now. Whales seemed to be spouting all about the ship. Then, like the passing of a comet, a scream came athwart the deck, and left a path. Three bodies were dragged hastily into the shelter of the break of the poop. Heavy crashes and ship-long shivers told that hits were being scored on the hull.

The ship's twelve-pounders opened up. The shore guns had revealed their own exact location; soon three of them were silenced. But the others were scoring steadily. This could not last.

The captain kept jangling the wire to the engine room. With belching smoke, bellying sails, the ship raced closer. Presently the hull-thuds ceased. The shots were screaming through the rigging now. One whanged the smokestack. One found the mainskysail and it exploded like a paper bag. Then everything was far above. There was peace under a screeching sky. Sailors looked up open-mouthed, grinned at each other.

The pilot was jubilant. "We're under it!" The shore guns, high on hills, were trained on the channel. The *Wyoming* was too close in to be hit. But there were still the three warships.

These could not expect to be attacked by a single ship. What the enemy did not expect was just the thing to give him. The *Wyoming* altered her course a few points to bear down directly upon the anchored ships.

The men were in high spirits. They caught the audacity of the quarterdeck—of the captain, squared off, grimly biting his mustache; of the tall fellow at the wheel, eyes glinting under shaggy brows.

The ship being now tight under the lee of the land, the wind failed. The sails relaxed their bulged muscles. "Better so," the pilot said. "We can do a nicer job of steering with only the engines."

"Won't take much maneuvering," said Captain McDougall, "to sail by on the outside of the three of them and rake the steamer, then come round to starboard, pass between them and the shore, and take the barque and brig."

Again the pilot must be diplomatic if he would have his way. "Yeah, that's easy," he said, "only I know what you'd rather have me do. Think I can't do it, like as not."

"What's that?"

"Steer right into the nest of them. Right plumb in the middle. Then we can use all our guns. Port broadside on the steamer, starboard broadside for the sail ships. Make it a real surprise party."

He saw indignant protest coming from the captain and hurried on. "Can't fool me, Mac. I can see it in your eye."

"Garn!" said the captain, bit his mustache, and looked through his glass. "Tight squeeze. Sure you can do it?"

"Make a stab at it—if it's orders."

"It's orders!" McDougall's walnut face wrinkled into a grin. "Hell's navel!" he ejaculated, and spat over the side.

They were near enough to see the name of the Japanese steamer—*Lancefield.* Probably bought from the British.

"Purple awnings over the deck, with gold crests," said

McDougall, squinting through his glass. "What's the meaning of that?"

"Must be dignitaries on board. Perhaps the prince himself."

"Right. Some big-wigs are going down the companionway to a boat alongside. Must be planning a dash to shore . . . No, they've decided we're too close. Climbing up again, losing a bit of their god-awful dignity. Awnings are coming down. Sailors hoppin' round the deck. Running out guns—on the port side. That's good. They just can't believe we'd be so rude as come between them and the other ships. By the time they wake up . . ."

Stern guns, one on the barque and one on the steamer, began firing. The *Wyoming* remained gun-dumb until she had reached the heart of the nest. Then she stopped her engines. There she lay like a rat in a trap.

But a very vicious rat that suddenly clawed out with broadsides left and right at steamer and barque and bit with her forward pivot-gun at the brig. The range was only thirty yards to the ships on the beam, a hundred yards to the brig. The shock told most upon the barque. She replied promptly, but so wildly as to suggest the confusion on her decks. Her foremast tottered for a moment, then crashed down upon the port guns.

There was no time to exult, for a tremendous salvo came now from the *Lancefield*. The pounding of the shots on the hull was like the beating of an African drum. Shrieks ran through the rigging. A hail of splinters and bolts fell on the deck. The American gunners returned the fire. Still the *Lancefield* rode evenly and sent over another broadside, worse than the first. Two of the *Wyoming's* twelve-pounders were silenced, and the men behind them.

Now the drift had brought the *Wyoming* alongside the brig, which gave all it had—but an answering broadside burst its hull and it began to settle by the stern.

But the *Lancefield* was still in fine fettle. Her Japanese gunners were well trained and had quite recovered from their surprise at the tactically unreasonable behavior of their enemy. Such unreasonableness must be punished. To the rote-routinized, by-the-book Japanese mind, there is no sin greater than irregularity. The Nipponese went at their work to save the world for rule of thumb.

Captain McDougall vibrated with the trembling of his ship under the terrific drubbing.

"Dahlgren," he bawled, "fire!" But Sims, his veteran gunner entrusted with the precious eleven-inch Dahlgren, hadn't let loose a shell yet. He figured and fiddled, squinted and readjusted. Sims was always a tinkerer. Everything had to be just right for him, down to the last hair. Once preoccupied, hell let loose around his head would not disturb him.

He was not disturbed now by the bombardment, by four unobeyed commands to fire, nor by sizzling promises of court-martial.

When Sims was good and ready, he fired. The shell struck the *Lancefield* precisely at the water line, tore through her side, ripped into her boiler, and exploded. A volcano of smoke and steam rose. The ship filled rapidly, slewed, heeled over. Her crew took to the boats. The loaded boats were excellent targets, but . . .

"Let be," said Captain McDougall, rang up steam, and sailed for Yokohama.

He stopped only long enough, when he was well out of the straits, to consign five dead to the sea.

A substantial indemnity was demanded for these five dead and for the six wounded and for the shot and shell expended and for forty-one repairs to the pock-marked hull, dented stack, and torn rigging.

The shining example of the American punitive expedition was followed by fleets of French, Dutch, and English ships. At Shimonoseki and Kagoshima, drastic punishment was inflicted, and a bill for three million dollars expenses was handed to the Japanese government.

11

FEVER OF GOODWILL

More American, British, French, Russian warships came.

They were not needed. No people adjust themselves to the demands of necessity more quickly than the Japanese.

It had become plain that killing foreigners did no good and only brought terrific vengeance. The lesson had been forced home by the *Wyoming*, and the foreign fleets that had punished the Prince of Choshu and the Prince of Satsuma.

These princes, two of the most powerful in Japan, changed their front. Instead of attacking foreigners, they set out to make friends with them, employ foreign experts, hurry to learn in the shortest time possible what made the foreigners so strong. Once their arts had been learned, it would be time enough to think of wiping them out. Meanwhile, they must be humored.

The mikado issued no more orders demanding the expulsion of foreigners. The shogun befriended them.

Attacks upon foreigners were not at an end, but the police caught the culprits now as often as before they had failed to catch them. Offenders were severely punished. The execution of Mamiya and Seiji in December, 1864, marked the beginning of this policy.

The whole nation caught the fever of goodwill toward foreigners, imitation of foreign ways, duplication of foreign battleships, cannon, steel mills, steamers, and everything else down to buttons, beer bottles, and Peekskill stoves.

The next few years rose like steps, steps of progress and prosperity for both Japanese and aliens, steps of the sort once so happily described by Job as "washed with butter."

The white man in Asia now seemed secure. All foreigners rode on the crest of the wave of the public passion to imitate the West.

•

The revolution had come.

The year 1868 saw the overthrow of the last of the shoguns, who for two and a half centuries had usurped the authority of the mikado. The mikado was restored to power.

The underlying conflict was not, however, between shogun and mikado, but between the shogun's circle of princes and the mikado's circle of princes. The latter included the powerful daimyo of Satsuma and Choshu, who had received such a drubbing from the guns of foreign ships.

The scales had been shot away from their eyes, and they saw their way to power. They acquired foreign armaments with amazing speed, marched upon and demolished the shogun's armies, and raised themselves, as it were, by the bootstraps, attaching themselves to the mikado and then elevating him to supreme sovereignty.

The old word *mikado* was abandoned. Kyoto, ancient seat of the mikados, was also abandoned.

The sixteen-year-old Emperor Meiji set out from Kyoto in

triumphal procession along the historic Tokaido toward Yedo, now renamed Tokyo.

There was an epidemic of renaming. There was a national turning up of noses at old things. What could not be remodeled was at least rechristened.

The emperor's procession was unlike any royal progress ever seen in Japan. A few years earlier no third-rate prince would have been satisfied with such modesty, but the new rulers were making a fetish of simplicity. The company numbered only a thousand. There were no brilliant colors, no dancing steps. The soldiers had dressed as they pleased. Some carried their swords strapped to American trousers. Some wore French or British naval caps. All carried foreign rifles in addition to their swords.

The emperor rode in a plain white wood palanquin. Many of the people had brought out mats to kneel on. They were sorely perplexed when the heralds, instead of intoning the usual "Down on your knees," commanded, "Stand up."

In Tokyo the emperor was ensconced in the palace formerly occupied by the shogun. Broad parks, great walls, deep moats surrounded him. But the gates were thrown open to foreign diplomats. Even some of the great foreign merchants were summoned, and looked upon the face of the Son of Heaven, which had always in the past been screened from public gaze.

An American constitution was framed by statesmen who had been pupils of the American scholar-missionary, Dr. Verbeck. It provided that "all officers shall be changed after four years service. They shall be appointed by a majority of votes given by ballot."

The Magna Charta of the new Japan was the emperor's Oath, which promised a congress or parliament and equal opportunity for all men. It lifted Japan's eyes from centuries of introspection and directed them overseas. "Knowledge shall be sought for throughout the world so that the foundations of the empire may be strengthened."

Young men and women of fashion scorned things Japanese and bowed down in sometimes ridiculous reverence before anything foreign.

•

The new Japanese dandy wore no topknot, his hair was cut short except for a generous bang plastered tightly above the left eye. This was the New York mode, according to the *Police Gazette.* The back hair, formerly trained to turn up to the topknot, was now held down by scented hair oil.

The new man's cheeks were slightly cut by the unwieldy American razor. He owned a shaving mug decorated with his name. He had also acquired a mustache cup, though he had no mustache. All attempts to raise one had failed, the Japanese face being infertile soil for this adornment.

He wore the latest in paper collars and a shirt that buttoned up the back. His tie was the clever ready-made bow that clung to the collar button. His American coat and "spring bottom" pants were close fitting. A silk sash with tassels held up the trousers. The shoes were congress gaiters with elastic sides.

A heavy gold watch chain divided him and held in leash a watch of generous proportions, which he wound every night with a key. On the other end of the chain was New York's most modish toothpick made of solid gold and studded with rubies.

He blew his nose on a linen handkerchief and deposited it carefully in his pocket, much to the disgust of his unenlightened countrymen who used a square of tissue paper for this purpose and threw it away immediately after using.

He startled bystanders by scratching highly combustible sulphur matches, which threw off sparks in all directions, and tried not to make a face when he smoked a cheroot.

He wrote with a modern quill pen instead of a writing brush. He read foreign novels that filled his head with a tornado of seductive ideas. He lost interest in the nape of the feminine neck, supposed by the Japanese to be the seat of passion, and began to look for the contours of breasts and thighs. This led him logically to a study of foreign women. Their gowns were not so secretive as the kimono. He warmed to their frank, lustful appearance. But when he made advances, he did not find them as bold as they looked.

He spent money like water. Americans were good spenders, and he would not be outdone. He was popular with foreigners because he was a good fellow, knew English, and could always be relied upon to set 'em up for everybody. His natural inquisitiveness led him to make a thorough investigation of every foreign drink, new and old, and all possible combinations thereof. When closing time came there were always willing seamen to carry him home because his servants had standing instructions to give a purse of *ryo* to each.

He must have anything and everything he could afford of the imports from America. He enjoyed the relaxation afforded by Mrs. Winslow's Soothing Syrup. He bought a Connecticut lamp fed with Penn petroleum. He invested in condensed milk, beer, clocks, pictures of Abe Lincoln, umbrellas, and that unique foreign invention, buttons.

He bought soap, supposing it to be a confection, but was disappointed when he ate it.

He was charmed with himself when he looked into a western mirror which made him look so much better than had the old ones of steel.

He wore glasses, whether or not he needed them.

He went to an American photographic studio and came away with a handsome daguerreotype portrait of himself.

He bought California butter, but, not fancying the taste of it, used it to grease his wife's sewing machine.

He bought a chair but used it rarely. He did not understand why anyone should tolerate a chair when he could sit in comfort on the floor.

•

All these products, and more, Japanese artisans began to imitate and export for sale in America and Europe at a fraction of the price in the lands of their origin.

The industrial revolution was under way in Japan. The nation that had known no sound louder than the chiming of temple bells woke to the scream of the factory siren, the roar of modern machinery, the rumble of train and tractor, the booming of dynamite in her once silent mountains.

The woes that had accompanied the dawn of the industrial revolution in England, Germany, America, were repeated in Japan. Goods were shoddy, unreliable, deceptive. They won a bad reputation. Wily Japanese manufacturers countered this handicap by copying not only the foreign product but even the label so that it appeared to have been made in New York or Chicago.

In one year before the First World War, the United States bought seven million toothbrushes from Japan, eight hundred thousand tablecloths, two hundred and thirty-three million cigarette mouthpieces, sixty-seven million paper napkins, two million imitation Panama hats, and millions of dollars' worth of silk.

Experts from Switzerland, Germany, England, and America were engaged to install and operate the machinery—then dismissed as soon as the Japanese learned to do it for themselves.

Japanese millionaires, or *narikin* as these newly rich were called, sprang up overnight in astonishing numbers. A Japanese publication reported: "The narikin are making their objectionable presence known in every way. Fine mansions are being built, motor cars are racing, geisha are attired more gaily, and summer resorts are crowded with those 'who spend money like water.'"

A noted *ryoriya* (Japanese restaurant) in Kobe refused to serve any dinner below fifty yen (twenty-five dollars) a head.

It was the day of big profits. A Japanese steamship company declared dividends of 360 percent. A metal refining company declared 200 percent. Japan commenced lending capital to other countries.

The workers in the new factories did not share the prosperity of the owners. They were paid starvation wages. In many factories the cost of dormitory accommodations was taken from the wages, and a system of fines still further reduced the amount actually paid. The result was that factory workers, instead of making and saving money, were frequently left not only penniless, but in debt to the factory at the end of a few months.

•

Nevertheless, country life was being swept into the cities. Every year a third of a million people were brought from the freedom and healthful conditions of the country to the congested factory quarters of the city.

Agents of the factories scoured the rural districts for recruits. Ignorant youths of the countryside were told of the wonders of the city—the great buildings, the parks, the theaters, the festivals and celebrations. Promises were made concerning fine wages, short hours, good treatment, and so on, promises which in most cases were never fulfilled. One can almost sympathize with the agents, for theirs was a tremendous and difficult task, the task of refilling the ranks of thousands who were annually ground to pieces by the factory system. Any one district was likely to be exhausted of girls in three years; and a Japanese authority stated that the supply was beginning to run out all over the country.

So great was the scarcity of labor that according to the *Japan Weekly Mail*, actual kidnaping methods were sometimes employed:

> The metropolitan police have recently learned that kidnapers have been selling children to various factories at the price of five or six yen each. This revelation came through the finding of two children wandering in Honjo about a fortnight ago. When the two children, both eleven years old, were found by the police, it was ascertained that they had both been kidnaped in Akita prefecture, and were sold to a factory in Honjo for five yen a head. The two boys escaped from the factory and were wandering in the streets when they were discovered by the police.
>
> It is reported that many young men have been brought to Tokyo by kidnapers and, although not bad when they first arrive in the capital, they mingle with youths of bad reputation, especially after their escape from the factories to which they have been sold.

Many factories were little better than prisons. Dormitories were erected within the factory grounds, and the workers were kept under strict observation and rarely were able to make good an escape. But if factory life was so delightful as the agents made it appear, why should anyone wish to escape?

The large cotton mills ran in two shifts day and night, so that each worker had a working period of about twelve hours. In the silk factories and in the weaving factories the hours were more extreme, running from twelve to sixteen a day. Rest periods and meal periods were cut short. Thirty minutes was nominally allowed for lunch; but it would be a courageous worker who would dare to displease the foreman by taking so long a time. Lunch was frequently eaten during five or seven minutes while standing, or without even leaving the running machine. The brunt of this régime fell hardest upon the women and children. Little girls, scarcely in their teens, must rise every day at four-thirty and work from six in the morning to six in the evening; and, when the pressure of orders was heavy, up to eight or nine or ten o'clock at night.

Nor were the conditions of work entirely delightful. Many of the factories were dark, crowded, poorly ventilated, excessively hot; and in the cotton mills the air was filled with tuberculosis-provoking dust, and modern methods of artificial moisture to arrest the dust were not employed. Accidents were frequent, because of the lack of proper safety devices. One factory in Osaka with a thousand employees had an average of fifty accidents daily. Girls were often subjected to rough and insulting treatment at the hands of foremen. From ten to thirty operators slept in a single room.

"The dormitories," an investigator reported, "are frequently upstairs over the noise, steam and foul air of the factory itself. Although the large cotton factories allow a little more space per girl than the smaller factories, hygienically considered, they are the worst of all. This arises from the fact that the girls are divided into day and night shifts; both use the same rooms and bedding from one year's end to another. Furthermore, in winter the bedding is so thin that the girls have to sleep close together and share quilts to keep warm. The frequent change of personnel results in the same bedding being used by several different girls in the course of a year. Since the night shift sleep in the day they shut the blinds, and consequently the bedding is rarely if ever sunned. Inevitably tuberculosis and skin diseases are transmitted from one person and generation to another."

Such treatment was not confined to the women workers. A description of the appalling conditions among the men employed for the work on one of the new power plants was given by the Reverend Christopher Noss.

> The contractor sublet the job to conscienceless exploiters of labor of the type of those who have built the railroads through

the lonely wildernesses of Japan. Men out of a job were gathered in Tokyo by means of fine promises of big wages and easy work and sent to Odera in carload lots. Arriving, they were handed over to bosses armed with stout staves, and put to digging. Many, being unaccustomed to the work, fainted and were beaten to death, their bodies were thrown into the fills or bundled into cement kegs and buried in the mountains. Their food was vile. At night their clothes were taken from them and they were penned up. In order to discourage desertion the contractor paid them, not in cash, but in tickets, making such generous deductions for expenses that the portion remaining to the laborer amounted to three and a half cents a day (ordinary wages for such work being from thirty to forty cents without board). There was a constant ebb of the manpower through desertion, death, suicide, and deliberate murder by the bosses, and almost every other day a fresh carload of fifty was brought in. An unsuccessful attempt to escape meant almost certain death. Yet refugees came in every day to Wakamatsu on the one side and Sukagawa on the other. One poor fellow dropped dead in Wakamatsu City Hall before he could tell his tale. Scores perished before the authorities could get their red tape unwound and begin to take notice. Three hundred were done to death.

Sixty percent of those recruited from the country districts never returned home. Broken in health and morals, they drifted from one factory to another; many of the girls turned to prostitution. Of those who went home, one out of every six had contracted tuberculosis. This disease was introduced by factory workers into rural districts where it had previously been unknown. The death rate among factory women was almost three times as high as the ordinary death rate among women. In the great manufacturing city of Osaka the number of deaths equaled the number of births. More Japanese died of tuberculosis in one year than were killed in the war between Russia and Japan.

Accidents in Japanese coal mines were frequent. Counting the number of men killed for each million of tons mined, the following record shows the mortality rate during 1901 to 1910:

Great Britain	4.40
Austria	5.05
Belgium	5.56
United States	5.83
France	7.19
Germany	7.55
India	9.00
Japan	22.71

And so with the other industries of the New Japan. The bugaboo of the newborn steel industry was a tremendous accident rate; of the pottery industry, lead poisoning from the glaze placed on the dishes to make them impervious to moisture and give them a polished surface; of brass founding, brass chills, zinc ague, metal shakes, and like ailments, all due to inadequate elimination of the zinc fumes from the zinc used with copper to make brass.

But who worried about these things (except the victims)? Industry was flourishing, wealth was pouring in thanks to exports, the government was secure. Nippon began to look for new worlds to conquer.

12

GO WEST, YOUNG MAN

Japan moved to extend her power westward. In this she was following the example of her mentor, America.

America had forged her way from the Atlantic shore to the Pacific.

She had placed a protecting hand upon Hawaii.

She had just bought Alaska, thereby, in the eloquent words of three congressmen, "assuring our control of the North Pacific," "extending a friendly hand to Asia," "building a bridge by which American civilization may proceed to the relief of six hundred million souls of the Orient."

An American diplomat in China had suggested the seizure of Formosa; Mr. Harris suggested buying it.

American warships, sent to extract a trade treaty from Korea, killed two hundred and fifty defenders of the forts in Chemulpo Bay but came away without their treaty.

A doughty American sea captain raised the American flag over the Marquesas.

Washington talked of taking over the Fijis because of their debts to American merchants.

The acquisition of Samoa was urged to plant American power in the South Pacific as firmly as Alaska had planted it in the North Pacific.

Americans had already noticed the Philippines, and a German economist had predicted that the United States would some day fall heir to the Spanish empire in the Pacific.

There seemed no reason why the success of America in Japan should not be repeated in the myriad islands of the southern seas. The Pacific should become, for trade purposes, at least, if not in a more real sense, an American sphere of influence.

•

Japan saw her golden opportunity to do likewise when Europe, concerned with its own problems which would come to a climax in World War I, had little time to devote to world trade.

Japan took up the task. Her salesmen penetrated China, Malaysia, India, Africa, South and North America, selling every conceivable sort of manufactured article from toys to hypodermic syringes.

She tangled with the great bear, and, to her own surprise, won the Russo–Japanese War. That victory encouraged her to undertake further conquests, both mercantile and military.

She began modestly by seizing the Bonin islands, the Loochoos, and the Kuriles.

The fact that Nipponese traders venturing into Formosa were inhospitably eaten by the savage tribes made it "necessary" to take over that great island.

Korean impoliteness led to the incorporation of Korea as part of the Japanese Empire.

The vast expanses of Manchuria and Mongolia looked good as possible homes of the crowded Japanese. So they were bloodily acquired.

Three million square miles of the Pacific dotted with two thousand Micronesian islands were taken from Germany without a shot being fired—because Germany was too busy fighting a war in Europe.

Flushed with victory, Japan tackled giant China. When the Sino–Japanese conflict broke out, many Japanese expected a decisive victory within two months. Japan sent a million men under arms to China. Instead of two months it was fourteen years before Japan acknowledged defeat and withdrew her troops.

•

It would not be fair to imply that this history of slaughter was due merely to Japan's overweening pride in her own prosperity and power. There was another cause, far more deep-seated.

The roots of militarism could be found in Japan's two-acre farms.

For five years we lived in the farm-and-fishing village of Hayama on Sagami Bay. Walking back into the hills one day, we turned in at a small, thatched farmhouse to ask the way. Rain was falling and the farmer and his wife insisted that we come inside.

The little house consisted of but one room, half of it floored with wood without the luxury of *tatami* or mats, the other half a step down and unfloored.

In the corner of the earth-paved half was a stall for the horse, but there was no horse. Beside the stall was the family bathtub, a stove for heating it incorporated within it. Rakes, hoes, and plows hung on the walls. In the raised portion of the room, life centered around the *kotatsu*, a square hole in the floor in which a few live coals lay on a bed of ashes. Suspended from above, a pot hung over the coals. The smoke circled upward and lost itself in the already smoke-blackened thatch.

The room was clean. Even the dirt floor had been swept and sprinkled. But it was a poor, bare, cramped place and the only furnishing was a Shinto *kamidana*. It was a shelf made roughly of a piece of board and fastened to the wall at eye level. On it there was no miniature temple as there usually is on the god-shelf, but only the *ihai*, erect wooden shingles bearing the names of deceased members of the family.

But what we noticed particularly was that a very small and new-looking *ihai* stood in front of the others, and before it glowed a small lamp consisting of a wick burning in a saucer of rapeseed oil. The woman saw that we had observed the *kamidana*. She appeared to be close to tears.

"You are in a very sad house," she said with an attempted smile.

"It was a child?"

"Yes."

"How old was it?"

"Only two weeks."

"What was its illness?"

"Oh, it was not ill. You never saw a more healthy baby."

"Then what happened? An accident?"

The man and his wife exchanged glances.

The farmer said, "You probably do not need to do such things in your country. But here there are more children than there are means to support them. So *mabiki* was necessary."

It was the first time that we had personally encountered *mabiki* and it was hard not to show that we were shocked. *Mabiki* means thinning out. It originally referred to the thinning of a row of vegetables. But used as the farmer had used it, it meant infanticide. Poverty-stricken families must be thinned out so that the survivors may live.

Another euphemistic term for child-murder is *modoshi*,

sending back. The unwanted child is sent back to the spirit world from which it came. If a girl comes when a boy is fervently desired, she may be "sent back."

But had these gentle-looking folk done this with their own hands? They seemed to feel the question that was in our minds.

"The baby broker took it," the farmer said.

"Then perhaps she is still alive." Girls are often bought by agents for the Yoshiwara—not only teen-age girls, but babies which may be had at a very low price because of the expense involved in caring for them until they become old enough to be of service.

But the farmer shook his head. "No, it is not alive. It was a boy."

"But didn't you want a boy? Everybody wants a boy—to continue the family, and worship the ancestors."

"I have a boy. He works in Tokyo. There is not enough work on this small farm for both of us. I have two girls. They are in the Yoshiwara. More boys are no good to me. More girls I could use. We prayed it would be a girl. The agents come through this country every few days looking for girls. They pay for girls. We have to pay them to take the boys."

I thought of the time I had paid a man to take a brood of kittens and drown them because of disinclination to do it myself. It is just so that the baby broker operates. For a few coins, he will take surplus infants and give them a painless escape from an inhospitable world.

A surprising angle of this tragic affair is that the very farmer who pays the baby broker to take his boy infant may turn to the "child merchant" and buy a boy, say, twelve years old to help on his farm.

He perhaps needs help at once and cannot wait twelve years for it. But the greatest reason is that he can purchase a grown boy for much less than it would cost to bring up one. The "child merchant" kidnaps boys in the cities for this purpose.

Officials stoutly denied that the traffic in children existed. I have heard them expatiate on the joys of country life in Japan and the simple happiness of the farmer.

"The peasant gets all the real satisfactions of life," a white-collar worker in the War Office assured me, "and he doesn't appreciate them."

And in April, 1944, American government monitors overheard a domestic broadcast of Tokyo Radio sharply criticizing Japanese farmers for their "love of luxuries and gaieties!" The broadcast warned that unless the peasant population returned to the practice of saving a quarter of their income for emergencies they would face "unavoidable famine" and find it difficult to escape the "greatest hardships." Just how the average farmer who is over his head in debt can save a quarter of his nonexistent net income for emergencies was not explained. Foreseeing catastrophe, the authorities evidently determined to throw the onus of blame upon the peasants rather than upon the militaristic-industrialist government that had bled them white.

What are the actual "luxuries" and "gaieties" of the peasants? Here are some of them.

The peasant has the luxury of raising rice but not eating it. It is commonly said in Japan that only the rich or the ill eat rice. A very aged and frail peasant may be allowed some—and his neighbors will say, "He must be far gone. They're feeding him rice."

The peasant may raise tobacco but not smoke it. Before the tobacco leaves are ripe, government inspectors come and count them one by one. After they are picked, cured, and delivered they are counted again and the farmer penalized for any that are missing. If he wants to smoke he must buy back his tobacco for eighteen times what he was paid for it.

If he has a good imagination he may enjoy a sense of luxury as he stands in the middle of his silkworm room and hears hundreds of tiny jaws transforming mulberry leaves into potential roll upon roll of lustrous silk. But he cannot afford to wear his own silk. The coarsest cotton must do for him.

The gaieties of the cities come to the country people only through the pages of an occasional newspaper or magazine. The farmer must keep his nose in the mud to make city life possible. The nation's industrial structure has been built upon the back of the peasant.

Japan in her eagerness to become a strong warrior power granted large subsidies to industry and raised the money for these subsidies by taxing the peasant. In addition to government subsidies, industries enjoyed tax remission. Just before the war Imperial Agricultural Society figures showed that landowners paid from 31 to 50 percent of their income in taxes while manufacturers paid 18 percent and merchants 14 percent. Thus the manufacturer and trader paid roughly only half the tax levied upon the man least able to pay, the farmer.

And these figures do not take account of another injustice: the practice of assessing the tax on a farm family as a unit, as if it were a single individual instead of a group of from two to ten persons each of whom should be considered a wage-earner. An income that might stand a 50-percent reduction if the balance were to support only one person means starvation if it must be divided among several. And yet the government, thus penalizing farmers for having children, propagandized them on the need for more and more children to make Japan strong.

The Japanese farmer was deep in debt. Mortgages grew from $65 per farm family in 1914 to $300 per family in 1937.

On his debt the farmer must pay 20 percent and more in interest. Sharply contrasted with the farmer's rate of 20 percent was the 1½ percent charged to shipbuilders.

As might have been expected, great numbers of farmers lost their farms and worked as tenants under conditions no better than serfdom. Seventy percent of the peasants owned only a part of the land they tilled or none at all. The best land went to large landlords. Peasant-owners were largely restricted to poor hillside soil. Ownership steadily passed into the hands of a few persons until half of the land belonged to only 8 percent of the landowners.

The tenant must pay one-half to two-thirds of the produce of his farm to his landlord as rent! From what he has left he must pay his farming expenses.

Add to all this the difficulty that as the population increased the amount of land from which the farmer must get his living grew smaller. Farmers make up approximately 51 percent of the population. Less than 20 percent of the surface of the California-sized Japanese homeland is cultivable. Japan has only one-half acre per head of population, the lowest ratio in the world.

In Japan the average size of the farm is two acres. The average American farmer has more than 150 acres.

But the two-acre average for Japan included the thousand-acre farms, the number of which was increasing; which meant that at the other extreme the number of poor little half-acre and quarter-acre farms must also be increasing.

Japanese farmers have remarkable talent for extracting large yield from little ground, as their American competitors in California know to their grief. The farmer in Japan produces thirty or forty bushels of rice per acre; our Louisiana rice fields, though farmed with the help of machinery, do not do half as well. The Japanese farmer gets record yields also of wheat, barley, and vegetables. His troubles are not due to lack of hard work.

The more the farmer produced, the more was taken from him.

"All the traffic will bear" seemed to be the government's motto in fleecing the farmer. For example, in 1936 the rice crop was one-eighth larger than in 1929 and the price was higher, yet the farmers, thanks to government maneuvering, actually received $300 million less for their rice.

In a survey made by the Ministry of Agriculture in 1934 it was found that 99 percent of the peasants working farms of five acres or less operated them at a deficit. They managed to earn enough to live by odd jobs other than farming. Later many of these outside sources of income were cut off.

The production of silk in farmhouses died out when rayon and nylon took its place in the American market. The farm income from this source in 1934 was only 20 percent of what it had been in 1929. This had been the chief subsidiary farm industry. Its decline was a catastrophe to the peasant.

In Ibaragi prefecture I found farmers selling their daughters to café owners as waitress-prostitutes. In Echigo it was unusual to see a young girl. An observer reported that Yamagata prefecture was "denuded of its feminine youth." Six prefectures in northern Japan were periodically visited by famine when unfavorable weather cut short the growing season and caused crop failure. We read such news items as this from the Tokyo *Nichi Nichi:*

"Conditions in the Tohoku district are horrible. The number of peasants who are dying of starvation reaches 70,000. Mothers are exhausted and children perishing. School children faint daily at school from emaciation."

In the island of Hokkaido it was reported that "thousands of children are too weak to attend school because of lack of food."

Japan made wars, not merely for the fun of making them, but to obtain more room for her 35 million overcrowded and desperate peasants.

13

THE HATE CAMPAIGN

Challenged by America to quit her wars of aggression, Japan retaliated by preparing to confront America herself.

The first step in this preparation was to inflame Japanese opinion against Americans. The army, which actually ruled both the emperor and the nation, went about this task with great deliberation.

We saw it happening. And felt it. When we had first arrived we had been treated with the utmost courtesy. The farmers and fishermen of Hayama village stopped us on the street to chat, invited us into their homes, entertained us at dinner, showered us with little gifts.

But the longer we stayed the fewer friends we had! The hate-America program was working. The police, under army orders, summoned to the police station any Japanese seen speaking to us.

"Why did you talk to the foreigners?" "What did you say to them?" "What did they say to you?" "If you wish to avoid suspicion, have nothing to do with them."

Every few days we were visited by a police or army official and questioned. He examined any manuscript on which I happened to be working (frequently holding it upside down). He grilled our servant and our neighbors. Time and again I was hailed to the police station to explain what was considered suspicious behavior.

•

Other correspondents fared worse. James Melvin Cox, English correspondent for Reuter's, was arrested for espionage. After he had been detained for some days he "fell" from a third-story window at the headquarters of the military police in Tokyo and died two hours later.

The correspondent for International News Service was arrested and jailed for two months.

The AP correspondent was grilled for seven hours and ordered to leave the country. The man sent in his place had hardly settled down when he too was commanded to get out.

An English professor from Tokyo sat at my table. He was A. W. Medley of the School of Foreign Languages.

He looked out into the pines of the emperor's beach home where Hirohito spent every summer.

"Your heavenly neighbor," he said, "nearly got me into trouble."

"How was that?"

"One of my students asked me about the Sphinx. I explained that the Sphinx was symbolic of the sun god from whom the Pharaohs claimed descent.

"The student seemed shocked. He said, 'You mean that the rulers of Egypt were descended from the sun goddess?'

"I immediately saw the trap I was getting into and tried to get out of it. I explained that this was not my claim, but the claim of the Pharaohs. And it was a sun god, not the sun goddess.

"He said, 'There is only one sun, and the deity of the sun is Amaterasu, the sun goddess. I never heard of this sun god. And if the Pharaohs were descended from him that would make them divine! Do you believe that?'

"I reminded him that I was not telling him my beliefs, and I said, 'Didn't you know that the Pharaohs were considered divine?'

" 'I never heard it,' he said, 'and I don't believe it.'

"A student is rarely so impolite to a teacher. I saw that he was getting badly worked up. I said, 'Don't worry your head over it. It is all ancient history. Many kings used to think themselves divine. It was called the divine right of kings. Surely you've heard of that?'

"He said, 'No, I have not and I am afraid I don't wish to.'

"I thought the thing would end there. But, would you believe it, he went to the head of the school. I was brought up before the board and accused of teaching heretical doctrine.

"I said, 'I was merely explaining some of the folk beliefs current in Egypt and elsewhere. It was just a bit of history.'

"The head told me, 'Professor Medley, we are trying to cooperate with the government. It is the wish of the government that history should be—shall we say, sifted—and the harmful parts removed. To intimate the divinity of other rulers would be to plant the seeds of doubt in the minds of students as to the unique character of our imperial line.'

"And I was told that one more such offense would mean my dismissal and the information would be turned over to the police."

Wilfrid Fleisher, American editor of the English-language newspaper *Japan Advertiser*, was forced to sell his paper to Japanese publishers at a nominal price and leave. He had printed a picture of the Crown Prince feeding a horse. The picture was slightly blurred and therefore constituted "an offense to the imperial family." In vain Fleisher pointed out that the photograph had been taken by Domei, the Japanese official agency, which had also made the cut.

Antiforeign sentiment was acerbated by headlines such as these in the Japanese press: "Roosevelt Peace Enemy Number One"; "America under Bolshevik Influence"; "Roosevelt Lies"; "America, Britain, about to Attack Japan."

•

Missionaries who had spent a lifetime in Japan and were among Japan's best friends were driven out. The new "Christian structure" in Japan must "conform with Japan's national thought"—the emperor must occupy the same position in the Japanese Christian Church as the Pope in the Roman Catholic Church.

The Japanese public was warned to beware of all association with foreigners. "The army is determined to take firm action against such unpatriotic Japanese." The few foreigners allowed to remain lived in a vacuum.

The army encouraged the formation of large hate organizations, the fascist Black Dragons, the Blood Brotherhood, the Death-Defying Troops, the God-Sent Troops, the Students' Union for Saving the Nation, and dozens of other groups with equally fire-breathing names. The chief rite in all these groups was the prayer meeting! The new nationalism had all the fervor and fire of a Methodist camp meeting.

The correspondents tried to warn the outside world. But the American and British public remained blissfully indifferent. War?—it just couldn't happen. And if it did, Japan would be defeated within a few weeks.

Then came Pearl Harbor—and four years of war.

14

HOW TO USE AN EMPEROR

One major reason why the Japanese were able to stand up against Allied military power for four years was that they had been thoroughly inculcated with the belief that their emperor wanted them to fight.

The opposite was the truth. The emperor did not want war. But faced with the army's threat that he would otherwise be forced to abdicate the throne, he signed the imperial rescript authorizing hostilities. He himself was a man of peace.

For five years the emperor of Japan had been our next-to-next-door neighbor.

Our wood-and-paper house was wedged in between a fish store on one side and a charcoal store on the other. Just beyond the latter was the palace wall. From our second story we could look over the wall into the imperial garden where pines half concealed the summer palace. From the palace the garden sloped down to the beach of Sagami Bay.

As the only foreigners to live near the palace, and the only Americans to remain in the village throughout the year, we were subjected to close scrutiny. Regularly once a month the police called *"Konnichi wa"* at the gate and entered with much hissing to drink tea and ask questions.

In these conversations we studiously avoided any reference to the emperor. The devout Japanese resented light talk concerning the emperor as the Christian does concerning the person of Jesus Christ. He was quick to detect any attitude not completely reverential. On the other hand, he had the yearning of a religionist that others should share his faith.

Our apparent lack of interest in the chief topic of Hayama village at first set our friends at ease, then stimulated their determination that we should hear about their emperor. And hear we did. Police officers of the village, sentries who stood like wooden soldiers in the pillboxes punctuating the palace wall and barked like sea lions in salute but relaxed when off duty, fishermen who helped the emperor collect marine specimens, tradesmen and farmers who brought supplies to the palace, carpenters who built the emperor's conning tower, visiting physicians, biologists, teachers, and musicians contributed, always discreetly, to our mosaic of homely details of the private life of the Son of Heaven.

Discreetly. For example, there was never a description of the emperor's appearance. Diffidence on this point was evidently due to the influence of the ancient tradition that no one may look full into the Heavenly Countenance and live. Now men looked, and lived, but still considered it sacrilegious to speak of what they had seen.

But we had plenty of opportunities to see for ourselves. Hirohito (whose name, by the way, is pronounced Hiroshtoh) is somewhat better built than most Japanese of his time. He does not have the usual squat frame and tendency to bowlegs. He had a horseman's balance and a swimmer's suppleness. When he swung across the beach or sprinted up the bank to the garden it was quite evident that he was not suffering from an overloaded stomach or an overtaxed brain. He was and is a good physical specimen.

His face was *yakimashita,* as the Japanese would say (literally, "broiled"), by sun and weather. Slightly prominent white teeth, better than most in this land of over-refined rice, contrasted with the dark complexion and short black mustache.

Although he was commander-in-chief of the army, his mouth was neither the hard thin line nor the tight purse of the Japanese military. His lips were full and sensitive. When he was interested they stood open, receptive and vulnerable, not sealed as were the lips of the hard-hitting and the self-made who brought him papers to sign.

Nor was his head square and efficient. It was slightly longer than broad, the head of a poet or professor or artist. It was a head of gentle dreams and intellectual delights. Its air of detachment was accented by the thick-lensed glasses. The eyes behind them had been weakened, as most really studious Japanese eyes are, by the intolerable burden of mastering the Japanese written language. The shortsighted eyes were brown. The hair was black and rebellious.

The general appearance was that of a student or of a gentleman with hobbies. He sought to learn, not to dictate. Oracles spoke in his name, but he was not an oracle. While he showed no evidence of being a great thinker, he had an inquiring mind which sought out information regardless of whether it was of direct use to a head of state. He was not a pragmatist, but somewhat other-worldly. One day when he retired from the shore to the palace he left behind a copy of *Aesop's Fables.* Although we did not touch it, a guard threatened us blackly, snatched it from our polluting gaze, and bore it in through the gate as if it were a holy wafer.

The books in his ample library ranged from Confucius to Spengler. Philosophy, economics, and history were well represented. There were many books in English; the emperor reads English easily but speaks it with difficulty. He had some choice illustrated volumes on the subject of his hobby—marine life.

Black-suited lecturers with briefcases full of wisdom came almost daily to the palace to address a class of one. Adult education had an advocate and example in the emperor. He took regular courses in economics, zoology, literature, and art. He made copious notes and kept a journal.

Even if he were not a man of simple and studious tastes tradition would compel him to live simply. The Hayama house provided for him is plain. Many a *narikin* (new-rich) has a better one. The "palace" is a palace only because it houses royalty. It is a purely Japanese building, erected by the Emperor Meiji and lacking the most modern conveniences. Its outer walls are of unpainted boards weathered a dull gray. Inside, the wood is the best in Japan, *hinoki*, tree of the sun, a cypress. It also is unpainted. Japanese builders consider it almost blasphemous to cover the beautiful natural grain of wood with paint.

The floor is paved with straw slabs of *tatami*, no different from those found in more humble homes. However, in this case there is a slight concession to foreign luxury, and occasional rugs are used on the *tatami*. Shoes are of course left at the door and slippers are worn. Sliding paper doors separate the rooms. Outside doors of thinner paper *(shoji)* may be drawn back to make the room part of the garden.

The Emperor Meiji, who opened Japan to the world and was more modern than the moderns, furnished the palace with western furniture and bath. The tables and chairs remain and the royal couple sleep in twin beds.

Our maid, wife of a fisherman of the village, had frequently been employed in the palace as a cleaning woman. She complained of the dust-harboring propensities of the dining room table legs and commiserated those Japanese who, for dignity's sake, must sit on high chairs at a high table when they might eat comfortably on the floor.

The house is innocent of the common utilities of an American home such as the electric refrigerator, electric clock, electric stove, heating plant with thermostat, cooling system, electric washing machine—all the things that an American housewife puts behind her as mere necessities and then goes on to covet a dozen other power gadgets, from air-conditioner and dishwasher to radio-phonograph with FM and television and that new method for the electrocution of all insects that dare to enter the sacred precincts of the American home. There are no screens on the emperor's palace and mosquitoes are not few along the shores of Sagami Bay. A net is hung over the imperial beds at night.

The simplicity of the emperor's private life is the more amazing since he is one of the richest men in the world. I do not refer to the fact that under the constitution he owns all Japan. That is theory. But his actual personal holdings are vast.

It was Bismarck who advised the Japanese statesmen to give their ruler prestige by making him peerless in the wealth of his personal possessions; but it was the idea of the Japanese themselves to prevent him from using this wealth.

Thus they make him a paragon of virtue. We may doubt that he likes being a paragon. Probably he and his wife and children do not care any more for discomfort than most people. But he must pose as the great example.

The people, knowing that their emperor has unlimited wealth, yet lives like one of them, can be persuaded to eat the bitter cake of frugality and like it.

If the squeezed farmer begins to protest, he has but to be reminded of the example of his Heavenly King.

Under this philosophy, low standards of living become a cult, an ideal. Persons who have a little more than others are ashamed of it and hide the fact. The outside of the Japanese house is purposely made less attractive than the inside. Within the house, the best wood is in the ceiling where it will not ordinarily be noticed. Art objects are not displayed in the rooms but kept in a cupboard or *godown*. The "front yard," pride of the Western home, is in Japan put behind the house where it cannot be seen by the passerby.

Students sometimes tear holes in their uniforms in order to look poor. Children of well-to-do families are not allowed by their parents to wear clothes better than those of their poorer schoolmates.

The great example is potent. The Japanese soldier is not ashamed of his coarse uncouth uniform because he knows his emperor's is little better.

It might not even fit so well since no one dared measure the imperial person. No hand should be laid upon him. Certainly a tailor would not be allowed such a liberty.

Exception might be made in the case of a physician if it should be desperately necessary; but the Emperor Meiji's pulse was taken through a silk cord around his wrist. And Meiji was the most democratic of Japanese emperors.

Even members of the royal house were sacrosanct, to their own disadvantage. Typical was an incident in 1869 when the Japanese doctor besought a foreigner by the name of Dr. Boyer to prescribe for the princess, who was suffering from a disease of women.

"Have you made a thorough examination?" Dr. Boyer asked.

"No. It is impossible to do so in the case of such a high personage as the princess."

"I could not prescribe without examining the patient."

"Very sorry. It is against the custom of the country."

And the recovery of the princess was left to chance.

•

One day a police officer, hissing more politely than usual, asked me to step over to headquarters.

"What for?"

"To have a cup of tea."

Leaving a rather perturbed wife, I walked out of the house with the officer, passed the charcoal store and the little post office, skirted the palace wall where sentries in the boxes unbent enough to show malicious glee at the spectacle of a foreigner being escorted to the police station, crossed the main street, and entered headquarters.

From one room came unearthly shrieks and the sound of blows. But it was not a torture chamber, only a gymnasium. Police off duty were indulging in *kendo,* fencing, a sport which seems to make a heavy demand upon the vocal cords.

However, I reflected uncomfortably that the shouts would effectively cover any cries from victims suffering the sort of "questioning" for which Japanese police were notorious.

In an upstairs room sat the captain behind his desk. He rose, greeted me, indicated a chair.

Sure enough, we were to have tea. The cups were already on the desk. But what particularly caught my eye was a copy of *Reader's Digest* lying open to an article signed by me.

I knew that the issue had been barred from general distribution in Japan because of this article. Only a few days before the wife of a missionary in Tokyo had said to me with some annoyance, "So you're the man who kept me from getting my *Reader's Digest.*"

I sensed trouble. The tea was good and the captain was very polite. Still I could not forget the fate of James Cox, tortured so severely that he jumped out of an upper window of the Tokyo gendarmerie to his death. But apparently this was to be just a friendly tête-à-tête.

"You like Japanese tea?"
"Very much."
"You like Hayama village?"
"Very much."
"Why did you take a house near the palace?"
"Because I found one vacant there."
"You did not take it because it was near the palace?"
"No. I took it because it was near the beach."

The conversation seemed to reach a dead end. The captain offered me a cigarette, then:

"You wrote this article?"

"Yes."

He scanned a paper covered with Japanese characters, evidently a translation of the article.

"It is about your trip through the *Nanyo* [Mandated Islands]. You say something about fortifications."

I was getting a little warm. "That's true."

"Do you think it was courteous of you to speak in such a way when you are allowed to live near the *Tenno?*"

"I don't know what that has to do with it."

Another dead end. The captain walked to the window, looked across into the palace grounds, then returned to his desk.

"Perhaps you do not understand our *Tenno.*" There was a note of appeal in his voice. I was beginning to like this fellow. He was evidently not one of the strong-arm squad. He just wanted to convert me. "Have you read the constitution?"

"Not very carefully."

He smiled. "We have to study it in police school. I wish you would read it—carefully. It was written by Prince Ito. A very great man, Prince Ito. He saw your mistakes."

"My mistakes?"

"The mistakes of your country and *Igirisu* [England]. You put the people first. We put the *Tenno* first. Will you read the constitution?"

I promised that I would.

And I did. The captain was right—it helped me to understand the emperor and the Japanese.

Ito's constitution specified that "the emperor has the supreme command of the army and navy." That was a new thing. In the past the court had been strictly civilian. The provision sounded harmless enough. The president of the United States heads the armed forces. But the Japanese used the idea to sidetrack the government entirely.

This was how it worked.

Since the emperor was commander-in-chief, it was taken for granted that the chief of the general staff might go directly to him for authority. He did not need to trouble himself with the Diet or cabinet or premier. He was a military man and went to his military superior.

The chief of the general staff became thereby the most powerful man in Japan. His power was of course controlled by the armed forces, but by them alone. With the emperor in his pocket, he was able to dictate not merely military matters, but political, social, economic, and foreign affairs. Through him the armed forces became in effect a political party, directing the entire life of Japan.

The ace in the hole was the emperor. His seal, always available to the general staff, decided any issue. Time and again the militarists, by using the emperor, defied premier, cabinet, and Diet.

The government proposed in 1918 to evacuate Siberia; but at the very time when the premier was making the promise, the general staff, unknown to the premier, was rushing more troops to Siberia.

That too was made regular by Ito's constitution. Ito says of it:

> The exercise of warfare in the field . . . as the exigency of circumstances may require, may be entrusted to the commanding officer of the place, who is allowed to take actual steps his discretion dictates, and then to report to the government. This is to be regarded as a delegation of sovereign power of the emperor to a general in command of any army in order to meet the stress of emergencies.

Act first; ask permission later. The attack on Manchuria was made at 10 P.M., September 18, 1931. News of it did not reach Tokyo until 2 A.M. In the cabinet meeting that morning Foreign Minister Shidehara objected to action in Manchuria and demanded that it be checked. The cabinet supported him. But, in the conference of army chiefs held that afternoon, it was declared that the army need not consult the cabinet regarding war measures and that these must be left to the judgment of commanding officers in the field.

The same sort of thing happened when Japan attacked China on the night of July 7, 1937, at the Marco Polo Bridge. The Japanese people and the government did not learn until the next morning that they were in for trouble with China —trouble that lasted many years.

In every case the emperor was effectively used to quiet public protest. His signed approval of steps already taken with or without his knowledge made the action right—and constitutional! This use of the emperor was the abuse of the public. But the public was not aware that it was being abused.

How it could be so fatally deluded is hard to understand until we look at the amazing scheme of miseducation that had warped the minds of a normally sensible and kindly people.

Every citizen from childhood up was inculcated with the doctrine of complete obedience to the will of the emperor.

•

"How do you do it?" I asked Ogawa, teacher of history and morals in our village school. "How do you teach children to worship the emperor?"

Ogawa sucked in his breath and raised his eyes to the ceiling. That was his way whenever the discussion turned to matters sublime.

"Perhaps," he said, "you will come to the school on portrait-unveiling day? Then you will see for yourself."

The school was a large low structure standing a half mile from Hayama village on the road to Zushi, the broad, paved royal road used by imperial processions.

A curious little building stood alone between the school

and the street. It was about ten feet square, beautifully designed, and built of fine stone. It had no windows, but only a very solid-looking door. It reminded one of a vault or mausoleum.

The sole inhabitants of this building were two pictures and a scroll. The pictures were photographs of the emperor and empress.

On the morning of my visit the portraits had already been removed, with ceremony, to the school auditorium.

Ogawa slipped me into a back seat. The auditorium was full of children. Although the meeting had not yet been called to order, there was an air of paralysis in the room. I thought of an American school auditorium with its whispering, rustling, and smothered laughter. Here two hundred children scarcely breathed.

Their eyes were fixed upon a cabinet on the stage. It reminded one of a church altar. The doors of the cabinet stood open, but a curtain with heavily tasseled draw cords concealed the holy of holies. No one was on the stage.

Presently an army officer stepped to the front of the floor, but not up on the stage, and called the assembly to attention. Everyone stood. An army man, by the way, was assigned to each school. He was nominally subordinate to the principal, but actually "advised" both principal and faculty, and they did well to follow his advice.

He snapped an order in that raucous unintelligible way that is the pride and joy of the Japanese military man. Every student bowed. It was not a bow, but a right-angle cramp. All of the body above the hips lay strictly horizontal. From the rear nothing could be seen now but row upon row of uncomely buttocks. In courtesy, I emulated the pose but could not hold it long. Everyone else remained in this position for fifteen minutes. That alone should be sufficient to make any child remember the emperor.

Of course no one could any longer see the cabinet—unless he peeked. The one who did saw the principal, in a fine state of dither—for one false move would necessitate suicide—ascend the platform and approach the cabinet, stopping every few steps to bow profoundly.

Arriving at the cabinet, he grasped the draw cords and drew apart the curtain. He was already bowing again so deeply that he could not have seen what was revealed.

There now looked benignly out upon the bowed backs of the audience the be-mustached, small-chinned emperor and his pretty empress, dressed in Shinto ceremonial robes. The pictures were ordinary black-and-white photographs about a foot square, cheaply framed.

The army officer now read an imperial message in a hard, strained voice. After this, the principal drew shut the curtains. Then, bent double, he walked backward across the platform and down the steps, a feat requiring no little skill. It was easy to imagine him practicing it many a night after hours.

Back in the audience and still bent double he furtively wiped the perspiration from his face with a paper handkerchief.

At a signal, the students straightened, turned, and marched soberly out of the auditorium.

I was amazed to see that many eyes were wet with tears. One boy broke into uncontrollable sobbing and had to be taken in charge by a teacher. I must admit that even the cynical foreigner was moved.

•

"You see how we do it?" It was Ogawa.

"Yes," I said sadly, "I see how you do it."

Every school in the empire had copies of the imperial portraits. Some were very reluctant to receive them because of the responsibility involved. A fireproof and earthquake-proof resting place must be provided for them. They might be kept in a safe in the principal's office, but it was obviously better to keep them in a fireproof building all their own so that, if the school burned, they might escape injury. The stories told of principals committing suicide, when they failed to rescue the portraits from the flames, are not fiction.

A Tokyo primary school attended by seven thousand children burned. After the fire an American asked the Japanese principal whether all the children had escaped unhurt.

"You will rejoice to hear," said the principal, "that the emperor's picture was unharmed."

Whether any of the pupils were injured was of secondary importance.

Harakiri was the penalty not only if the portraits were burned, but if they were lost, torn, or even soiled. Of course no one would steal them for their intrinsic value. But the thief might blackmail the principal, exacting a large sum as his price for returning the pictures.

Bowing to the imperial pictures began in 1891, just two years after Ito's constitution had raised the mikado to an eminence unknown in two millenniums.

But the full possibilities of emperor-worship were not realized by Ito and his contemporaries. It remained for the army in 1936 to solemnize the cult and surround it with grave penalties.

The picture ceremony was religious worship. It could not even be compared to prayer in a Christian church. That was, for most in the congregation, merely one of the formalities of a church service. The veneration of the imperial pictures was more comparable to the superheated emotion of an evangelistic revival.

•

"Before you leave you must see our new *kito-jo*," said Ogawa, and took me out to a corner of the playground where a new shrine of sweet, fresh wood had just been erected. *Kito-jo* means "praying place."

"It is for worship of the sun goddess, ancestress of our emperor."

"How is it used?"

"Mainly by individuals. Anyone who is troubled may come here. He is usually helped. You have no idea how useful it is if any one of our pupils breaks the rules. He is sent out here. He comes back with a proper spirit."

The strangulation of the Japanese people by rules, rules, rules, was clinched by this device.

"And young men who enter the army are sent here to give thanks. Sometimes they are not as thankful as they should be." I knew that. Japanese boys sometimes resort to extraordinary measures to escape the draft. "But this puts them in the proper spirit."

"Putting people in the proper spirit seems to be the main function of your school."

"Oh, yes," he said, suspecting no irony, "that is most important."

This picture of Japan's educational system was verified by a Japanese who received his high school education in Japan and his college training in the United States. Kenneth Kurihara wrote in the *Far Eastern Survey:*

"The fundamental objective of elementary school education in Japan is inculcation of loyalty to the emperor and the empire. Spartan discipline and 'the national spirit' are the next important items on the agenda. Whatever else the school children learn in classrooms is secondary."

Thus knowledge was subordinated to propaganda.

Going back to Ogawa. "It is essential," he said, "to start the day right. Every morning we all assemble on this field and do the 'worshiping-at-a-distance.'"

"What is this 'worshiping-at-a-distance?'"

"We all face Tokyo if the emperor is there, Hayama if he is here, bow, and remain so for sixty seconds. During that same minute millions of other students all over the empire are doing the same thing. It is very inspiring. That is the 'worshiping-at-a-distance.'"

"What else do you do to inculcate the—proper spirit?"

"Well, there are my courses in history and morals. And, ah, yes, the reading of the Rescript. That will be done next Wednesday. Would you like to come?"

•

I had not supposed that anything could be more paralyzing than the portrait ceremony. But the rescript ceremony outdid it.

The Imperial Rescript on Education was as holy as the Lord's Prayer of the Christians. It required all subjects "to guard and maintain the prosperity of Our Imperial Throne coeval with heaven and earth."

"Coeval with heaven and earth" was explained as meaning that the imperial line goes back not merely to the first emperor, but to a time millions of aeons more remote when the heavens and earth were separated. "No other nation can make such a claim."

But the point of the dagger was in the apparently harmless rhetoric of the words, "The way here set forth is . . . infallible for all ages and true in all places."

This was exploited to the full by the army as a divine imperative that the imperial way be extended to all places, that is, to the entire world. Thus Japan's educational creed established, as the ultimate aim of all education, world conquest.

•

"We do not ordinarily admit foreigners to this ceremony," said Ogawa. "You will be very careful about your deportment."

I appreciated the distinction, and promised to be careful.

Ogawa was evidently not quite sure of me. "If anything incorrect should happen," he said, "the principal would have to kill himself. So would I." The statement was quite calm and matter-of-fact. He meant it.

Again I was given a back seat. Again the deathlike hush. But this time the platform was occupied. All the faculty, with the exception of the principal, were seated there. The cabinet had been replaced by a lectern.

At a signal everyone rose. There was a long wait—but no fidgeting, no whispering. Out of the stillness at last came the sound of slow footsteps in the corridor. Grave and measured, they came nearer. Finally they reached the door—and there stood, or rather bent, the principal, in frock coat, his white-gloved hands grasping a tray raised to the level of his bowed forehead. The tray was covered with a white cloth and on the cloth rested a sumptuous lacquer box.

Everyone bowed toward the box and then straightened.

The principal resumed his arduous progress toward the platform. Unable to look ahead, he stepped warily. The consequences if he should bump against the corner of a desk, or brush the tray against the wall, or slip on a dropped pencil, were too awful to contemplate. The perspiration came out on my own forehead. I have no doubt that everyone in the room was suffering for him—except possibly some rebels who had felt his wrath and were secretly glorying in his discomfiture.

Up the steps he felt his way, and to the lectern. There he deposited his precious burden. We all bowed again, and again straightened. His large white gloves moving like a magician's over the box, he removed the lid and drew out something wrapped in purple silk.

The audience bowed.

He drew off the purple silk and disclosed something wrapped in white silk.

Another bow.

Hesitatingly, as if he hardly dared penetrate the last mysteries, he took off the white silk.

He now held in his hand what appeared to be a parchment roll. It looked like a Hebrew scripture or a college diploma. But now we were bowing down again, and this time we stayed down.

He opened the scroll and began to read. This must be an agonizing experience since the mispronunciation of one word would mean at least dismissal and possibly more serious consequences. "I have known a school principal to commit suicide because, at a ceremonial reading of it, he misread one of the characters," testifies schoolteacher Phyllis Argall. Nor was the document easy to read, being written in archaic Japanese. After each such ceremony a detailed report went from the military officer in the school to military headquarters.

At the end of the reading we straightened, only to bow again as each wrapping was replaced on the document and it was put into the box. Then the tray was lifted to brow-level and the principal undertook the hazardous journey across the platform, down the steps, along the aisle, out the door, down the corridor, and outdoors to the sacred vault.

The audience sang the national anthem to the accompaniment of a small wheezy organ.

The rescript ceremony safely over, the army officer immediately cashed in on the emotion it had generated by making, in a strident voice, an impassioned appeal for all-out support of the emperor and the army. With Hitlerian fervor, he screamed louder and louder. But he was evidently making himself ridiculous to only one member of his audience. All others seemed to rise with him from pitch to pitch of excitement. At last he reached a shrieking climax with:

"What is your dearest wish?"

And in one shrill cry the children gave the required response:

"To die for the emperor! *Tenno heika banzai!*"

•

The meeting was over. The children were trembling and sniffling as they went out. The teachers, distributed among them, were watching them. I had noticed that before the officer began his harangue the teachers had come down to stand here and there in the assembly. When I had a chance, I asked Ogawa about this.

"Our children are intensely patriotic," he said proudly. "Sometimes it leads them to do rash things. A few months ago after a talk like this, one of our boys would have stabbed himself with his jackknife if a teacher had not stopped him."

"Do you think such hysteria is good for the children?"

But he did not understand and I despaired of making it clear. You can't explain paranoia to a paranoiac.

Once there was no competition between the rescript and Jesus Christ. Later, in the chapel of a Sendai mission school a stained-glass window had to be curtained because the Lord and his saints must not be allowed to look down upon the sacred writing of the emperor.

Formerly the rescript might be kept in the school safe with other papers. Now it should have, if not a separate building, at least a safe of its own.

And this safe is no ordinary one. Teacher Phyllis Argall describes the one in her school. The rescript, wrapped in silk, reposed behind a curtain screen, behind a wooden door, behind an iron door with combination lock, and all this was "shielded from public gaze by a wooden structure about six feet high, painted black, a white silk curtain covering the opening."

Such a compartment reminds one of the screened repository of the Koran in a Mohammedan mosque. Was that where the Japanese picked up the idea?

Certainly every effort was made to copy from existing religions and go them one better.

The mission schools are forced to knuckle down to the

emperor or go out of business. Inspectors visited the schools and asked such questions as these:

"Which is the more worthy of reverence, Christ or the emperor?"

"Which is the more important, the Imperial Rescript on Education or the Christian Bible?"

In 1940 the Bible was banned in the schoolroom because its doctrines were said to be "detrimental to the moral education of the Japanese."

Children of mission schools, as of all other schools, were required to make regular expeditions to Shinto shrines and bow to the imperial ancestors.

The mission schools were given the choice of abandoning their principles or closing. Most of them closed, long before Pearl Harbor compelled them to do so.

If the emperor myth had been expounded only in assembly it would have been bad enough. But it was a daily theme in every classroom. Ogawa explained to me how it was worked into courses on reading, writing, and even arithmetic. As for his subjects, history and morals, the emperor stood at the center of them.

Ogawa showed me some of the textbooks used not only in his school but in the higher schools and the universities.

Here are a few random excerpts. First, from a nursery catechism:

"What do you love best in the world?"

"The emperor, of course."

"Better than father and mother?"

"Yes. He is the Lord of Heaven, the father of my father and mother."

"What will you give the emperor?"

"All my best toys, and my life when he wants it."

Children in the primary grades learned from the *Textbook of Ethics for Ordinary Primary Schools* that "Amaterasu sent down Ninigi-no-Mikoto and caused him to rule over this country. The great-grandchild of this Prince was the Emperor Jimmu. More than 2,570 years have elapsed since the accession to the throne of this Emperor. His successors throughout successive generations have ascended the throne."

Of course all these statements were false and the writers knew they were false.

Such fairy tales were fed not only to primary children. High school students found in their *Japanese History for Middle Schools* the detailed story of the gods from Izanagi to the first emperor *presented as history* and capped with the solemn conclusion:

"The foundations of our imperial rule, which shall not be moved forever, were in truth laid at this time."

And lest teachers take these fantasies lightly and fail to impress them upon their pupils, they were enjoined as follows in the official handbook, *Instructions to Teachers:*

"It is required that by means of these lessons the august, divine influence of Amaterasu be extolled, the descent of our Imperial Family made clear, and the source of our national organization, which is without peer in all the world, made known. The teacher should carefully explain this national constitution, which is peerless in all the world."

An "educator" shudderingly imagined what things would be like without an emperor:

"If there were no emperor, there would be no nation. Without him there would be no subjects, and our territory would cease to exist.... He is god of light; he is manifest god. His authority is unique. He is the absolute ruler determined by the Divine Ancestor."

Teachers were helped to expound the "eternal truths" of the *National History for Primary Schools* by an official commentary which told them:

"We subjects who live under such an illustrious Imperial family are for the most part descendants of the gods."

"Ogawa-san," I said, "why do they say 'for the most part'? Aren't all Japanese subjects descendants of the gods?"

Ogawa was slightly embarrassed.

"Well," he explained, "you see, there has to be a distinction between native Japanese and foreigners who have taken Japanese citizenship—I mean, Koreans, Chinese, and so forth."

"And Englishmen and Americans," I added. "So, to take an example, if my wife and I should become Japanese subjects, that would not make us children of Izanagi."

"I'm afraid not."

"But if we foreigners are not descendants of the gods too, then what are we?"

Ogawa took a long sip of tea before he answered.

"I believe you have your own theory of evolution," he suggested mildly.

I bowed to his logic and embraced my ape ancestors. After all, I preferred them to his gods.

•

How could Ogawa think otherwise about Nipponese preeminence when his *Handbook of Ethics* declared:

"There are many countries in the world but there is not one that, like our great Japanese Empire, has one Emperor of the same dynasty through the course of the ages. We who have been born in such an exalted country . . ."

Lest we think that bombast was entirely limited to the Japanese, let me quote from an old American textbook entitled *Universal History:* "The only historic race is the Caucasian, the others having done little worth recording."

Shades of India, China, and Japan!

No, racial conceit is not a monopoly of the Japanese, but they seem to have more than their fair share of it. What is more important is that it was skillfully used as a weapon of national policy.

Education was perverted from its proper objective. Learning no longer was of first importance. The military ideal of education was summed up in a War Office directive: "Education of a very intellectual type must be abandoned; stress must be laid upon moral training."

It is hardly necessary to say that such terms as "moral training," "morals," and "ethics" as used in the Japanese school system had not the meaning we give them but signified one thing only—the emperor cult.

The last traces of liberalism in the universities were stamped out. It was announced that the Tokyo and Kyoto Imperial Universities, "in harmony with the times," would establish courses on "History of Japanese Ideology" and "The History of the Japanese Spirit."

Japanese education had come a long way—down—since it was so bravely launched in the days of the Restoration. Now it was in the hands of a modern inquisition. "Inspectors" haunted the schools. Students informed on their professors. Waseda University students burned the books and wrecked the homes of Japanese professors considered too liberal. A missionary teacher, who was accused (falsely) of failing to remove his hat when the emperor passed, found it expedient to go back to England for a holiday. Professor Kume was dismissed from the Imperial University for questioning some of the dates of the early mikados, and another member of the same faculty lost his chair for suggesting that the ancestors of the mikados may have been Koreans. A radio lecturer was deluged with protests because he used certain respectful words in referring to the British monarch—words his hearers thought should be reserved for the Son of Heaven.

The master of the First Higher School in Tokyo, Mr. Ichimura, was dismissed because "he did not bow his head low enough to the picture of the emperor on the occasion of the latter's birthday."

Even a minister of education was not immune. Ozaki, when holding that post, remarked in a lecture, "But suppose, just for the sake of argument, Japan were made a republic thousands of years from now, although I never for a moment fancy it possible, then it would be likely that . . ."

One would think this a very carefully guarded hypothesis. Yet, for even supposing such a remote possibility, Ozaki was forced to resign and barely escaped prison.

Professor Minobe's textbooks describing the emperor as an organ of the state were accepted and taught in all universities for twelve years—then the army suddenly became conscious that this was most heretical doctrine, banned the books, and forced Minobe to resign from the House of Peers. And the army sought to counteract the evil doctrine with an official pamphlet making it clear that the emperor was not an organ of the state, but the state itself.

A lecturer who spoke of the early myths without due respect spent six months in jail.

Eighteen students who questioned a myth got three months' imprisonment. For disrespectful reference to the emperor himself the penalty would be death.

A school wanted to put on a performance of *Hamlet.* It was barred because it derogated royalty. Hamlet, you remember, was rude to the king.

Every school must preserve all examination questions and answers and turn them in to the police for inspection.

Professor-hounding rose to such a pitch that in 1938 a jingo newspaper listed practically all the professors of the law department of Tokyo Imperial as dangerous thinkers.

We think of literacy as a liberating force. "Literacy" and "democracy" seem to belong together. Yet, in Japan, one of the most literate nations on earth, literacy was used to enslave the people to false gods, and the school became a channel for ignorance and superstition.

Dominating every classroom, every teacher, every student, was the emperor hoax.

•

Why did the Japanese lose the war? No soldier in the world was more courageous. None more energetic. None more conscientious in the performance of duty.

And yet he failed. It was not merely that the equipment of his enemy was overpowering. In unnumbered instances where the equipment on both sides was about equal, the Japanese were defeated.

Even against the very poorly armed Chinese the Japanese failed.

I believe the explanation lay in "the Japanese spirit," *Nippon seishin*. Japanese leaders staked their hopes upon it. It was considered the great strength of Japan. Experience proved it Japan's fatal weakness.

"The Japanese spirit," said General Araki, "is the spirit of blind devotion to the emperor."

But there was just one drawback to blind devotion. *It was blind.*

Blind men do not make good soldiers. True, they are easily led. They are amenable to discipline. They obey their officers. Many an American officer has sometimes wished his men were as pliable as the Japanese. But it is the pliability of ignorance and dependence. If the officer is killed, the men are lost.

It is, for them, almost as if their emperor had been killed, for they have been taught, "The voice of your officer is the voice of your emperor."

Complete reliance upon the emperor was so thoroughly inculcated that the soldier's own initiative was numbed. To his mind there was only one right way. It was *Kodo*, "the emperor's way." The man who contrived a new way of doing a thing ran the risk that it might not be *Kodo*. In that case, he was guilty of the gravest sacrilege and disloyalty.

There were tremendous advantages in the emperor cult. By forcing all the people into subservience to one man, a remarkable unity was achieved. Unity is valuable, but not at the price of individuality.

The unity of Japan was accomplished by mass hypnotism. Free will was repressed, thoughts controlled, actions regulated, eyes fixed upon the Son of Heaven until the steady stare bemused the brain. Araki was past master of this sort of enchantment. A magnetic orator and a dealer in the most golden of generalities on the ancient glory of Japan and divinity of the emperor, he became the idol of the officers and his technique was passed down until it reached every recruit.

A hypnotist fixes your mind upon one thing to the exclusion of all else. Araki did that. The one object was the emperor-god. The result was that the Japanese soldier was like a horse wearing blinders. He looked straight ahead and went straight ahead—but he was unaware of anything on either side. A mental "flanking movement" would defeat him.

•

How peculiarly fixed the Japanese soldier's mind was upon the emperor appeared in conversations with prisoners. In *Yank*, an army weekly, Sergeant H. N. Oliphant recorded several such dialogues:
"Why were you fighting in the first place?"
"For the emperor."
"Are you fighting for anything else?"
"No."
A private was asked:
"Why did you fight and kill Americans?"
"Because of the emperor."
"Do you believe that the emperor is God?"
"Yes."
"Why do you think the emperor is God?"
The private replied that all Japanese knew that.
A pilot was questioned:
"Why did you do it [attack American ships]?"
"For the emperor."

"Why do you think the emperor is making Japan fight?"
"Japan is fighting for Eternal Peace."

•

"The Japanese spirit" as taught in the army was not quite the same as taught to children in the schools. There it took the form of intense love of country. In the army it became intense hatred of the outside world. The second was laid firmly upon the groundwork supplied by the first, hate upon love.

Hate is blinding. There have been times in history, even recent history, when a blind furious hate has won a battle. But in general the method belonged to the ancient days that Araki held so dear. The modern battle is pretty much a matter of cold planning and execution. The mathematically calculated attack accomplishes more than the *banzai* charge.

The most serious error of the Araki military schools was the death doctrine. It can be expressed nobly, as in the aphorism: "Duty is weightier than a mountain, while death is lighter than a feather."

It had enough of fineness in it to make it fool some ignorant boys who had some fineness in them. Life is a good deal to give up. Any boy knows that, but it easily leads him into the false notion that the obverse is also true: that by giving up life he is accomplishing a good deal. No matter how he gives it up. The mere act of getting rid of it is a contribution to the war effort. Death is an end in itself.

On the day he entered the army he was taught: "Our highest hope is to die for the emperor." He was likely to hear it every day thereafter, though usually condensed to the first three words, "Our highest hope." They rang always in his brain. They became an obsession.

His family heard them too. Just after he was recruited a letter went from his commanding officer to his relatives. It asked them to be careful not to block his road to an honorable death.

"We want to be able to teach him in such a way that he may be able to realize the highest hope of a member of our race."

Many a recruit's wife killed her children and herself so that the soldier would have no reluctance to die. Many soldiers conducted their own public funerals before leaving for the front. There is quite a bit of the actor in Japanese character. No doubt the soldier got a melancholy pleasure out of burying himself.

•

From the barracks near our home in Hayama village frequently came this cheerful chant:

"Whether I float as a corpse under the waters or sink beneath the grasses of the mountainside, I will willingly die for the emperor."

Suicide squads were trained in schools of *Keshitai*, Do and Die. The chief was in Hokkaido under the command of the rabid General Hashimoto. There were courses in the suicidal use of bombs, torpedoes, mines, and airplanes. The most spectacular manifestation of this training was in the *kamikaze*, divine-wind, or special-assault corps, made up of pilots who strapped themselves into the cockpit and crashed into enemy ships. These tactics were in a way effective. And yet, the non-Japanese viewpoint on this question would be that any man who had the nerve to do this would be more useful alive than dead.

To make the prospect of dying more attractive, dividends were attached to it.

According to an army manual, "To die for the sake of the emperor is to live forever."

It was a curious fact that in a *banzai* charge men went to death with life on their lips. *Banzai* means "long life." *Tenno heika banzai* means "His Majesty the Emperor, may he live forever."

But when the soldier shouted that he was thinking of himself as well as the emperor. For he had been carefully taught that by becoming a soldier he had become part of the "mystic coalition," the supernatural union of emperor and army. The soldier was the "four limbs" of the emperor. The Son of Heaven was always with him, and soldiers even claimed that they found hairs of the emperor's white horse in their pockets!

The emperor was in every man. And that meant that if the emperor lives forever, so will he.

Emperor-filled, he too is a god. He can do no harm. His every act is perfect. Said a Japanese radio commentator, "Since the Heavenly Emperor is a God, the Japanese army under His Majesty also is just and righteous."

And the same spokesman went on to assure his listeners that when the Nipponese took Manila, the Filipinos cried, "The angels have come; the angels that we have awaited so long have descended."

Neither the Japanese radio listener nor the Japanese soldier would see anything funny about this. For it was understood that when a man joined the army he sprouted wings.

"No matter how much of a wrongdoer," declared a Japanese newspaper, "no matter how evil a Japanese subject may have been, when once he has taken his stand on the field of battle, all his past sins are entirely atoned for and they become as nothing. The wars of Japan are carried on in the name of the Emperor and therefore they are holy wars. All the soldiers who participate in these holy wars are representatives of the Emperor. . . . Those who, with the words *Tenno heika banzai* on their lips, have consummated tragic death in battle, whether they are good or whether they are bad, are sanctified."

That is the payoff. Every private was promoted at death,

promoted at one leap to the emperor level.

The emperor himself worshiped him! What a kick the abused, slapped, pushed-around Private Suzuki got out of that idea. Yes, his soul would be enshrined in the Yasukuni Shrine on Kudan Hill in Tokyo and thither the emperor would repair to bow in worship before the pantheon of soldier gods, including himself.

For the tablets which stood row on row in Yasukuni did not represent dead men. They represented living gods. Twice a year, during a week-long ceremony, the names of war dead were placed in an ark and this was carried in torchlit procession to the music of flutes up the long approach to the great temple and set down before the altar. Then in most impressive ceremony the dead were deified. It was a great moment for Suzuki.

That was the beginning rather than the end for Suzuki. He was thereafter one of the great guardians of Japan. Petitions would be addressed to him.

The defenders of Attu who died to a man became deified spirits which, according to a Tokyo newspaper, tampered with American radio instruments, calmed the seas so that the Japanese could escape from Kiska, appeared spectrally in the fog waving Rising Sun flags and shouting *Banzai.* And even after the last Japanese was gone from Kiska—this still according to Tokyo—the Americans had to fight for three weeks against the spirit army.

Also it was claimed that in the South Pacific warrior spirits "tangled with the enemy, causing many of them mental derangements and others to kill themselves as a result of nervous breakdown and morbid fear."

And what made the fight so bitter on Okinawa? "Ghostly troops from martyred Saipan could be plainly seen approaching through the morning sky to help us defend sacred Japanese soil. Our officers and men worshiped them in humble gratitude."

Thus the position of a disembodied spirit is one of power and importance. All this, if you really believe it, adds up to a good reason for throwing away your life.

•

The result was that many impressionable soldiers became actually *eager* to die. They were vexed if they stayed alive too long. This abnormal psychology applied by no means to all soldiers, but to a surprising number, as any Yank who saw them die rather than surrender would testify. They looked for an excuse to finish themselves off. As one of them is made to say in a novel by Captain Tadayoshi Sakura:

"I had been fully resolved to die on Takushan, but still I was left behind by a great many of my friends. Surely this time in this general assault I must have the honor and distinction of offering my little self to our beloved country. With this idea, this desire, this determination, I started for the battle."

Note that the hero's chief desire is to die, not to kill the enemy. Of course it is preferable to spend one's life to good advantage, to sell it dearly. That is why the militarists encouraged the death doctrine. But the propaganda failed at this point. Many death-seekers overlooked the importance of taking along with them as many of the enemy as possible. The heavenly rewards were the same no matter how they died. The main thing was to die.

Many Japanese blew themselves up with grenades when they saw the enemy approaching. They could have thrown the grenades at their opponents. Scores of Japanese prisoners tried to kill themselves. They could instead have tried to kill their captors, or they could have tried to escape and fight again.

Suicide charges took the place of scientifically plotted maneuvers. In such attacks the men sometimes actually wore white robes of the sort used in Shinto funerals. To come out of such a charge, dressed in the death robe and still alive, would be unthinkable. They made every effort to die without too much regard for the amount of damage they were able to inflict upon the enemy.

This death doctrine proved costly and disastrous to the Japanese army. It often meant the loss of ten or twenty men to the Allied one.

It was too easy a way out. It takes no talent to die. In any battle the difficult thing is to stay alive, not to get killed. Sneaking out the death door is close to moral cowardice. But, more important from the army's standpoint, it was uneconomic.

Thanks largely to Araki the Japanese army was highly emotional. The Japanese soldier could weep tears for the emperor more easily than he could add up a column of figures. Even the officers were "turned on" with *Nippon seishin* to the neglect of basic knowledge. In the Japanese counterpart of West Point there were no courses in economics, government, and international law, but endless disquisitions upon the sacred mission of Nippon. It was more of a theological school than a military academy. Viscount Saito admitted to Ambassador Grew: "The army knows very little about the world."

The death-defying valor of the Japanese forces made the war last four years—but when the cream of Japanese manhood had been skimmed off, defeat was inevitable. Two million lost their lives—or gave them—and millions more were crippled by war injuries, by maladies picked up in the barbaric isles of the South Pacific, by food shortages in the wake of bombardment of Japanese cities, towns, and villages.

15

"MOVE OVER, GOD, IT'S MAC"

But a Supreme Being, in the person of General Douglas MacArthur, undertook to set all right.

We were once more in Japan, this time to study the achievements of the American Occupation. They had already been eloquently described by MacArthur, acting as Supreme Commander for the Allied Powers in Japan:

> The greatest reformation of a people ever attempted.
>
> One of the great revolutions of all time.
>
> Probably the greatest the world has ever known.
>
> A spiritual revolution ensued almost overnight, tore asunder a theory and practice of life built upon two thousand years of history and tradition and legend. . . . This revolution of the spirit among the Japanese people represents no thin veneer to serve the purposes of the present. It represents an unparalleled convulsion in the social history of the world.

The military purpose, which is to ensure that Japan will follow the ways of peace and never again be a menace, has been, I think, accomplished.

[The Japanese] could not rearm themselves for war within one hundred years.

Japan should be the Switzerland of the Far East.

The new Japanese constitution is the most democratic in the world.

History may finally point to the Japanese constitution as the Magna Charta of free Asia.

The Emperor's function is about that of the Stars and Stripes in the United States, or the Union Jack in England.

[Land reform in Japan] is the most successful experiment of its kind in history.

If we moved out tomorrow and any group tried to restore the old conditions they would be hanged to the lampposts.

I believe sincerely and absolutely that it [democracy] is here to stay.

The Japanese have got the spirit of the Sermon on the Mount.

The sweeping nature of the Supreme Commander's statements was characteristic. A common expression of those who worked under him was: "Move over, God, it's Mac." While a shade suspicious of this grandiloquence, we hoped to be convinced that MacArthur's interpretation was accurate. What normal person would not welcome a spiritual revolution anywhere in this corroded world? And what greater satisfaction could an Occidental have than to know that his way of life, freely taught to a defeated enemy, had profoundly moved and improved existence on the darker side of the world?

America, Britain, and Europe were pretty well convinced that the Occupation was doing a great job. Anyone not personally on the Japanese scene was bound to be persuaded by the reports in the press and on radio that a transformation was taking place in Japan.

Western readers and listeners must depend for their news of Japan upon foreign correspondents in that country. During the period of the Occupation the newsmen in Japan were under strict control of the American military.

Newsmen entered Japan only under a special military permit. Once in, they remained only on sufferance. They were subject to prompt dismissal if they became "poor security risks"—that is, if they unfavorably represented the works of the Occupation or dared to criticize the Supreme Commander or his aides. If having fallen from grace they left the country, they found it difficult or impossible to return.

The newsman caught in this predicament was quite likely to lose his assignment to a man more adept in treading thin ice. Any newspaper that refused to compromise faced the loss of its representation in Japan.

By such methods of intolerance and intimidation, both the individual correspondents and the newspapers behind them were whipped into line.

Only a few powerful journals resisted the pressure. *Time*, which had for years endured the ban of Argentina's Perón rather than lick the boots of that dictator, was equally frank about SCAP (Supreme Commander for the Allied Powers). It gave generous space to achievements of the Occupation but did not mince words in discussing its faults. It found a chief fault to be the suppression of news:

> U.S. correspondents who have written dispatches critical of the commander or of Occupation policies have soon learned what it is like to be unpopular. Some got the deep-freeze from MacArthur's staff. Others who left Tokyo on visits, or assignments in the Far East, had to wait weeks and slice through

endless snarls of red tape before they were allowed to return to Japan.

The distinguished military analyst, Hanson W. Baldwin, spoke frankly in *The New York Times.* Concerning the Occupation he commented, "What it needs most, but can tolerate least, is criticism."

The Christian Science Monitor dared the thunderbolts with statements such as the following:

> Many of the repressive or regulatory techniques favored by the Japanese have been applied at Occupation headquarters in the treatment of American and other foreign correspondents . . . While practising censorship, Occupation spokesmen blandly talk of "freedom of the press" and point out that it is guaranteed in the new constitution—which most Japanese know was written primarily by Americans.

In another article the *Monitor* reported that "the Japanese complain that the MacArthur supervision of newspapers, books, radio and movies is worse than Tojo's."

"Every American newsman and magazine writer in Japan," declared *Look,* "knows the consequences if he sends to this country facts that displease General MacArthur or the all-powerful members of the high command. He will find all official avenues closed tight against him. Besides that, he will very shortly be forced by some means to leave the Far East, with no possibility of returning." General MacArthur, said the magazine, "has misled the American people."

Frank Hawley, a noted classic scholar and correspondent for the London *Times,* was expelled from Japan in June, 1950. The memorandum of expulsion signed by General MacArthur declared that Hawley was no longer welcome in Japan and ordered his immediate departure. Hawley had incurred official wrath by his statement that SCAP's ban on public demonstrations was a violation of the new American-written

Japanese constitution which declares, "Freedom of assembly and association, as well as speech, press and all other forms of expression are guaranteed."

The correspondent for *Newsweek*, charged by SCAP with associating "with the wrong kind of Japanese," was barred from Japan for almost a year.

Tiltman of the London *Daily Herald*, Bill Costello of CBS, Jessup of McGraw-Hill, had difficulties.

Dozens of such incidents led to an open revolt of the Tokyo press corps. The correspondents drew up a manifesto charging that men who merely reported facts were subjected to persecution by SCAP. They requested that the American Society of Newspaper Editors investigate "intimidation, coercion, and censorship in Japan."

When a committee of correspondents complained to SCAP's press relations officer he warned them: "Every time [you] have pressed for a clarification of policy, the policy has grown tighter."

No wonder Senator Knowland, after a personal investigation of the situation, charged that MacArthur was setting up an "iron curtain" to ward off all criticism of the Occupation.

"Ever since the surrender," wrote *Fortune*, "Americans have had the comfortable illusion that while the rest of the world was in a fearful mess, this Occupation was just about an unqualified success. Yet on the briefest investigation this belief turns out to be moonshine, and each deeper probe merely confirms and darkens the bad news."

But these were voices crying in the wilderness. Ninety-nine percent of the American press was uncritical of the Occupation or, like the Hearst papers, gave it incessant and overwhelming praise. Hundreds of press handouts from SCAP headquarters were printed verbatim. General MacArthur's personal reports and directives got Page One every time, and their ringing eloquence convinced millions that we were truly accomplishing in Japan "the greatest reformation of a people ever attempted."

Even more amazing than this mesmerism of the outside world was the fact that the Japanese themselves did not know what was going on in Japan.

They read and rejoiced in MacArthur's announcement, made at the beginning of the Occupation, that a "free, uncontrolled and unfettered press" was being established in Japan. On the basis of this solemn declaration they had a right to believe that what they now read in their papers or heard over the radio was the truth.

Japanese editors who took seriously the promise of an "unfettered press" were soon disillusioned. They ran into snags of censorship at every turn. No slightest criticism of the Occupation or of any of its personnel was allowed. Criticism of the new constitution was banned. It was a constitution for the Japanese and it might have been supposed that the Japanese had a right to discuss it—but no. Nor was any comment other than favorable permitted of the Land Reform Bill. Any suggestion that the industrial trusts had not been fully abolished was blue-penciled by the censors.

No mention must be made of past offenses of statesmen approved by SCAP for a place in the new government. The fact that the militarists were still active underground was not to be printed. It might disturb the people's faith that Japan was now and forevermore a democracy. The golden age of labor had supposedly been ushered in by SCAP, and news of labor unrest, strikes, wage demands, were suppressed.

Nothing but glowing words might be written about the United States. Lord Bryce's *Modern Democracy* was edited to retain his praise of America but omit his criticism of American politics. Parts of Leo Tolstoy's *War and Peace* were deleted. Even a volume of Hans Christian Andersen's *Fairy Tales* was banned because of its description of a naval fight.

Papers were encouraged to extol democracy and condemn the sort of emperor-worship and hero-worship that had proved so injurious to Japan in the past. The ban on hero-worship was subject to one exception. When the people chose to make General MacArthur their hero, no objection was raised. Reading nothing but praise of the general, and having no way of knowing that the chorus of approval was not spontaneous, the people gave themselves up to an adulation that became fanatical.

This worried the wise editor of a great Japanese paper. Knowing that hero-worship and democracy were not compatible, he assumed that SCAP would approve his effort to check it. He wrote:

> Japan used to abound in ardent Hitler worshippers.... When the Japanese-American war started they switched their worship to General Tojo, and, after the surrender, to General MacArthur. Japanese teachers have traditionally been bent on inspiring the children with this habit of blind worship for the ruler ... a tendency constituting the worst enemy of democracy....
>
> The proper way for the Japanese to repay General MacArthur's sincere efforts to democratize this country and his wise administration is not to worship him, but to rid themselves of subservience and strive, with high self-esteem, to assume the actual authority of government by themselves. Only then will the Supreme Commander be assured that the object of the Occupation has been achieved.

It might be supposed that SCAP's reaction to this editorial would be a profound "Amen." Instead, when one of the first copies of the paper reached headquarters, the presses were ordered stopped and the copies already printed were pulled from the delivery trucks and destroyed. General Willoughby, speaking for SCAP, said, "The article is in bad taste." Some felt that the bad taste lay not in the article but in the suppression of it.

There was a similar personal reaction when the Japanese

news service *Kyodo* received dispatches from the United States reporting the formation and activities of anti-MacArthur-for-President clubs at the University of California, Harvard, and University of Wisconsin. SCAP killed this news as "of controversial conjecture" and unsuitable for publication in Japan. A Japanese businessman visiting the United States was astounded to find that, contrary to the impression in Japan, the entire American public was not solidly back of MacArthur for President.

The maze of taboos became so bewildering that Japanese editors mustered up the courage to protest. They were delighted when SCAP in 1948 announced the end of censorship —but bewildered anew when censorship before publication was replaced with censorship after publication.

Now the editors were left to themselves to figure out what was fit to print. If they guessed wrong, they were likely to have their publications suspended. An editor was sent to prison for two years for making such a mistake. Editors felt it necessary to step more cautiously than ever before. The new system, instead of liberating the press, completed its suffocation.

•

All of this, we are willing to suppose, was motivated by the highest purposes on the part of the Supreme Commander. He sincerely desired to transform Japan into a democracy and believed that the way to do it was through thought control. The Japanese were to have only the highest thoughts, see nothing of the seamy side of life or of the Occupation.

In a way, it worked. The unremitting flood of good news kept the people quiet, made them acquiescent and obedient. This pliancy was interpreted by MacArthur to be the birth of a new spirit in Japan.

It was not a new spirit, but a rebirth of the age-old spirit of subservience to dictatorship. Seen from a distance as MacArthur saw it—for he never permitted himself to mingle with the people—it looked like democracy.

But the army, necessarily autocratic from top to bottom, is hardly the best teacher of democracy. People cannot be pushed or herded into democracy. Democracy is not achieved by putting blinders on citizens so that they can see neither to the right nor to the left.

At first the word "democracy" had a tremendous vogue in Japan. No one knew what it meant; everyone had his own idea.

A schoolteacher thought it meant equality and that meant that boys and girls in the sixth grade should be examined together by the instructor in hygiene.

"But they will be stripped naked," the instructor objected.

"We have been living in a world of false modesty," said the teacher. "This is the age of the equality of the sexes."

The children were stripped and examined. Infuriated fathers and mothers called a meeting of the PTA and the teacher was dismissed. He believed he was a martyr to democracy.

A girl joined a group to study freedom and democracy. She came upon Patrick Henry's inspiring line, "Give me liberty or give me death!" Greatly moved, she wrote a will declaring her purpose to die "so that democracy might live," then drowned herself in Tokyo Bay.

To many young people, democracy meant freedom to do anything they pleased regardless of others and regardless of consequences.

Every newspaper, every magazine, every radio station extolled the beauties of democracy, but carefully ignored its faults and difficulties. The picture of it was too highly colored, too devoid of tone and shadow. People became hysterical about it.

But one extreme invites the other. The curve of devotion to democracy was up during 1945 and 1946, fairly level during 1947, then descended ever more steeply and plunged abruptly after the end of the Occupation in 1952.

In the beginning, every political party sought to be known as democratic. The Socialists renamed themselves the Social Democrats. The middle-of-the-road party called itself the Democrats. The rightists became the Democratic Liberals. The Communists did not change their name but they also claimed to be the chief champions of democracy.

By 1952 the democratic label was no longer an asset. The Social Democrats were once more Socialists. The Democrats now called themselves the Progressives. The Democratic Liberals were now just Liberals.

In 1946 books on democratic institutions were in great demand. For the right to translate and publish such books, Japanese publishers paid royalties 50 percent higher than the average. By 1949 the reaction had set in and, as reported in *The New York Times*, "a noted professor, an established author on such subjects, reported that his publisher had told him the sale of anything favorable to the United States was doubtful, but if he would venture some criticism of democracy or say a few kind words for the Communists, public acceptance was certain."

This did not mean that democracy was done in Japan. Far from it. It meant that the Japanese had found it was not something that could be thrown on like a coat. It must grow from the inside. It had been growing in Japan, with occasional setbacks, for the past hundred years. Now it was retarded rather than advanced by the effort to impose it by force.

The Japanese were at first carried away by MacArthur's manifest idealism, by the contagion of his overoptimism, and the surprising goodwill of the occupying forces. Later they came back to earth. They began counting their gains and losses.

Certainly their form of government was more subject to popular control than it had been. Japan owed a lasting debt to the able General Courtney Whitney and brilliant Frank Rizzo, chiefs of the Government Section of SCAP, who were instrumental in the extension of the suffrage, the writing of a new constitution, and the elevation of the Diet to a position at least theoretically superior to that of the cabinet, premier, or emperor.

But Japanese governing classes never had much faith in the wisdom of the common people. To them, government by the people seemed dangerously close to mob rule. Nor did the people have much confidence in themselves. In every case, the "free elections" returned ultraconservative leaders. There was no sign of the emergence of a people's party.

Half of the members of the postwar cabinet were men who were purged for wartime activities, now depurged and restored to favor. The premier, Shigeru Yoshida, acted without consulting the Diet or waiting for its decisions. He did not defer even to his own party. He summarily hired and fired state ministers.

The Occupation believed in states' rights. The states or *ken* and the cities were given a large measure of self-government.

This self-government idea was carried too far. It might be proper for Texas or New York to conduct most of its own affairs without dictation from Washington. But why the government of a nation smaller than California should be distributed among units no larger than California's counties was not clear. Public dissatisfaction with this system was turned to advantage by the premier, who concentrated power in his own hands rather than in the Diet where it belonged.

Another reform that nullified itself by being carried too far was the decentralization of the police force. Formerly all police were controlled from Tokyo and were a dangerous tool in the hands of the military.

To correct this situation MacArthur ordered the national police abolished, leaving every town and village to establish its own police force. The result was complete inability to handle any national crisis such as a strike or a Communist riot. Also the expense of maintenance of separate forces was too great and in 1952 there was a return to the prewar police system.

The national government used to reach into every village through the *tonari-gumi*, neighborhood association. This was an association of villagers for mutual help, but because it was used to kill self-government in the village and enforce the will of Tokyo, it was abolished by the Occupation. However, it seems that nothing adequate was put in its place, for when a public opinion poll was taken in 1951 it was found that 65 percent of the villagers questioned favored the lifting of the ban upon the neighborhood association, while only 18 percent were opposed. These groups were therefore revived.

With the passing of the Occupation, all its reforms were critically studied. An Ordinance Review Committee appointed by the Yoshida cabinet examined, with an eye to repeal or amendment, laws originally adopted in accordance with SCAP directives. Many were abolished and others modified.

•

"It's all going back," a missionary told me sorrowfully. "Back to the old ways of nationalism and emperor-worship." Commented the London *Times*, "The forces of old Japan are again gathering." While the progressive *Nippon Times* sadly remarked, "Signs of Japan returning to where she was before the Occupation began and the eventual undoing of many of the postwar reforms are very much in evidence these days."

The people were indifferent. Reforms which they did not fight to gain they would not fight to hold. The postwar Japanese government was not, as promised in the Potsdam Proclamation, "established in accordance with the freely expressed will of the Japanese people." The people merely submitted to reforms imposed by alien authority.

I asked the famous Tokyo teacher and editor Florence Wells, "Will the changes stick?" Her reply was significant: "Those that return Japan to what she was will stick."

Japan in the twenties had been moving steadily toward democracy. The trend was reversed by the conquest of Manchuria beginning in 1931 and the ensuing wars in China and the Pacific. Insofar as the Occupation helped to restore Japan to the pattern of preaggression days, the changes would stick. But American ways of life imposed upon Japan by Washington could no more be expected to endure than would Japanese ways dictated to citizens of the United States by Tokyo.

A healthy appreciation of this fundamental truth was shown by General Ridgway when he inherited MacArthur's job in Japan. A memorandum from GHQ to all members of the Occupation laid down a radically new policy:

> Many of the social customs and manners that you observe in Japan today were already old a thousand years before Columbus discovered America. So don't come barging into Japan with any idea of revolutionizing their customs, or of remolding their daily lives into a carbon copy of your own. In the first place, it can't be done. In the second place, Japanese customs and social mores are adapted to the kind of life the Japanese must live.

Here at last was sound common sense. That this policy was to guide American conduct not merely in Japan, but the world over, was promised in the fourth of the nine principles stated by President Eisenhower in his inaugural address in January, 1953:

"Honoring the identity and heritage of each nation of the world, we shall never use our strength to try to impress upon another people our own cherished political and economic institutions."

When democracy develops in Japan we may be sure it will not be the democracy of Britain and America. It may be inferior to our brand in some ways, better in others. It will take account of Japanese traditions two thousand years old. It will be based upon cooperation rather than competition. The Japanese do not like our individualism. They regard it as selfish and antisocial. They cannot understand the principle of "every man for himself." A Japanese will never act alone if he can help it. He prefers group action. He calls in his friends, his neighbors, even his rivals, to advise him and work with him.

Who shall say that this philosophy is a poorer basis for democracy than the principle of devil take the hindmost?

Besides objecting to an egocentric society on moral grounds, the Japanese considered it too expensive. It might be feasible in a land of great natural resources such as the United States for each man to go his own way, but Japan, they believed, was too poor to afford it.

In western society great stress is laid upon happiness. The Japanese regard the pursuit of happiness as unworthy. They consider it even immoral, and as a goal of life it is not likely to enter into the Japanese conception of democracy. They place the emphasis on duty. If happiness comes to them in the performance of their duty, they accept it gladly. But it is a byproduct, not an end in itself.

Of paramount importance in the Japanese democracy will be *on*. Perhaps the closest English equivalent of the word is obligation. A Japanese feels acutely any debt of gratitude he owes to anyone who has helped him and will not rest until it is paid off. Even then he is not satisfied until he has placed his former benefactor in his own debt.

He finds his greatest enjoyment in giving. He does not understand our conception of sacrifice, for he has no feeling of sacrifice when he gives. Nor does his religion promise him any reward or merit for giving. He does not do unto others in order that they shall do the same or a little better unto him. His democracy, when it comes, will be a democracy of mutual helpfulness.

It will be slow in coming, for feudal traditions are still

strong. Probably no people change so quickly on the surface and so slowly beneath as the Japanese. They adopt the new without rejecting the old. Isolated from the continent, with a remarkably homogeneous people who all think alike, Japan is deeply conscious of its own history. Its religions, language, drama, arts, have persisted through centuries.

Equally persistent has been the subjection to autocratic control—in early days to that of the emperor; later, to that of the shogun speaking for the emperor; in war times, to that of the militarists manipulating the emperor. For two thousand years the Japanese subject did not dare call his soul his own. It belonged to his emperor, or to anyone strong enough to usurp the power of the emperor. The inbred docility of the Japanese made them like rubber in the hands of the Occupation.

Like rubber, not clay. Clay can be molded and will hold its form. Rubber can be pressed into shape but will spring back when the pressure is removed.

16

DESPERATION BUT NOT DESPAIR

War's end had left Japan in a desperate situation which continued until well after the Occupation. But there was never a lack of courage.

Two million of her finest had been killed and six million disabled. Thanks to bombing raids, ten million Japanese were homeless. Tokyo alone had lost two-thirds of its housing.

People who had fled from the cities to escape American air raids now returned—and found no place to live. Thousands camped outdoors among ruins of their homes destroyed by bombs and fire. Others erected tin shacks, or slept in railway stations, or under bridges. Others found refuge in broken sewers, or burrowed underground.

Food consumption dropped from 2,200 calories per capita before the war to 1,300 after. The average in America was three thousand.

Wrecked roads prevented shipments from the country. The country itself had little to provide since much of its manpower had been destroyed.

Motorized fishing boats could not put out for lack of fuel. Sailboats dared not, since they must cross heavily mined bays to reach the open sea. The great Inland Sea, favorite fishing area, was a jungle of floating mines dropped by American airmen. B-29s had strewn a total of 10,703 sensitive mines in the waters of Japan. They were made to explode of their own accord in response to magnetism, sound waves, or sudden change of aquatic pressure as ships approached them. They comprised 4,472 magnetic mines, 3,027 acoustic mines, and 3,204 aquatic pressure mines. Of these, 7,182 mines were laid in the Inland Sea. The acoustic and aquatic pressure mines died after six years but twelve hundred of the magnetic mines remained active for another decade.

Industrial production was a poverty-stricken 10 percent of prewar levels.

Shops that had not been destroyed were closed for lack of goods. One enterprise that did thrive and thrive mightily was the black market. Prices were prohibitive, skyrocketing at the rate of 120 percent in a year. Inflation meant starvation for many.

Japan could no longer depend for food upon the lands overseas that she had controlled at the beginning of the war: Manchuria, Korea, North China, Indochina, Thailand, Indonesia, Okinawa, Formosa, the myriad islands of Micronesia. All gone. To add to her troubles, the several million Japanese who had lived in these far-flung outposts now flooded home, arriving hungry and destitute. And in an already overcrowded country, soldiers returning to their wives pushed up the population from 72 million in 1945 to 80 million only three years later.

Japan had to import to live. In 1948 her imports were double her exports. Food, fertilizer, and other goods from the United States cost a million dollars a day, in spite of eight hundred thousand tons of food contributed free by America.

From her meager resources Japan must rush help to the

mangled and starving survivors of Hiroshima and Nagasaki, struck by atomic bombs.

•

We visited what was left of Hiroshima. It had been one of the seven largest cities of Japan.

The mayor took us to the roof of the City Hall where we looked down upon the city as upon a map. Not far away was the Atomic Bomb Dome, the gutted Industrial Museum which is being preserved in its ruined form as a memento of the blast.

The bolt from the blue at a quarter after eight in the morning of August 6, 1945, destroyed seventy thousand houses and wiped out 60 percent of the city at one stroke.

The Japanese government estimated the number of killed at seventy thousand and the injured at 130,000. Mayor Hamai takes exception to these figures, claiming that those killed numbered more than two hundred thousand if the fatalities resulting from the injuries and diseases caused by the atomic blast are also taken into account.

"One out of every two persons then in Hiroshima perished on that historic day or immediately after it."

An American newsreel cameraman who flew over Hiroshima following the surrender said, "The city was just a flat expanse of emptiness. You could play billiards on it." But the ashes had hardly cooled before rebuilding began.

We came close to one of the personal tragedies of Hiroshima when we entered our hotel. An unexpected "Good evening" in English came from the family room behind the vestibule.

A woman with an abundance of blond hair surrounding a deeply lined face introduced herself as Wanda Yamatoda.

"The proprietor of the hotel isn't used to receiving foreign guests," she said, "so he called me in to find out what you would like."

We explained that we were used to Japanese inns and would give no trouble. But we invited her into our room for a talk.

Wanda was an American who had married a Japanese and had come with him to Japan in 1941. Of course that was just the wrong time to come. In December of that year the war broke. Her husband went to war and came back to die of cancer. His widow, left without means of support, suffered great privations.

Worse than that, being an American, she was in constant danger of arrest and torture. Other foreigners of her acquaintance disappeared without a trace.

She was taken to police headquarters and questioned as to just what she thought of the Japanese and their policies. She had reached the point where she hardly cared what happened to her, so she told them exactly what she thought, good and bad. They were very angry, but one stood up for her. "She's right," he said.

There were more of these inquisitions, but her independence and frankness won respect and she was never subjected to actual torture.

When the atom bomb fell upon Hiroshima she was inside a building more than two miles from the center of the blast. Others were killed all about her but she was unhurt.

"Sometimes I think it would have been better if I had died then."

Now she was teaching English and was getting along well enough. She had never taken to Japanese ways and had given up trying. She had a careless almost gay manner and laughed frequently but there was an aching sadness back of her laughs. She could not afford to return to America. There was no American community in Hiroshima. Still young, but lost-eyed and wrinkle-faced, she was a sorely displaced person, a victim of war though not of the atom bomb.

Still more pitiful were Hiroshima's armless or legless or faceless *mutilés*, or those mentally deranged. Men were restoring the buildings of the city, the stores, temples, schools, but could never wipe out the physical and psychological legacy of those ten seconds on August 6, 1945.

•

It was not only the people of the cities who felt the devastation of war. The countryfolk also suffered.

One day during a two-month sail in a chartered Japanese junk down the Inland Sea after the minesweepers had cleared it of its greatest hazards, we were driven ashore by a thunderstorm. Cold, wet, hungry, we had visions of spending the night in a comfortable inn.

But there was no inn—only a farmhouse dimly visible through the scudding rain. I looked at Mary.

"Let's try it," she shivered.

We walked a narrow, muddy ridge between sweet potato plots to the house.

"Komban wa," we called. "Good evening." We did not knock. It is considered discourteous to pound a Japanese door.

It was necessary to call twice again before we were heard over the cry of the storm. Then a door slid back and the master of the house peered out.

We explained our predicament and were at once invited to come inside. In the *genkan* or vestibule, we removed our shoes, stepped around the screen that is supposed to prevent evil spirits from entering the house, and padded over the resilient *tatami* into a large room lighted by a single electric bulb. It is hard to find a spot in Japan that electric wires have not penetrated.

The room was bare and poor. Its only decorations were a crude scroll hanging in the sacred alcove, and a small Shinto shrine on the god-shelf. The *tatami* were in bad repair and the paper doors were torn. There were no glass doors outside the paper doors, but there were heavy *amado*, storm doors of solid wood, that more or less successfully kept out the rain and wind. The roof was of thatch supported by smoke-blackened rafters.

The man was perhaps in his fifties. His face was weather brown and work lined and both his shirt and trousers were patched. His feet were bare and as tough and gnarled as oak stumps.

He profusely begged our pardon, as if the storm had been his fault. He did not seem quite to know what to do with us and called his wife.

She came in with many bows and smiles and apologies. She had reached the early old age of the woman who has borne many children without letting it interfere with her work in the fields.

She took one look at our sodden figures, exclaimed, *"Ma! Taihen desu! Chotto matte!"* (Oh! Terrible is! Little wait!) and scurried out to get us a change of clothing.

While we contrived to get out of our wet clothes and into the worn but clean *yukatas*, she made tea and we could hear rattlings that told us the fire was being stirred up under the family tub.

There were no cakes with the tea, but it was strong and hot and sent the blood once more coursing through our dishrag veins. Then, one at a time, we soaked in the near-boiling water of the three-foot-wide and three-foot-deep wooden tub. We returned to the big room, our lobster-red skins glowing with comfort and radiating steam.

Dinner was served. There being no table, it was brought in on trays and set before us as we sat on the floor. The woman apologized deeply because there was no rice. The meal consisted of sweet potatoes and sliced raw fish. There was more tea. It was a profoundly satisfying meal.

Then we talked.

•

The man's name was Ando. He owned two acres. I wanted to know whether the Occupation's program of land reform had helped him. I had been asking the question of farmers all the way down the Inland Sea. Ando-san's reply was typical.

"Makasa [MacArthur] tried to help us. We are very grateful. Now for the first time in my life I own land."

"You used to be a tenant?"

"Yes, on this same land. For thirty years I farmed it, but it was not mine. Of everything that grew I must give sixty percent to my landlord. Now it is all mine."

His wife sighed. Ando-san reproved her with a look.

"So life is easier for you than it used to be?"

Ando-san smiled a wry smile. "*Sa!*" he exclaimed thoughtfully, with a glance at his wife. He was plainly anxious to avoid giving offense. "It is good to own your own land. It is a very good feeling."

"Everything is harder," broke in his wife. "The taxes. The inflation. The government."

Ando-san was keenly embarrassed. "You will pardon my wife," he entreated. "She mourns the loss of her daughter."

"Your daughter has died?"

Ando-san hesitated. "You must understand that we are very poor. My wife was ill and needed medicines. A man came from Osaka, visiting the islands, looking for girls. He thought our Yuriko good-looking. He offered two thousand yen. We refused, but Yuriko insisted upon going."

Two thousand yen was the equivalent of $5.60. No one said anything for a moment. The storm beat upon the *amado.* I could not bring myself to inquire what Yuriko was doing in Osaka. Nine out of ten girls recruited in this fashion are destined for the houses of prostitution.

"She was your only child?" I asked.

"Oh no. We had four boys and two girls. Three of our sons were killed in the war. One died of troubles of the chest. Two years ago our elder daughter . . . went to the city. And now Yuriko." He laughed softly in apology for burdening his guests with his troubles. *"Shikata ga nai."* (It can't be helped.)

"But you managed to live on this land for thirty years. And now your income should be much larger since you no longer have to pay sixty percent of your crops to a landlord."

Ando-san nodded gravely. "That is true. Now all that we earn is our own. That is democracy. It is better than the old way. But I am afraid we still have many things to learn before we can do everything in the new fashion. We used to be able to go to our landlord for help when we were in difficulty. We have gone to him twice since the war and he has said, 'Why come to me? My land has been taken away from me and now I am as poor as you. I cannot help you.' He used to own twenty-five acres, and eleven of us tenants farmed his land. He could buy fertilizer and seed in large quantities at a very low price. He could afford to keep an ox and a horse and would let us use them. He had a pump to pump irrigation water to all of the farms. Since the land has been redistributed there is no pump and some of the plots on the slope are not being farmed because the small holders cannot afford to irrigate them. And then the taxes! In the old days the landlord paid the taxes. Now we must pay them, and they are six times as high as they were. And this terrible inflation makes us poorer as fast as we get richer!"

"They have given the women the vote," his wife put in. "But there is no one to vote for who will protect the rights of the farmers. Each party has a landlord party. Our government has no sympathy for the farmers. The good changes the Americans made—little by little they are being changed back. But you must be very tired after your hard journey and here we chatter on and on about our foolish troubles!" She rose briskly, slid open a closet door and began to take out padded *futons*.

•

"The most successful experiment of its kind in history," was MacArthur's appraisal of his land reform program. The judgment was perhaps a little premature. It was like declaring a horse the winner the moment it had left the post. Only time would tell whether the experiment would end in success or failure. Strong interests were determined that it should fail.

Certainly it was a "noble" experiment. Its intentions were the best. The land reform law was passed by the Diet in October, 1946, by order of SCAP. Its purpose was stated to be "the wide extension of the ownership of agricultural land, so that cultivators may receive the fruits of their labor, thus promoting stability among farmers, increasing productivity, and fostering democratic tendencies in rural communities."

It ended the autocratic power of the absentee landlord. He must sell his lands, all except two and a half acres, to the government at a sacrificial price, and the government would then resell them on reasonable terms to individual farmers. These new landowners would be allowed twenty-four years to pay for their land.

Before the law went into effect 46 percent of Japanese cultivated land was operated by tenants. By December, 1949, only 11 percent was tenant operated. More than 4 million acres had been bought by the government and distributed to former tenants.

To study the effects of land reform the Natural Resources Section of SCAP conducted in 1947 and 1948 a competent survey of thirteen fairly typical villages.

"Most new owners," according to the report of the survey, "found taxes high, delivery quotas heavy, and the continuing inflation burdensome."

"The problem of inflation was on the tongues of villagers everywhere," runs the report. "Frequent references were made to the phenomenally large amount of yen now needed to purchase a plow, a bicycle, a power-driven thresher or a calf."

The slivering of the holdings of "large" landowners into still smaller fragments had raised serious problems. The plots were too small to farm economically.

This problem was further aggravated by the provision of the new Civil Code that all children and relatives have the right to share in the inheritance of land. This meant that if a farmer died leaving, let us say, a wife and five children, his already tiny farm must be divided six ways so that each survivor might have a share.

This was democracy gone wild. Most of the people of the thirteen villages chose to cling to the old custom by which the eldest son inherits the land while the younger children seek employment in town or city. The sound horse sense of the people nullified the law. Children legally entitled to land refused to exercise their rights. The survey report states:

"The majority of young people interviewed in youth association meetings favored the continuance of the traditional methods of inheritance. Because the elder brother is obligated to take care of the aged parents and look after the welfare of the younger children until they reach maturity, it was only proper, they argued, that he should inherit the family property." And it was the common opinion that the subdivision of the already pitifully small holdings was impractical.

Village young people are steady. They are not swept about by every breeze from America or Europe as are the young folks of Tokyo. The revised Civil Code allowed a young man and girl to marry without the consent of their elders. But the finding of the investigators was: "There is no evidence that the incidence of parental selection has materially declined in the thirteen villages since the surrender."

As for divorce, "Until the revised Civil Code was promulgated, Japanese women were not able to sue for divorce, and divorce action was considered to be a prerogative of the husband. Under the revised Civil Code, however, wives can sue for divorce on the same grounds as can husbands. Nevertheless, the post-surrender divorce proceedings recorded in the villages were all initiated by men."

Among the farmers of Japan as a whole there was disillusionment and reaction. Owners who could not bear the burden of high taxes and high prices and the responsibilities of ownership were selling their land and once more becoming tenants. In 1950 according to the Japanese Agriculture Ministry, one hundred thousand farmers disposed of portions of their property. In 1951 transfers of farm lands were 2.6 times as frequent as in 1950.

"In Tohoku," reported the *Nippon Times*, "the rate of sale has increased to five times compared with 1949, in Kinki twelve times and in Chugoku twenty-eight times."

Large numbers of the farmer-owned cooperatives went broke, because of lack of experience, and the refusal of banks to lend money.

•

The "slave market" was the most reliable barometer of rural welfare. Rarely, except in times of national disaster due to earthquakes or famine, had so many farm girls been sold into prostitution.

In 1951 four thousand girls from rural communities were sold into prostitution, some for as little as $2.80.

More than half of these girls came from families earning

only eleven dollars to fourteen dollars a month for an average family of six.

The girls of such families were sometimes sold for as little as a sack of potatoes or rice. Highest prices were paid for girls possessing enough beauty and talent to qualify them as "entertainers." They brought an average of forty dollars with a maximum of about two hundred dollars.

Under a new law girls thus sold might renounce their debt at any time and go home. Actually they rarely did so. The pressure of custom and the feeling of obligation were so strong that they stayed until they had worked off their debt. The company or house employing them could so manipulate their expenses that they never cleared themselves.

The reason the land reform program, though valuable, fell far short of being "the most successful experiment of its kind in history" was that it did not touch the basic problem.

The basic problem of the Japanese farmer is *too many people on too little land.*

The average size of the Japanese farm is two and a half acres. Compare that with 3 acres in China, 3.6 in Korea, 10 in the United Kingdom, 47 in the United States, and 80 in Canada.

The Japanese who has two and one-half acres is lucky. Nearly one-third of Japanese farms are one acre or smaller.

Japanese agronomists calculate that the size of the average farm would have to be tripled to give the typical farming family a fair livelihood. Another way of saying this is that there are three times as many people on the farms as there should be.

17

THE USES OF ADVERSITY

Misfortune has played a large part in the good fortune of Japan.

It was historian Arnold Toynbee who propounded the theory of *challenge and response.* From his study of the history of the rise and fall of nations, he concluded that much depended upon a nation's response to a severe challenge.

Such a challenge could make or break. If the people were weak-willed, the difficulty or danger would be too much for them. If they were strong, surmounting the crisis would make them stronger.

Many nations of the past—for example Egypt, Greece, Rome—languished, not because of defeat in war, but because of self-defeat due to luxury, soft living, loss of moral fiber.

In the case of Japan, there was enough toughness in Japanese character to override adversity and by dint of strenuous effort come out the better for it.

Certainly, Japan has had the discipline of disaster. Cataclysms, like everything else in this methodical country, have come with almost clocklike regularity. Storm, fire, flood, drought, deluge, tidal wave, earthquake, and eruption—they have followed each other like scheduled classes in a school of misfortune.

"I wish there would be an earthquake!" says the new arrival in Japan. He soon has his wish. "Not bad at all," he comments, greatly pleased with the novel rocking sensation.

The second one does not please him quite so much. The third makes chills go up and down his spine. The fourth brings out the goose flesh. He thinks, "I wish they would stop that."

But there is no way to stop an earthquake. And the newcomer's increasing uneasiness is due to his growing realization that there is nothing he can do about it, that this is something beyond his control. There is no way of telling whether the shock will be trivial or fatal. Perhaps only a vase will fall from a shelf. Perhaps the house will collapse and kill all the inmates.

This is a land of the unpredictable and unexpected. It is in a peculiar sense in the lap of the gods. And they are nervous gods—trembling, stormy, explosive.

Japan is a geological and meteorological novelty. It may owe its very existence to seismic and volcanic outbursts—these, say the geologists, raised it up out of the sea. That Japan once lay at the bottom of the ocean appears from the fact that on the mountaintops one may find fossilized sea shells.

According to Japanese legend, Fuji and her lesser companions rose in a night. According to geology, it took a few million years more than that. But according to anyone's casual investigation, it is plain that the upheaval was tremendous. Japan is a land on edge. It is 85 percent mountainous and two dozen of its mountains are between eight thousand and twelve thousand feet high.

Japan is an island floating upon a sea of fire. Recently fifty-eight of her 192 volcanoes have been active. There are nearly a thousand hot springs. The seismograph records four earthquakes a day, one severe earthquake every thirty months, a disastrous shock every lifetime. Typhoons are frequent. Also tidal waves. Floods. Conflagrations.

Dean of disaster is the beautiful Fuji. Robed in virginal white, she is a devil at heart. Herself dormant, Fuji is a volcanic and seismic center. The fires still burn below and burst forth through other volcanoes or shake the earth with quakes many miles away. Fuji has been constituted a Shinto shrine, and thousands of pilgrims climb it yearly to beseech the spirit of the mountain to have mercy.

The name *Fuji* is an aboriginal Ainu word with two meanings—"Goddess of Fire" and "to burst forth." In either sense, the name is appropriate. Standing 12,400 feet high, the majestic cone represents the greatest "bursting forth" that has ever occurred in Japan. It has the shape of a perfect ant hill, and, like an ant hill, it was formed by material forced out from beneath. It has been compared to a titanic crucible out of which in past ages the surrounding country has been poured. Its most recent great eruption was in 1708; then, in the words of a priest whose temple stood at its base, "Fuji-no-yama suddenly opened in a place overgrown with splendid trees to vomit fire. . . . Showers of stones and ashes lasted for ten days, so that fields, temples, houses were covered with ejected matter more than ten feet deep. Millions of dwellers in the neighborhood of Fuji lost their homes and many of them died of hunger."

Today only steam spurts from holes in the crater's rim; pilgrims cook their eggs in the jets. But Fuji may become weary of speaking only by proxy, through the mouths of other volcanoes. The people fear her, knowing well how dormant or supposedly extinct volcanoes suddenly throw off all reserve . . . how Bandai, for example, awoke from a thousand-year sleep to blow off her snow cap and kill four hundred persons.

So the Goddess of Fire, who is supposed to sit in the white-hot center of the snowy cone, is worshiped more devoutly than any other deity in Japan with the exception of Amaterasu, the Sun Goddess. Contrarily, the Sun Goddess is besought to bring heat, while her subterranean sister is begged to withhold it.

Of the fifty-eight active volcanoes, Asama has been most vicious in modern times. She has been greatly disturbed and seems to be preparing for a major catastrophe. The crater has been boiling furiously, now and then spurting streams of red-hot lava. Showers of incandescent rocks have killed climbers. Ashes and cinders pour down upon the roofs of houses twenty miles away and the violent quakes make life uneasy in the nearby resort, Karuizawa, where British and American residents of Japan spend their summers. The volcano is twice as high as Vesuvius, has a more deeply buried Pompeii near its base, and a greater record of activity.

Asama means "Without Bottom" but the name is a misnomer. The crater's bottom may now be seen at a depth of six hundred feet, and is steadily rising. This gradual filling of a crater is usually a prelude to a major eruption, and seismologists have already given warning that the catastrophe of 1783 may soon be repeated. At that time forty-eight villages were buried a hundred feet deep by a great river of boiling lava. The river then cooled and hardened, and today you may walk a hundred feet above the houses and the bodies of the victims, forever imprisoned below.

•

We climbed Asama and shall not soon forget the experience. Not that the climb would be difficult to the hardened mountain climber—but the fact that it must be made at night, and that the trail is easily lost, and that the mountain gives constant promise of annihilating the human midget, lends spice to the adventure.

Being ignorant of the way, we attached ourselves to a

group of Japanese students—but soon found that they were no wiser. We were soon quite off the trail, clambering up through lava boulders, and skidding in cascades of cinders. While escaping the day's heat, we encountered a chill night fog. It drenched us so thoroughly that we could wring the water from our clothes. The darkness was profound, illuminated only by the occasional flash of an electric torch. The fog smothered even this, and the light of a climber fifty feet away could not be seen.

Now and then we would climb out of a cloud. It lay below us against the mountainside like a sea against a shore. Roofing us was another sea and into it we would climb.

Dawn found us fogbound, lost, and shaking with cold. We huddled in the lee of a big rock, the swift, cold tide of cloud sweeping by us. The rumbling mountain had taken to hurling out red-hot stones which went sizzing through the liquid air above us. This should have been terrifying, but in our chilled condition the thought of being struck by a few hot stones was not altogether unpleasant. From our pockets we collected scraps of paper, made a small fire, and warmed our cramped hands.

Where to go? The obvious answer would seem to be "Up!" But Asama is not a cone, and the top of the mountain consists of miles of hills. Therefore the way to the crater is quite as likely to be down as up.

Suffice it that we found it. We came suddenly to an abrupt brink and looked down into a cloud-filled void. We could see nothing, imagine anything. A deafening roar smote us. Down there a Titan was hurling hills, tossing up sky-rockets made of incandescent boulders, splashing about in his morning bath of boiling lava. Or was it the sound of a thousand trains going over a thousand bridges? There was also a fluid note in the tumult, reminding one of Niagara Falls—but the fluid in this case was liquid rock. Again, it could be a foundry, Vulcan's workshop, but equipped with all the most ear-splitting modern machinery. What grinding, gritting, bursting, rending! One of the students spoke to me. I could see his lips move but could not hear his voice.

Belches of sulphurous smoke seared our eyes, made us gasp for air. The changing wind would at one moment cook us in hot steam, then chill us with a bath of cold fog.

We scattered, lost to sight instantly, each bent on some bit of exploration along the rim. There were nine of us . . . when we came together again there were only eight.

One had seen it happen.

"He left this letter," he said when we had descended to a spot of comparative quiet.

The letter was to the boy's mother. We did not open it, but his fellow-students could guess the message.

"School was pretty hard for him," they said.

•

Even when one knows that there are three volcano-suicides in Japan every day of the year, it is a shock to have one come within close range. At least it is a shock to the foreigner—but to the Japanese, suicide is an orderly and recognized procedure, and our companions were only a little quiet as we went down the mountain. We went rapidly, for the Titan did not seem to have been appeased by the pathetic human sacrifice, and we did not forget that six descending pilgrims had been hurried into eternity only a few days before by a volley of hot stones. Another had been caught on an island in a stream of lava . . . the island became smaller, the glowing river kindled his clothing. . . .

Many of Japan's most vigorous volcanoes are on islands. Mihara, a few hours' boat ride from Tokyo, is a favorite suicide resort. Sakurajima smokes as a constant reminder of its most brilliant achievement, the burying of a whole town of ten thousand people. Mount Niidake recently trapped on its tiny island a party of scientists who came to investigate it.

The flanks of Uracas, a cone which rises abruptly out of the sea, often gleam at night with streaming lava, and ashes strew the decks of passing steamers.

Other volcanic islands rise out of the sea, stay long enough to collect a few inhabitants, then sink. Near San Agostino an island two and a half miles in circumference rose in 1904 and disappeared in 1906. Smaller islands frequently pop up, get themselves onto a chart, then mock the chart by vanishing. South of the Ogasawara Islands there are many submarine volcanoes which at times capsize schooners by their sudden explosions, spewing up great rocks, and leaving nothing at last but a few floating spars and the stench of sulphur.

There is one profitable by-product of Japan's volcanic energy—the hot-spring business. Thousands of hotelkeepers have reason to thank the fiery gods responsible for 954 hot springs to which bathers make pilgrimage by the hundreds of thousands. These springs are of many sorts: simple thermal, carbon-dioxide, alkaline, salt, bitter, iron, vitriolic, sulphur, radioactive. Farmers near spas use warm water in their fields, thus hastening growth; others economize on manure by fertilizing with water from ammonia springs.

The city of Beppu has steam heat. Live steam is diverted into the stoves for cooking purposes. There are hundreds of *jigoku* or "hells" where one may enjoy boiling himself in bubbling mud. Even the sand of the sea beach is steaming hot and one witnesses the remarkable spectacle of thousands of human heads projecting from the beach. The bodies are baking below.

•

Less spectacular, perhaps, than the volcanoes, but more deadly, are the earthquakes. The earthquake of 1923 earned distinction as the greatest natural catastrophe of history. Half of Tokyo was destroyed by the quake and ensuing fires, and all of Yokohama. Official figures disagree as to the number of lives lost, the estimates ranging between 96,000 and 157,000. There was far too much confusion to make an accurate count possible. It is known that in a single square in Tokyo 33,000 people were turned by the holocaust into 150 cubic feet of ashes; an Earthquake Memorial Temple built upon the spot now enshrines the ashes.

On that fateful day there were 222 shocks between noon and midnight. A Japanese friend tells me, "So much dust was jarred out of the walls into the room that I couldn't breathe. I ran out and climbed a tree. Foolishly, I tried to count the other trees in the yard. But I couldn't tell whether there were four or five—they were moving so fast."

The earth split and burst. People in the country ran to the shelter of bamboo thickets—for the bamboo roots go deep and intertangle in such a way as to hold the earth together. But it was necessary to crouch low, for the trees beat together, sometimes flailing each other into kindling wood. The quake upset kitchen fires—the cities were soon in a blaze. Thousands fled to the shore of the Sumida River. Other thousands came behind them. The fire followed, and the struggling mass was pushed over into the river.

There was occasional comedy relief. The walls of the Grand Hotel fell away and exposed a lady in her bath on an upper floor. She gesticulated wildly but would not step out of the tub; young gallants climbed up and rescued her, tub and all.

Thousands who did not lose their lives lost everything else. There were estimated to be three million sufferers in all.

Japan outstrips Italy, her nearest competitor, in number and violence of earthquakes. During the ten years following 1923 there were 21,845 quakes strong enough to be felt—besides tens of thousands detected only by the seismograph. The death toll is heavy, the nerve toll heavier. The Japanese do not become used to earthquakes; they heartily dislike and fear them.

What causes earthquakes? Seismologists say that they are due to volcanic disturbances beneath the earth's crust, the steam generated by the infiltration of water to the deep fires, the burning out of subterranean caverns followed by the collapse of these hollows, the slipping of submarine mountains. Earthquakes show affinity for great depressions, and the Pacific basin is the deepest depression on the globe. Therefore the great circle comprising Japan, the Philippines, New Zealand, and the South American and North American coast up to Los Angeles and San Francisco is subject to earthquakes.

If earthquakes cannot be bridled, can they at least be foretold? Japanese seismologists have naturally given more study to this problem than scientists elsewhere, and they are now having a fair measure of success in predicting earthquakes in specific localities several months in advance by recording changes in terrestrial magnetism. But there are still plenty of surprises to lend spice to life in Japan.

•

When disaster does not come from below it comes from above. Rain is the angel and devil of Japan. It makes crops grow with unexampled speed, but it annually causes devastating floods. Rain has made "peaked deserts" of many mountains, despite the efforts of reforestation men, and down these bare slopes rush deluges which swell rivers, sweep away bridges, flood the country, make thousands foodless and homeless. Floods, together with tidal waves and typhoons, drown six hundred a year. Even Tokyo, one of the driest spots in Japan, has more than twice the rainfall of London. In the western mountains, winter snow forms to a depth of eighteen feet, covering the low houses so that tunnels must be dug down to the doorways. This snow melts in spring with dire results. Flood control is expensive—even the wealth of the United States has not accomplished it.

What the malicious gods above cannot do with rain, they accomplish with wind. Wind means fire. The glow of a forgotten coal becomes the holocaust of a city. Japanese cities are built of wood, favorite food of fire. Japan has eighteen thousand fires a year, destroying twenty thousand houses. In certain parts of Tokyo it used to be taken for granted that the average house would survive for only three years. Modern fire-fighting equipment has changed that . . . but still there are city plans drawn up for new thoroughfares, fatalistically awaiting the inevitable fires that will open the way for their execution. Fire in Hakodate took two thousand lives and left 150,000 people homeless.

•

Earthquake and fire affect chiefly the cities; they do little damage to the farms. The typhoon is impartial. It destroys all alike.

Consider, as a study in calamity, the account a young farmer gave me of his experiences as everything he had worked for was wrecked in one night by a typhoon.

He tossed in his floor-bed. Outside in that dark fury, his farm was being ruined. There was nothing he could do about it—only lie and wait for morning.

The house shook as if in a perpetual earthquake. Heavy tiles were torn from the roof. A rending crack now and then told the fate of another tree.

Flying timbers that struck the house could only mean that other dwellings of the village were being torn apart. His own house might collapse at any moment.

Although the house was hermetically closed for the night, as is the Japanese custom, wind blew through the rooms. A burning wind, straight from the South Seas. A wind heavy with sand and salt . . . although the nearest ocean beach was a mile away. He could feel the sand on the covers and the saline spray of the sea on his lips. A bad night for sailors as well as for farmers!

The roar of the wind was no mere roar. It was more like the ear-splitting shriek of a high-powered circular saw. If his sisters called from the next room he could not hear them. He had better see how they were.

He went into them and turned on the light. They lay tense, staring up from their pillows. Japanese women do not weep, wail, or indulge in hysterics. They are used to living on the edge of disaster.

"The worst of it is past, don't you think?" Fujiko said.

"Bound to blow over soon," replied big brother Dokyo, perhaps adding bitterly within himself, "and take everything with it."

His entire farm, two acres, wiped out in one night!

After his parents' death, his younger brothers had gone to the city to make a living. It was his duty, as elder brother, to stick to the farm. And, for a Japanese, to question Duty would be like cross-examining the emperor.

So Dokyo had no thought of deserting his farm . . . even when he looked out through the greenish-yellow dawn and saw that he no longer had a farm. What had been his farm was a lake. In the midst of it was a powerful current marking the course of the river. But the river was flowing backward!

Then this flood was not riverwater nor rainwater, but ocean. Tidal waves, rolled up by the terrific wind, were rushing up the riverbed and overflowing to destroy scores of farms. Grain needs water—but too much is even worse than too little. And this water, when it finally did disappear after some weeks, would leave a heavy impregnation of salt and sand. It would take years to restore the land to its former condition.

As for the near future, there would be no more food out of the soil this autumn or winter.

He went to the kitchen. The girls were getting breakfast.

"Don't bother," he told them. "We'll have to get along on one meal a day now. We'd better have it at noon."

He did not add that soon even one meal a day would not be possible. But they sensed the truth.

"Well, at least we can feed the silkworms," said Natsuko.

Human beings may not be able to eat mulberry leaves, but silkworms thrive on them.

Dokyo opened a storm shutter. "Look," he said.

The mulberry bushes, projecting above the flood, were stripped. Not a leaf remained. The worms must die. There would be no silk this year.

•

There was someone in the village that morning who had a ready solution for the problems created by natural disasters. He had come on an early train from Tokyo. He had immediately asked which houses contained personable young girls. Late morning found him calling *"Ohaiyo!"* at Dokyo's door.

He was ushered in, leaving his shoes in the entrance. There were some general remarks about the storm. One does not state one's business abruptly in the Orient. The day's only meal was ready . . . courtesy demanded that it be shared with the visitor.

He helped himself liberally. When he had quite finished, he made known the purpose of his visit.

"You will be under great expense to restore your farm," he said to Dokyo. "Draining the flood, clearing the land, buying fertilizer, seed, new shrubs and trees. Your sisters will wish to help you. Fortunately I am able to be of service to you. I represent interests in Tokyo. Your sisters are attractive and I believe I can use them. It might be possible for us to pay our top price, two hundred yen for each."

The girls were silent. True, it was their duty. Young people of Japan are expected to sacrifice themselves for their parents, and, after their parents' death, for their elder brother who becomes the head of the house.

"What interests do you represent?" demanded Dokyo suspiciously.

"You have guessed," smiled the oily man, "but I assure you . . . don't be hasty . . ." as spade-hardened hands closed on his collar and propelled him toward the door, "think of your farm . . . we might even make it three hundred each!" But he was now out in the rain. His shoes came hurtling out after him.

Of course that solved no problems but it was a great satisfaction to Dokyo.

Typhoons are annual visitors. An autumn typhoon in 1937 completely destroyed five hundred homes and was accompanied by a tidal wave which flooded thousands of homes and farms. The most serious typhoon of recent years was that of September, 1934. Arriving in Japan with a velocity of 130 miles an hour, it not only stripped and flooded farms, but killed three thousand people, injured nine thousand, wrecked eight thousand steamships and sailing craft, blew several trains from bridges, destroyed 292 schools, inundated 105,000 homes, and caused a total loss of $300 million.

As if that were not enough, there was drought in Kyushu which cost the farmers $30 million, floods in Hokuriku which incurred damage to the extent of $9 million, cold weather in Tohoku causing a $25 million crop failure.

The government is not idle in such emergencies. Extensive relief measures are forever in progress. Nevertheless, not only in the north but throughout Japan, the farmer's savings have vanished and his debt is steadily increasing; the average debt of the Japanese farmer now being three hundred dollars. And he must pay to the money lender from 10 to 20 percent interest.

The Japanese endure willingly that the nation may survive. They do not clench their fists or grit their teeth or go through any of the pantomime of endurance. These impossible people only smile. They answer catastrophe with *"Shikata ga nai"* (it can't be helped), and rebuild. Hardship only tempers the edge of Japanese purpose. Disaster in one form or another as the daily food of Japan has bred a stoical, bullheaded people who know how to fight because they have had a hard drillmaster, Brute Nature. There is also a Mother Nature in Japan, gentle, lovely, artistic to a high degree. The charm of the Japanese environment, together with the rigor of physical forces, must have had much to do in the molding of that curiously two-sided individual, the Nipponese . . . esthetic and indomitable . . . a man compounded of cherry blossoms and iron.

18

UP FROM THE ASHES

A month before Pearl Harbor, our most respected military analyst, Major George Fielding Eliot, predicted that if Japan dared start a war, superior American forces would bring her to terms within two weeks.

It took four years.

He was right about the superiority of our forces. Wrong in not taking into account the toughness and resilience of the Japanese.

These qualities, born of adversity and intense nationalism, are also the qualities back of the sensational reconstruction of the country's economy since the war. Japan's former enemy helped her to override the shock of defeat. But America has poured aid into other countries without the same results. Japan must be given the chief credit for the swiftest surge of recovery and achievement in history.

Of the 132 nations of earth, Japan is now the third greatest manufacturing power—following America and Russia.

No nation, not even the United States or U.S.S.R., builds

so many ships, or ships of such incredible size. Fifty-one percent of the world's ships are built in Japan.

And what monsters! The world was thrilled when the 55,000-ton *Queen Elizabeth* slid down the slipway into the Clyde. In 1970 visitors to Japan watched without great excitement the building of a mammoth drydock at Tsu intended for a 500,000-ton tanker. When completed, the ship will not slide into the water. That is old hat. The dock will be flooded and the ship floated out.

Already, 300,000-ton Japanese ships are commonplace. Set vertically on its stern, such a ship would be taller than the 102-story Empire State Building. It carries more than two million barrels of oil which, stacked, would be 192 times higher than Everest.

In a year, Japan's most serious rival, West Germany, builds a thousand ships—Japan, seven thousand.

We walk through the busy shipyards of Uno where giant vessels are getting their final fitting before being dispatched to Danish, Norwegian, Philippine, and other foreign purchasers.

For Japan is building ships not only for herself but for customers all over the world. This is a really stupendous fact when one considers that 80 percent of Japan's merchant fleet, once the world's third-largest, was sunk during the war. Japan was left with only one passenger liner, five oceangoing merchantmen and a few hundred small coastal vessels.

And under the surrender terms she was forbidden to build any ships for herself larger than five thousand tons or faster than eleven knots.

But SCAP lived and learned and in 1949 this policy was reversed. The reason for the change of heart was that it was costing the United States too much to ship goods to Japan in U.S. bottoms. About twenty-five cents out of every rehabilitation dollar that America was spending on Japan went to defray shipping costs. In December, 1949, restrictions were removed and Japanese shipbuilders were given the green light.

They went at their job with typical Japanese energy. Starting almost from zero they have, in only two decades, passed all rivals.

•

To build ships, they needed steel. But Japan had no iron ore. It would have to be brought seven thousand miles from India or Australia. And coal, to turn ore into steel, must come ten thousand miles from the East Coast of the U.S. This would make it cost twice as much as in Germany or Britain.

And there was little flat land to spare for large steel plants. This difficulty was solved by reclaiming land from the sea.

To use less of the expensive coal, oil and oxygen were injected into the furnace, a novel practice which steelmen come from all over the world to admire.

Surmounting these problems, the Japanese can sell their steel products in the U.S. for $10 to $15 a ton less than their American counterparts.

West Germany, long famous for steel output, was passed in 1964, promoting Japan to third place behind only the two superpowers.

•

Steel, worth its weight in gold, is today the most useful of all metals.

Without it, Japan, traditional land of the ricksha, could not stand second to the U.S. as she does today in production of motor cars. In 1969 alone, Toyota made a sales gain of 80 percent; Datsun, 52 percent. Japan now has "motorcar fever."

She enjoys the highest auto-accident rate in the world. Drivers exult in speed. The taximan is dubbed the "Sedan Samurai" or the "Kami Kaze" (Divine Wind). During the last ten years bus output has doubled, trucks increased twentyfold, passenger cars, fortyfold. Millions of three-wheeled trucks are exported to Asian nations too poor to buy four wheels. At the other extreme, Europe's Rolls-Royces are rivaled by Japan's Prince Motors.

Motorcycles also take part in the *boomu.* Japan now leads the world in this field. And continues to gain. Honda sales go up 40 percent a year. Hondas have gained worldwide reputation by winning practically every race and trial. Close runner-up is Yamaha.

Steel trains speed over the tracks from Tokyo to Osaka at 125 miles an hour. These thunderbolts carry 200,000 persons daily. One leaves every fifteen minutes. They are clean, comfortable, serve good food, and arrive on the second. Trains on other lines do not move so fast, but they have the same habit of leaving precisely when they are supposed to leave and arriving strictly on time. You may set your watch when the train moves, or when it stops. There are plans to extend the high-speed system to all Japan.

Japan has more miles of track per area than the U.S. While passenger traffic languishes in America it thrives in Japan. It thrives too well for comfort on trains other than the Tokyo–Osaka bullets. On the Tokyo platforms of local lines 2,700 stout guards, appropriately called "pushers," jam people into cars by main force, tearing off shoes or sleeves, packing in the human cargo so tightly that one can scarcely move his arms or take a full breath. Progress!

However, I am unjust to first class. There, one may actually sit down, and even remove coat, shirt, and trousers for the sake of the inimitable comfort Japanese gentlemen seem to get out of sprawling in long underwear.

•

Aircraft rely heavily upon steel, and the Japanese rely heavily upon aircraft.

When the world's first experiments in military aircraft were begun by France in 1910, Japan sent officers to watch, and the next year saw French experts on Japanese airfields coaching Japanese aviators. In the early years American planes were used. Now Japan not only builds planes of her own but exports to the U.S. and France. Most recently the emphasis has been upon new types of aircraft including supersonic jumbos designed to excel the 747.

In 1970 Japan joined the U.S., the Soviet Union, and France in the satellite age and her "Lambdas" now patrol the skies.

Japan is as active below the earth as above it, but the results are disappointing since minerals such as gold, silver, tin, lead, zinc, nickel, and bauxite were somehow forgotten when the god Izanagi formed the islands of Japan.

There is copper, and one of the globe's greatest copper mines is Besshi, buried a mile deep in a mountain near the city of Niihama.

The mayor insisted that I must go through the Besshi Mine. Being already sated with caves of many sorts, I declined—and the next day found myself in the lockerroom at the mine's maw, removing my clothes lest they be damaged by the drippings, and donning miner's shirt and pants, canvas boots, and a black patent leather helmet equipped with a clasp to hold an open-flame acetylene lamp. The helmet was too small, the pants too short, and I had the general appearance of a slightly surprised visitor from Mars.

My wife would not accompany me, for three reasons: (1) she didn't want to; (2) the management didn't invite her; (3) the miners didn't want her, because: (a) they imagined a woman's presence in a mine causes accidents; (b) they go naked.

I was ushered into a trolley which presently plunged into a tunnel. As it did so, every man removed his cap in deference to the god of the mine. This is supposed to insure safe passage. The ceremony is repeated upon emerging into the blessed light of day.

Our train consisted of half a dozen cars equipped with seats but no walls or roof. The train roared through the tunnel of solid rock with such a din that if you wished to speak to your neighbor, mouth must be placed to ear and you must shout at the top of your lungs. The car rocked violently from side to side. I had reason to regret overtopping my Japanese companions by almost a foot. This brought my head within eight inches of the trolley wire. The wire packed six hundred volts. When I removed my hat because of the increasing heat I was sharply advised by an executive to put it on again. He shouted in my ear something about electrocution. The rough roadbed continually bounced us up and down, uncomfortably close to sudden death.

Trains of ore on the way out passed us. The air was stifling and the noise deafening. The tunnel seemed endless. My fingers ached from clutching the rungs of the seat to hold myself down.

We stopped and the manager said we had come a mile. The same trunk tunnel, he said, ran on for another mile.

The air was oppressive with a damp heat that fogged the lens of my Rolleiflex and blurred my glasses so that I had to remove them. To the flicker of our acetylene lamps, we walked, choosing between stepping on the slippery ties or in the mud between them. One of the Japanese volunteered the information that this obstacle race sends many men to the company hospital with broken legs.

Presently we stepped into a cage and dropped a third of a mile.

We came out into a cave as big as a church occupied by the enormous steel-built power plant whose heartbeat sends electric life throughout the great mine. This plant was buried two miles inside the mountain. Each of the huge machines had been made out of units small enough to be brought in through the tunnels, then assembled. An enormous blower labored to lift the stagnant air out of the tunnels—but since there were 250 miles of tunnels, this task was an almost impossible one.

Near the power room was the brain room, the main office of the mine, a place of desks and stools and walls hung with diagrams. Here in the heart of the mountain we were served tea! Everyone received it with much formality and polite sucking of breath, despite the fact that the attendant who served it was perfectly nude.

This however did not seem unreasonable in view of the heat. Our clothes were soaking wet with steam from without and sweat from within. Each of us had been furnished with a towel before entering the mine, and found full use for it. Our faces flowed, and water streamed out from under our helmets.

Near nakedness alternated with nakedness in the style show of the copper mine. Some workmen wore a G-string effectively, some ineffectively, most did not bother with it at all. When the manager summoned an engineer who had been working on the generators, the man came modestly holding his cap over his essentials.

Stark naked men repaired tracks, loaded ore cars, ran electric locomotives, operated the machines, dug into the walls with automatic drills, did carpentry, worked over books in the main office, bowed before a Shinto shrine a mile underground.

It is not quite correct to say that they were naked. Most of them did wear helmets. Many also carried a towel which was usually draped around the neck.

They looked as if they had returned to the age of primitive man, and it was extraordinary to see these cavemen lift their hats to us and bow as courteously as if they were dressed in afternoon suits and high hats at an imperial garden party. Not only did they salute the visitors, but they were continually lifting their hats and bowing to each other. Responding to their courtesy I nearly stepped into a shaft 160 meters deep.

The greatest shafts are the elevator shafts. The man who operates a cage covers a good deal of perpendicular territory in a day. From bottom to top his trip is two-thirds of a mile.

The Besshi Mine is a skyscraper inside a mountain. There are forty floors in this skyscraper. But unlike the floors in other skyscrapers, these are numbered from the top.

The first floor is the highest level, although this is still far below the top of the mountain. The fortieth floor is the basement—but only temporarily, for work will proceed to still lower levels. The distance from the fortieth floor to the first is 3,712 feet. That makes the Besshi skyscraper three times the height of the Empire State Building.

The 250 miles of corridors have taken 260 years to dig. Progress was slow when it was a job for chisel and hammer. Modern steel machinery has speeded up the burrowing, and the tunnels are now being extended at the rate of four miles a year.

Twelve hundred men are employed underground, six hundred above. There are fifteen hundred houses for the men and their families, six stores, four hospitals, one school.

There is a question whether there is more copper or more steel in this mine. The steel is in the form of giant turbines, locomotives, trains, elevators, and huge excavation machinery.

•

One watch does not require much steel but six million watches take quite a bit of it. The same can be said for radios, TV sets, cameras, typewriters, bicycles, sewing machines, pianos, and a thousand small articles that stream out of Japanese factories to all lands.

Thirty-six years ago I bought a watch in Kyoto's Daimaru store for five dollars. It still goes. Later, I put down a hundred dollars in Zurich for a Swiss chronometer. It became weary of life after five years.

I don't wish to disparage the timepieces that have made Switzerland famous, but must give credit to the Japanese product. John Gunther writes: "Not long ago a great airliner smashed into Mount Fuji, and everybody on board was killed. Most passengers carried watches, and it was discovered that every Swiss, American, British, French, or German watch had stopped dead at the moment of impact. But every Japanese watch survived the crash and was running fine."

Japan can thank her own camera buffs for the superiority of the Japanese camera. The amateur Japanese photographer is not content to make snaps in the manner of the foreign tourist. He may spend a whole day on a subject that would be disposed of by a visitor in a split second. He will study the scene from every angle, wait hours if necessary for the right combination of light and shade, probably set his camera on a tripod so that there will be no chance of jarring the image, consider what filter to use if any, shut down the lens to a pinhole if he wants great depth of field, open the lens all the way if he prefers a sharp image of one object or person against a dissolving background, and so on and on.

To meet his demands German cameras were ideal but they cost too much. So Japanese manufacturers buried themselves in research and came up with instruments that were better than the German, and at a fraction of the price.

American amateurs had scorned Japanese cameras as "cheap and nasty." Reporters covering the war in Korea used German cameras—but when they wanted special lenses they were unable to get them because of transport difficulties. Reluctantly they made shift with Japanese lenses—and discovered that they were excellent. That turned the tide.

Today, Japan is by far the largest camera-manufacturing country in the world. German photographers buy Japanese cameras. More than a hundred Japanese companies have opened European sales headquarters in Düsseldorf. Practically all innovations and improvements in camera making are Japanese. The Nikon has superseded the famous Leica.

Canon has produced an FO.56 lens, thirteen times brighter than the human eye. It is invaluable in X-ray photography since it greatly reduces the length of exposure of the patient and doctor to radiation.

The gastrocamera, for taking pictures inside the stomach, was not new with the Japanese. But the early machines were large and clumsy. The patient could not swallow the camera without anesthesia and the work had to be done by a specialist in the hospital. The Japanese developed a camera so small that it could be swallowed easily and any general practitioner could manipulate it, drawing out the camera again at the end of a wire and developing the film. No specialist was needed, no hospital required.

Japan, world leader in so many fields, unfortunately leads also in stomach cancer. The gastrocamera armed with a small flash can locate the cancer in a matter of minutes. In America the stomach ulcer reigns supreme and Japanese gastrocameras are important to locate and define the ulcer or any abscess or tumor within the stomach. A tiny pair of forceps from inside the camera will take a sample for diagnostic examination.

An endoscope inserted at the other end of the intestinal tract will do a similar job in the intestines.

The high quality of Japanese cameras is largely due to the fact that they must pass muster in the Camera Inspection Institute set up by the government. There is no court of appeal from its decisions. If faulty specimens are found, the entire line representing millions of dollars may be condemned. That puts camera makers high on their toes and insures a reputation for fine quality.

In motion pictures, Japan came to life after the death of Hollywood. She now makes more feature films than any other country, more than four hundred a year. For scientific purposes a camera has been devised with the incredible capacity of sixty thousand exposures a second, fast enough to photograph the movement of sound waves through the air.

Fine lenses are not limited to cameras. Binoculars, microscopes, optical goods of all kinds, are welcomed by specialists everywhere if they bear the words "Made in Japan."

The visitor is surprised to find television sets wherever he goes in Japan. Ninety percent of the Japanese sit before TV screens. Great numbers of Japanese sets are sold in the U.S. However, America still holds the lead, second world honors going to Japan. American makers will have a hard time to match the Japanese Sony, which instead of beaming its color through three small electron lenses which cause some blurring, uses only one big lens which does not diffuse, thus yielding a sharper picture.

Japan has outdistanced all rivals in the quantity and quality of transistor radios. Even radios carrying American trademarks have probably been made in Japan.

A few decades ago the abacus held undisputed sway in the shops and factories of Japan. Today the Japanese market for computers is the second largest in the world after the U.S. Large numbers of American computers are actually made in Japan. IBM looks askance at the rapid growth of the Nipponese computer industry.

Only ten years ago the U.S. bought 30 percent of all foreign electrical goods from West Germany; from Japan, almost none. Now she buys 50 percent from Japan, 6 percent from West Germany, and even that low percentage is dwindling rapidly. The Germans complain about the "yellow peril." They consider the Japanese too aggressive. The Japanese reply that the Germans are too complacent.

Japan makes a point of studying the needs of other nations, and meeting those needs. She herself prefers the *samisen*, the *koto*, and the *shakuhachi;* yet she is the world's leading piano manufacturer. Last year her piano exports totaled eleven million dollars.

Distressing to the West is Japan's growth of 33 percent a year in the chemical industry. Nowhere else is the rate more than 20 percent.

An astonishing chemical development from Japan is the birth of life from lifeless matter. This demolished the idea that living cells could be derived only from animate material. The magical chemical is urea and it has already been widely licensed abroad. Its possibilities still lie in the future. Its chief use at present is as fertilizer to put new vitality into plants.

It is no surprise that Japan leads in silk production, since the intricate method of its manufacture was known in the Orient before Christ was born. Not until A.D. 550 did the West learn how it was made, when two Nestorian monks brought the "art and mystery of silkworm rearing" from China in the form of silkworm eggs concealed in their bamboo canes. Japan got the secret from China in prehistoric times.

The origin of silk is a viscous fluid from two glands under the silkworm's stomach. The worms must be collected when very small, forty thousand of them weighing only seven-tenths of an ounce, and farm women have almost no time to sleep during the feeding period which brings this number up to a weight of six hundred pounds in a month.

The worms then spin cocoons, each fiber of which may be anywhere from twenty-five hundred to three thousand feet long. A Japanese writer says, "The combined length of four or five of them may be equal to the altitude of our Sacred Mountain, Fuji-san." The cocoons go to filatures where the fibers are unwound and made up into skeins. Eighty-five percent of the silk was exported.

Was. With the advent of synthetics, Japan promptly changed her tune and began producing rayon on a grand scale. Now she even fashions clothing from fiberglass.

Japanese cotton has swept the world—this in spite of the fact that she raises no raw cotton but must get it from the U.S. and India.

Manchester cotton men taught the Japanese how to spin cotton, and sold them looms. Soon Japan was able to make cotton shirts, send them halfway around the world, and sell them in the stores of Manchester for less than shirts made in Manchester.

But that wasn't the worst of it. A Japanese by the name of Toyoda invented a better loom. It would do more with less attention. While in a Lancashire mill one girl could tend eight machines, now in a Japanese mill one girl could tend sixty.

Lancashire stubbornly refused to believe it. It was only when all world markets were flooded with Japanese cottons at prices from a third to a tenth those of Lancashire, and the cotton capital of the globe had definitely moved to Japan, that Lancashire men went to Japan to study the cotton industry. They took no looms with them this time—instead, after they had inspected the Japanese mills, they paid a million yen for the license rights to use the Toyoda Loom in Lancashire.

By the time they got the new looms working, Japanese engineers had begun to improve the design to make their own looms more efficient. Their success is indicated by this amazing fact: Japan could buy raw cotton in India, pay the freight on it to Japan, process it, pay freight back to India, pay an import duty, and sell the goods in India for less than the price of cottons made in India.

To beat Lancashire where manufacturing costs are high is one thing. To beat India where costs are even less than in Japan is another thing, and gives sober warning to the textile industry throughout the world.

In an Imabari *ryokan* officials dinnered us from ten to one A.M. It seemed that we had hardly begun to sleep before there was a polite *"Ohaiyo de gozaimasu"* outside our door and the city fathers were ready to take us toweling—for is not Imabari the greatest towel city in Japan and the second greatest on earth?

We visited a goodly proportion of the sixty-three towel factories of Imabari. In this city woman's place is not in the home—it is in the textile mill. In one vast room 530 looms stretched away into the dusty distance. A factory of average size turns out a million towels a year.

Beside each loom hang cards perforated as for a player piano. By some mysterious art the perforations in these cards determine the pattern in the towel. The cards, all connected, pass through a mechanical brain above the loom and the holes in the cards regulate threads in the weave, altering according to the design. A fabric with no design needs no cards. A very intricate design requires thirty-five hundred cards.

In towel production America is first, Japan second. But Japan's export trade is greater because her towels are cheaper. She exports to South Africa, Southeast Asia, Iran, Iraq, Pakistan, Afghanistan, Hong Kong and India. A bid is being made for the American market as well as the European.

One would expect that towels made by so artistic a people as the Japanese would carry a beautiful oriental design. But the designs were painfully commonplace. We learned the reason when we visited the Ehime Prefectural Textile Laboratory where the designs are created.

"We get most of our ideas," the manager said, "from the Sears and Montgomery Ward catalogues. We consult them to find out what Americans like."

When I suggested that these institutions, though admirable, are not necessarily the last word in art and that the laboratory would do better to rely upon Japanese art sources than upon mail-order catalogues, my suggestions fell on deaf ears.

This overweening passion to give foreigners what they want is responsible for the tawdry and tasteless junk that clutters shops serving tourists in large Japanese cities.

Though Japan must get her raw wool from Australia, Africa, and the Argentine, she sells woolen textiles back to the same countries for less than they can buy them anywhere else.

Japan markets more fish than any other nation on earth.

One and a half million persons are engaged in the industry, and 450,000 vessels. The motorized fishing boat is the rule, and yet the age of sail has not vanished. Standing on a height overlooking the Inland Sea one may count half a hundred sails within view at one time.

Fishing vessels do not merely catch fish. They are floating canneries. The freshly caught fish are at once cut in pieces, canned, weighed, sealed, and steamed, all by machinery. The ship returns to port loaded with millions of cans ready to be exported at once to all lands, east and west.

We must end this chapter with an anticlimax. Agriculture is the Cinderella of the Japanese economy. The demands of industry are so great that young men of the country are drawn to the cities. Farm workers were once predominantly male. Now they are women. Still, they are not doing so badly. Because of extremely intensive farming methods made necessary by the small amount of arable land available, Japan gets per area ten times the yield in India.

California owes much to her Japanese immigrants. They came with a remarkable knowledge of soils, an expert way of using fertilizers, great skill in land reclamation, irrigation, and drainage, and willingness to put in the enormous amount of labor required in intensive farming operations. They reclaimed vast areas of the West. The *San Francisco Chronicle* conceded that "the most striking feature of Japanese farming in California has been the development of successful orchards, vineyards, or gardens on land that was either completely out of use or employed for less profitable enterprises."

But with all their skill, those now left on Japanese farms cannot feed their countrymen and Japan imports a large proportion of her food, mainly from the state she helped put on its agricultural feet, California.

19

CREATORS OR COPYCATS?

"The Japanese are imitators, like monkeys. They do nothing original."

This insult was at one time common enough. And it had some basis in fact. All sorts of foreign goods were stolen and reproduced without regard to patents. Foreign machines were duplicated even down to the trademarks.

A Japanese company offered to make dishes for an English firm cheaper than they could do it themselves. The English sent a cup to be copied, with an order for a thousand gross. The cup happened to be chipped in transit. The Japanese made a thousand gross, reproducing the chip in every cup.

The Japanese Navy Department wrote British shipbuilders for estimates on warships to be constructed in British yards and sent to Japan. Along with the preliminary estimates they required blueprints.

One British firm, suspecting fraud, sent a false blueprint in which the center of gravity of the ship was misplaced, making the vessel topheavy.

The Japanese said, "So sorry," and returned the blueprint —but not until after their draftsmen had copied it.

The Japanese-built ship slid down the ways, turned over, and sank. Why this happened the Japanese could not understand since they had faithfully followed the blueprint.

"Made in Japan" became the mark of the copycat. It was accepted as a warning that the article on which it appeared was shoddy stuff and would go to pieces under the slightest strain.

Becoming aware of their tarnished reputation, the Japanese makers left off the trade mark, or used the original, or credited the article to a fictitious firm in Germany, or Britain, or labeled it "Made in USA." We were delighted to find shoe polish so identified and only learned later that the label was true, yet false. The polish was made in Usa, a town in southern Japan.

But today Japanese manufacturers are careful to stamp "Made in Japan" in large letters on every product. It has become an assurance of superior quality.

The truth is that most nations have gone through the borrowing or stealing stage of development. The Cretans copied from the Egyptians. The Greeks copied from the Cretans. The Romans copied from the Greeks, the Germanic peoples copied from the Romans and there was a time within your memory that German goods were so shoddy that "Made in Germany" was the kiss of death.

The French learned embroidery, silk, glass, silver from Italy. Spain learned from the Arabs who for seven centuries occupied that country. Until the eighteenth century most arts practiced in England were of Continental origin. America copied modern industry from England and the scornful English assured themselves that they need have no fear of Yankee rivalry because Americans "are clever copyists but have no genius for invention." But within the next half century America became the chief source of inventions.

Imitation is the mark of an alert mind. Willingness to learn from others is scorned only by people who shut themselves off from the main currents of progress.

Japan still copies, but pays for everything she copies and then sets about trying to better it. America still copies, and much of what she copies is Japanese.

Since the 50's Japan has paid out a billion dollars for foreign know-how. At the same time her own researchers and inventors have taken their place among the most talented and innovative on earth. The Imperial Patent Bureau in Tokyo grants twenty thousand patents a year.

Among Japan's plethora of inventions is the laser-guided rocket, the typewriter with three thousand characters, a metal alloy lighter than aluminum, the taxi door that opens automatically when you reach your destination, the cultured pearl, paper bicycles, "silkool" from soybeans combining the qualities of silk and wool, felt made out of peanut shells, leather made of fish skins, really soft toilet paper and paper clothing, a magnet alloy for which Bosch of Germany paid a million dollars, the Toyoda Loom bought by England and considered the finest in the world, the Takuma Boiler, outstanding in its field, the pentaprism camera, the plastic motorcar, the rotary piston engine—but who can possibly list the twenty thousand a year that pour from lively Japanese brains?

A Japanese genius with his tongue in his cheek has even devised something better than the alarm clock. When it is time to get up, a balloon inflates under the sheet, throwing the occupant out of bed!

20

FIRST IN THE TWENTY-FIRST CENTURY?

I am no prophet. I cannot predict the future by the stars, or the lines in a Japanese hand, or by the GNP.

Nor can anyone else. But it is fair enough for knowledgeable experts, both Japanese and western, to extrapolate from the present what Japan's future *may* be. Therefore, with due allowance for unforeseen circumstances, we may consider some of their opinions.

First, the Japanese.

The Finance Ministry in 1969 published a "tentative estimate" that the per capita income of the Japanese people would become the highest in the world in twenty years.

Prime Minister Sato, after viewing the largest world's fair in history, Expo 70, exclaimed: *"Subarashii* [Terrific]! This is not a statement of the twentieth century but the twenty-first—a good expression of our national power."

The aspiring firm, Mitsumi Denki, adopts as a slogan, "Catch up with American industry and surpass it."

A leading Japanese newspaper editorially declares, "What

Japan intends is to become as big as the United States."

Another confesses, "Catching up with the Americans in the sphere of economics, including technology, production, and consumption, has become the burning ambition of the Japanese."

But certain well-informed European and American analysts, with the benefit of perspective, are even more sure of Japan's coming place in the sun.

"It would not be surprising," says Herbert Kahn, respected economist of the Hudson Institute, "if the twenty-first century turned out to be the Japanese century."

U.S. Commerce Secretary Maurice Stans says that Japan "could very well" move to the head of the class in the next twenty years.

Economist Peter Drucker comments, "Japan's success story is the most extraordinary in all economic history."

Time captions an analysis of Japan's rising economy, "Toward the Japanese Century."

A German industrialist describes the Nipponese advance during the last hundred years as a *wirtschaftswunder*, economic miracle. "It has been both the admiration and the envy of other countries of the world."

Haakon Hedberg, Swedish author of *The Japanese Challenge*, calls Japan "the economic super power of the 80s" and forecasts that Japan's per capita income will exceed that of the United States in fifteen years.

"Japan is the nation most likely to equal or surpass the U.S. in standard of living and industrial productivity in this century," writes James C. Abegglen, vice-president of the Boston Consulting Group, who has spent half his time in Japan since 1955. He agrees, "The twenty-first century may be Japan's."

"Within a generation Japan may well be the world's most affluent society," is the comment of the *Scientific American.*

"Japan's industrial complex, now the third largest in the world, will probably give rise within the next couple of decades to the world's second industrial state." The speaker is T. F. M. Adams, past chairman of the Tokyo Stock Exchange and present adviser to large American concerns seeking to do business in Japan.

The science editor of *British Industry Week*, P. B. Stone, expects that Yawata-Fuji will soon outstrip U.S. Steel's annual output of 28 million tons. That is now the world's largest, but only 6 million tons ahead, and Japanese production is growing more rapidly. As for shipbuilding, Japan at the current rate will soon build more ships than the rest of the world put together.

Fortune, making an industrial survey, finds that 71 percent of large American firms are not expanding, 73 percent are not increasing inventories, 69 percent are laying off personnel, and 61 to 83 percent will cut budgets, close marginal operations, and delay new projects if, as expected, profit margins slide. Japan, on the contrary, is forging ahead on all these fronts. While the New York Stock Exchange average was dropping 14 percent during 1969, the Tokyo index rose 32 percent.

•

Why?

Why has Japan progressed so far and so fast?

We have already seen some of the reasons: the world-challenging rescript of the first emperor which has never been forgotten, the instant learning acquired readymade from China, the stimulus of contact with the English, the Portuguese, and the Dutch, the two centuries of strict seclusion against the great powers that had already subjugated much of Asia, the awakening of Japan under the guns of Commodore Perry and the conclusion of treaties with America, England, and Russia, the restoration of the emperor and demise of feudalism, the generous treatment by Japan's conquerors after her defeat in 1945.

One great advantage of the Japanese is that having been

shorn of their outlying possessions they are once more a small nation. "All great things have been done by little nations," said Disraeli. There's a good deal of truth in it. A nation that allows itself to become a gigantic sprawl full of rebellious minorities faces serious trouble. It was true of Greece, of Rome, of the British Empire, and is true of the United States. In the small nation the people are close to their government —they are the government. The Japanese are a homogeneous people, merged during the last two thousand years into what they consider a single race, all thinking pretty much alike, all stung by defeat into a fever to prove themselves, out to demonstrate that General MacArthur was wrong when in his messianic wisdom he stated that the average Japanese man had the mental age of twelve. From top to bottom, from emperor to scavenger, they are imbued with a patriotism rare in this cynical age.

The island group is small enough so that all may read the same newspapers every day; attend schools that all teach alike without proliferating into a confusion of fads and fancies; join in what they have come to call "Japan Incorporated," meaning that there is no such thing as an "Establishment" apart from and antagonistic to the people, but all are united in a single purpose—the glorification of Japan. Of course there are some dissidents. But they have the same goal, and only hope to reach it in a slightly different way. They are not out to make trouble at the expense of their country.

An enormous force behind the present industrial surge is the *zaibatsu*. The *zaibatsu* is the group of enormous holding companies that control most of the business and industry of Japan. We would call them "trusts" and do everything in our power to break them up. The Occupation did just that. The half dozen great houses, each controlling from a hundred to three hundred industrial firms, were forced to give them all independence. Each was now on its own. Strangely enough, they did not appreciate their freedom.

The trouble was that they were now free to swim, but also

free to sink. They had not possessed the latter freedom under the *zaibatsu*. Formerly when a company got into difficulties the big conglomerate to which it belonged would help it out.

As soon as the western "know-it-alls" left the country, the Japanese set about re-forming the *zaibatsu*.

On my visit to the Besshi Mine, I asked a high executive whether it had not been better during the short period when the mine had been free of the domination of the Sumitomo conglomerate.

The executive shook his head. He could not speak English, but he could write it. He wrote in my notebook:

"Under Sumitomo we could work indeferently with profit or loss of this mine in a short time. Now we must operate fearfully in the care of share of stock."

In other words, it would be a matter of indifference if the mine should operate at a loss for a short time provided it were backed by powerful financial interests such as Sumitomo. As an independent company, however, it must rely "fearfully" on its own resources.

The mayor of Niihama when asked the same question explained that all industries of Niihama had been Sumitomo before the war. Then they had been broken up into many companies. None had enough capital.

The nearby Kamioka Mining Company had not only suffered but expired. For three years the huge copper smelter and sulphuric acid plant were a study in still life, not a wheel turning. The firm had formerly been a part of Mitsui. Now it is operating once more under the same umbrella. I asked the manager what he thought of the breaking up of the *zaibatsu*.

"I think it was wrong, because smaller units cannot function so efficiently."

Zai means wealth and *batsu* means clique. The name is apt, for the *zaibatsu* is the wealth-clique that owns and operates Japanese industry.

The *zaibatsu* is made up of a dozen great conglomerates,

the largest of which are Mitsui, Mitsubishi, Marubeni-Iida, and Itoh. A *zaibatsu* official describes Mitsui thus:

> A comparable business organization in the U.S. might be achieved if, for example, U.S. Steel, General Motors, Standard Oil of New York, Alcoa, Douglas Aircraft, E. I. Dupont de Nemours, Sun Shipbuilding, Westinghouse Electric, American Telephone and Telegraph, RCA, IBM, U.S. Rubber, Sea Island Sugar, Dole Pineapple, U.S. Lines, Grace Lines, National City Bank, Metropolitan Life, the Woolworth Stores, and the Statler Hotels were to be combined into a single enterprise.

Each of the subordinate companies fathers a horde of lesser companies. Toyota Motor Company has 120 subcontractors, each supplying some essential part of the Toyota car. These companies rely on Toyota. Toyota must foster them, keep them alive, help them financially when they require help.

Thus Japanese enterprise is a maze of interconnected entities. The top managers of affiliated companies form an overall board of directors meeting regularly to discuss matters affecting all companies in the group.

Such alliances in the U.S. would be accused of being in collusion, or in restraint of trade; but in Japan it makes sense. Every company is subordinated to the aims of the group as a whole. Any decision of the board of managers is carefully considered as to its effect upon every member firm. Care is taken never to "break his rice bowl." If one gets into trouble the others will bail him out.

•

The entire *zaibatsu* is attached to the government by a sort of umbilical cord. Far from censuring the great combines, the government urges firms into mergers to withstand foreign competition. It works so closely with the heads of industry that it is difficult to say where the government ends and the *zaibatsu* begins. Government experts are responsible for deciding new directions for Japan's industrial effort, opening up fresh opportunities, protecting every branch of business. In short, the whole economy behaves as one huge corporation, able to channel cash from low-growth to high-growth areas, capitalize rapidly growing but unstable ventures, dominate new industries by setting prices so low that foreign firms cannot compete. From Minister of Finance to the maker of hubcaps, all have a place in this common effort.

•

All: the government, the masters of industry, and the workers as well.

The most extraordinary feature of the entire scheme is the attitude of the employee. He too regards himself as a member of "Japan Inc." He takes pride in the fact that he is working to benefit his country.

The Japanese employment scheme is radically different from that anywhere else. The factory worker, technician, clerk, or manager is employed for life. His salary goes up according to seniority. He is a member of the family, and as such he has a strong sense of loyalty to his mates and his superiors. And his firm is strongly loyal to him. Twice a year it pays him a bonus amounting to from one to three months' salary. He has fringe benefits that would make a western worker dizzy. His actual salary is small compared with those in the West, but, as *Foreign Affairs* points out, big firms provide employees with apartments, dormitories, or homes, at one-fifth to one-tenth the prevailing market price, sell company-owned land to employees at bargain prices on long-term payments. Employers provide villas on the seashore or in the mountains where employees and their families can spend their holidays at low cost. Baseball, tennis, and swimming facilities, instruction in flower arrangement, traditional musical instruments, and the tea ceremony, etc. are provided free, also medical and dental services, and employees may enjoy the long sleep at no charge in company-owned cemeteries. There is an automatic pay raise once every year.

A few take advantage of this paternalism and loaf on the job. But very few. The Japanese are constitutionally hard workers. They take pride in doing more than is necessary. During the period from 1953 to 1965 working hours rose, whereas in all other industrial countries they fell.

Practically anyone who wants a job can get one and be secure for life. Japan has the lowest jobless rate of any industrialized nation. Unemployment is 0.8 percent, contrasting with from 4 to 6 percent in the United States.

A Japanese worker doesn't understand the western love of strikes. He has all he needs. His house is cheap, his wants are few, and his savings are large. Japan has the world's highest rate of personal savings, 21 percent of income as compared to 7 percent in the United States. He cannot understand what he hears of the lackadaisical indifference of employees in Britain and America. He would agree with Juan Montalvo, "There is nothing harder than the softness of indifference."

The whole tightly knit structure of government, *zaibatsu*, and worker helps us to see logic in the swift advance of the Japanese economy and the possibility of preeminence in the next century.

21

WOMEN, PROGRESS, AND PROBLEMS

There has been a revolution in the status of women—but no revolution in women.

They remain essentially the same gentle, affectionate, considerate, outwardly dependent, inwardly strong personalities they have always been.

But their standing in the home and in public has radically changed. This transformation has been most rapid since the war.

•

Ten years before Pearl Harbor we sat on the floor of the excellent Iketoku Inn of Kanonji talking with a young man of the town, Sasaki by name.

"You will be very comfortable here tonight," he admitted. Then he inquired timidly, "Would you prefer to spend the second night here—or in my humble home?"

We chose the latter, much to his delight and confusion—and to the confusion but probably not delight of his pretty little wife, Tora, who reminded us that a fisherman's house could not make us as comfortable as the hotel that had once harbored the Crown Prince.

We entered the house through an unfloored storeroom filled with coils of cables, fishing tackle, canvas, nets, tubs, and machine parts. Above were two *tatami*-floored rooms. These small rooms were home for eight people—Sasaki, his wife and son, and Sasaki's father and mother and grandmother and sister and brother. Since the house already accommodated eight persons it was not too difficult to find room for two more.

Two uncles lived apart but they and their families came over to spend the day. Curious neighbors dropped in—visitors from overseas are as rare as elephants in Kanonji. The room overlooked a street on one side and a *kamaboko* (fish-paste) shop on the other. People congregated in the street and courtyard, lifting their gaze to the upstairs windows; two boys climbed on a roof to see better; children slipped into the house, crept up the dark stairs, and peered into the room; schoolboys came with card, brush, and inkstone for samples of our calligraphy.

A young druggist, a friend of Sasaki's, came to show us his stamp collection. Another friend of the family, a young lady named Atsuko which might be liberally translated Hot Baby, asked questions about the profession of writing, for she aspired to be a journalist. She had been through primary, lower secondary, and higher secondary and planned to go to the College of Foreign Studies in Tokyo.

But when it came time to eat, all ladies, except my wife, disappeared as if by magic. They did not presume to eat with the men. Even enlightened and ambitious Hot Baby would not be persuaded. Tora, Sasaki's wife, brought up the ingredients for sukiyaki, a dish which must be cooked on the table before the guests. But since tradition did not allow her to remain at the table, she blushingly declined to do the cooking. Sasaki and Mary, armed with chopsticks, manipulated the meat, cabbage, onions, beancurd, and slabs of fish paste in the bubbling shoyu, water, and sugar in the iron pan over a charcoal fire. What was left after we were through was taken downstairs to be consumed by the women.

Though we did not take kindly to this sex discrimination we would have been most impolite to make an issue of it. It was not our business to dictate manners in our host's menage. We could only hope that the presence of the American woman at the feast with the men might prompt some new ideas.

Tora was a lovely person, but shy, and much afraid of doing the wrong thing. Poor girl, she was the minority party in this house. Japanese custom required that the bride move in with her husband's family. Tora must take instructions not only from her husband but from her mother-in-law, her grandmother-in-law, and her sister-in-law. And she must be circumspect in her dealings with little Kan, her three-year-old male child. She could not order him about as she would a daughter and she was expected to obey his every wish unless to obey would do him positive harm. He was already showing signs of awareness that he belonged to the master sex.

•

Our host invited us to walk out with him and see the town. Mary asked if Tora might go too. The request surprised Sasaki, but he gave Tora a stern nod that seemed to say, "You may go, since the foolish foreigner wants it, but mind you behave yourself."

The three-year-old heir to the household throne demanded to be taken along. He was a heavy, husky child and could have walked, but he preferred to ride. So Tora carried him.

She lagged some ten feet behind the rest of us. Mary

dropped back to join her. They chatted in low voices and Mary later reported the conversation.

"You don't need to come back," said Tora.

"I want to."

"But they tell me that in your country the woman even walks ahead of the man. *So desu ka?*"

"No. Beside him."

Tora looked at the passersby. "People here would think that very strange. And it would make my husband very uncomfortable. Doesn't it make your husband uncomfortable?"

"No. He seems to like it."

Tora shifted the boy from one arm to the other.

"Let me carry him for a while," Mary said.

The boy, finding himself in a stranger's arms, began to howl. Then he noticed a bright pin on Mary's shoulder and promptly tore it off. He howled again and his mother took him back. She tried to extract the pin from his tight little fist, but gave it up.

"I'll pay you for it," she said.

"No, no, it's all right."

"You know how it is with boys," Tora said apologetically.

"I'm not sure that I do. Are they so different from girls?"

"The boy only minds his father—or his older brother if he has one. The girl minds her mother."

"If a boy's mother forced him to behave, what would happen?"

"She might be divorced."

"How could she be—if her only offense was that she had tried to teach her son?"

"There does not have to be a reason. If the man wants a divorce—that is all that counts."

"But doesn't he have to go to court?"

"Very few go to court. It is not nice to wash dirty shirt before all people. So there is divorce by custom."

"How does that work?"

"It's as simple as getting married. If you want to get married, you go to the *shiyakusho* [town office] and the man says, 'This woman is my wife. Write her name on the register of my family.' Then when he wants to divorce her he goes again to the office and says, 'I have sent my wife away. Take her name from my register and write it again on her father's register.'"

"But does this happen often?"

"I know one woman in Kanonji who has been married thirty-five times."

"But if a husband did something very wrong—couldn't his wife divorce him? Suppose he took up with other women."

"A Japanese may have just one legal wife. That is the law. But he may have as many other women as he chooses, if he can support them. And of course he may go to the Yoshiwara whenever he wants to. Or attend a party and bring a geisha home with him. And if his wife does not bear him a child, she herself may urge him to lie with the housemaid, because she knows it is very important to him to have a son to carry on the family line."

"Does a man like to have an educated wife?"

"Some do. Some don't. If the wife is educated she had better keep it to herself. Of course if she has a good idea she can suggest that it is his and not hers. That usually works."

"Yes," Mary said, "it works in my country too."

•

In the more remote past, the lot of the wife was still more difficult.

The classic, *Greater Learning for Women*, taught that "a woman should look on her husband as if he were Heaven itself, and never weary of thinking how she may yield to him, and thus escape celestial castigation."

Education for a woman was considered quite unnecessary since she was "born to be guided by man."

If a man owed another as little as twenty cents and could not pay it he could give over his wife to settle the debt.

The woman must blacken her teeth and pull out her eyebrows to make herself as unpalatable as possible to men other than her husband. Wrote British Minister Sir Rutherford Alcock in 1863:

> When they have renewed the black varnish to the teeth, plucked out the last hair from their eyebrows, the Japanese matrons may certainly claim unrivalled pre-eminence in artificial ugliness. Their mouths thus disfigured are like open sepulchres, and their faces powdered with rice flour look as if plastered with pastry and white lead. Were it not for such perverse ingenuity in marring nature's fairest work, many among them might make considerable pretentions to beauty.

One might think that such disfigurement must have been hard on the husband, daily confronted by such a nightmare. But it was explained that "six months' married life serves to familiarize the ugliest features and efface the original impression."

Japanese women were never forced to submit to the cruel distortion of foot-binding which so effectually kept Chinese women from roaming freely, but the same purpose was served by the wooden *geta* elevated on cleats, making walking less than pleasurable.

The kiss, as practiced in the West, was not understood. An old lady said, "I have heard, my daughter, that it is the custom for foreign people to lick each other as dogs do."

A young lady from England asked her Japanese girl friend:

"What do lovers do when they are—well—very enthusiastic?"

"They gently turn their backs to each other."

"Every emotion is chained," wrote a nineteenth-century commentator, "with the shackles of politeness. A merry girl will laugh softly behind her sleeve. A hurt child chokes back his tears and sobs out 'I am not crying!' A stricken mother will smile as she tells you that her child is dying. A distressed servant will giggle as she confesses having broken your treasured piece of china. This is most mystifying to a foreigner, but it means only an effort to keep oneself in the background."

A widow was not expected to throw herself on her husband's funeral pyre as in India, but her last act of conjugal uglification was to cut off her hair down to the roots and bury it with her husband's ashes as evidence that she had renounced the world.

•

Now, what a difference!

In 1970 a Japanese educator said, "In the last twenty-five years there has been as much change in the condition of Japan's women as it took Europe five hundred years to bring about."

The old idea that grace is found in weakness is gone. Japan knows that if she wishes to have strong sons she must have strong mothers. She is getting them, and without loss of charm.

Instead of the mincing step made necessary by stilted geta and knee-binding kimono, there is the healthy stride of the *moga* (modern girl), product of school drill in athletics, inches taller and pounds heavier than her mother. She skis in the Japanese Alps, goes in for all kinds of competitive sports, takes prizes in the Olympics, races motorcars, pilots airplanes, drops from the sky in parachutes. On the tennis court Prince Akihito, heir to the throne, met the girl who became his mate and will some day be the first lady of Japan. And modern geisha play baseball.

The present-day girl may even fall in love. In former days, love before marriage was rare. Marriage was the concern of the parents—the daughter had very little to say about it. A *nakodo* (go-between) was assigned the job of finding a suitable mate. The boy must then be examined by the girl's parents while the girl must appear before the boy's parents. If the parents were satisfied, the marriage took place.

In some cases the two young people had known each other, perhaps in school; in others they were total strangers. Whether or not love developed after marriage was considered of less importance than perfect obedience on the part of the wife, complete freedom for the husband. Many such marriages were happy—but happiness was not the object of marriage.

•

Recently we witnessed a modern marriage. The bride wore the costume prescribed by hoary tradition for such an occasion—exquisite kimono, resplendent *obi*, antique coiffure overloading her modestly bowed head. The strip of white gauze across her forehead was the horn cover, *tsunokakushi*, for the dangerous female was supposed to be equipped with the devil's horns.

After the wedding the girl changed her clothes. She appeared in a miniskirt and bobbed hair, having removed the elaborate wig, horns and all. She and her husband had met on the golf links.

She was delighted with her new home, kept it spotlessly clean, worked tirelessly and lovingly to give her husband a happy home life. She had visited America and, while she gave it high praise, she deplored its "dirt, laziness, and superstition." If this assessment seems unfair, perhaps it is no more so than the first impressions of some American tourists in Japan.

Today the rights of the Japanese husband and wife are identical. Women have the vote. They can be and are elected to public office. They have taken seats in the Diet or parliament. Many towns have female mayors. Women have equal access to schools and universities. They walk beside their husbands, not behind. They get equal pay for equal work.

They have time to read a book—now that the electric range supersedes the difficult charcoal *shicherin.* The refrigerator, washing machine, electric rice cooker, the "instant foods" of supermarkets, ease the housewife's tasks. Every year the "BG" (easier on the Japanese tongue than "business girl") is more ubiquitous. The divorce rate is one-third that of the United States.

A good-husband contest was held in Kagoshima. There were sixty-five candidates. Each was given a questionnaire including such questions as "Do you encourage your wife to improve her talent?" "Are you interested in discussing current topics with your wife?" "Do you come home straight from your work, or do you prefer to go to a party by yourself?"

First prize went to a sixty-eight-year-old doctor who was judged to have been most considerate and cooperative. When his wife came home late from women's meetings he went to the station to meet her. He helped her with the housework, ate at the same table with her, and walked beside her on the street. Second prize went to a railroad official who was not only good to his wife but had removed discriminations against women workers. Upon receiving the prize he stated that now that he was publicly recognized as a democratic husband he could carry a bundle for his wife without feeling embarrassed.

Women in industry are protected by new labor laws. Overtime for women is limited, night work restricted, generous leave prescribed in cases of illness or maternity, equal pay required for equal work.

Women may be found in almost every sort of business or profession. There are today even women police—two thousand of them—something never known before in an oriental country.

In Tokyo girls may be seen walking hand in hand with their boyfriends on a summer evening, sitting with them under the trees at the edge of the imperial moat, going with them to dances and shows. They dress in *yofuku*, western clothes, which they wear with much more distinction than before the war. The kimono is rarely seen on the streets, but lives on in the home. Recently a Japanese garment expert came out with a "five-minute kimono" that can be slipped on as easily as an overcoat.

The kimono has been on the way out since 1868. On my first visit to Japan in 1915 I wrote about its "disappearance." It is still disappearing and will probably keep on disappearing for another century or more. It is one of the loveliest costumes in the world, transforms a kitchen wench into a queen, perfectly conceals Japanese bow legs, and though inconvenient for school wear or business is still prized by Japanese women for use at all dress-up functions.

In the country and smaller cities the kimono is more common. There, the new freedom is more than some women can cope with. In Tokushima a kimono-clad newspaperwoman joined a few male reporters and shyly looked on as they interviewed us. When we singled her out and urged her to come closer she retreated so abruptly that she stumbled over an anchor and sat down hard on the deck.

Now she was all blushing confusion. She would have run away in utter disgrace and mortification. Mary gently detained her until she had got over her fit of tears and giggling, then gave her an exclusive story "from the woman's angle" that she could take back in pride to her city editor.

The postwar path of the Japanese woman has not been completely paved with cherry blossoms. Some of her troubles and frustrations can be laid at the door of foreign troops still present in Japan.

It is not surprising that the delightful little "moose" of Japan should have turned the head of the woman-hungry soldier. The word *moose*, by the way, was the Yank soldier's invention derived from the Japanese *musume*, girl.

No invading army was ever more well-behaved than the Allied soldiers upon their entry into Japan. The Japanese were astounded. The men had expected massacre, the women had anticipated rape. Women and children had been sent in great numbers to the comparative safety of the country. But the invaders came in with smiles and bows, gave cigarettes to the men, candy bars to the children, and politely ignored the womenfolk.

Perhaps the ladies were slightly piqued by such lack of attention. At any rate there was soon a change in their attitude. Instead of keeping themselves out of the way, they set about putting themselves in the way of the conquering barbarians.

Most had no evil intent—they merely responded to kindness and courtesy. Acquaintance budded into friendship, friendship in many cases into adoration, for the Japanese female had never known such a considerate male. The age of chivalry which still cast a lingering glow over Europe and America had never touched Japan. Japan had its own rich virtues, but deference to woman had not been one of them.

It was heady wine for the Japanese girl, walking beside her foreign escort instead of six paces behind, going first through doors, seeing him carry the bundles and bare his head upon meeting and parting. Besides he had both the means and the inclination to give her a good time while her Japanese men friends had neither.

Etiquette required the Japanese boy to keep aloof and wait for his elders to arrange a meeting with some personable girl. No such inhibitions restrained the American, Briton, or Australian. And their freedom from such conventions was contagious; many Japanese girls met them on their own grounds with a frankness and intimacy that they would not have dared to show the men of their own nation.

Every man could have his moose. Thousands took advantage of the opportunity—and thousands still do, now that the Occupation has been replaced by the "Security Forces."

Many of the girls involved are of good family and the finest type of Japanese womanhood. They expect to be taken seriously. Many of the officers and men are just as fine and just as serious. This is indicated by the fact that up to March 19, 1952, eight thousand U.S. servicemen had married Japanese girls and taken their brides to America. Thousands of others had wedded Japanese brides with the intention of staying in Japan with them or taking them home later.

•

But for every one of these men who were willing to face the problems of interracial marriage, there were perhaps a hundred who did not care to wade in so deep. They wanted a moose but not a noose. To meet their needs the "*après-guerre* geisha" came into being. The after-the-war geisha was not necessarily a geisha at all but any girl willing to make herself agreeable through the long night hours without expecting any more lasting alliance. Some of them were actual geisha but they were apt to be expensive, usually costing ten dollars an hour. The highest type of geisha kept herself aloof from such traffic, jealously preserving her status as an entertainer and artist. But the fat wallets of servicemen caused many to slip.

A far greater number of the *après-guerre* geisha are taxi dancers, barmaids, waitresses, prostitutes, and "pompom girls." Pompom is a play on the Japanese word *ponpon* meaning the stomach, and pompom girls are those who go with foreign soldiers for the sake of food, cigarettes, dresses, and other material advantages to be paid for with "love."

Just who is the victim in these transactions is sometimes hard to say. The girls often give as good as they get. A Tokyo taxi dancer pulled the same trick on several dozen hapless servicemen. In the dance hall where she was employed she would dance with a likely looking prospect, pretend to be overcome by his charms, show great interest in learning his name and address, and date him to meet her at a certain rendezvous the next day.

When the time came, he would be there but she would not. While he waited for her she ransacked his quarters and made off with everything of value. Then she moved to another dance hall and repeated the routine.

The police finally caught up with her but not before she had made forty soldiers very red in the face.

As any foreign correspondent who was in Japan during the Occupation will testify, great care was exercised by the authorities lest anything but the "truth" should go to the outside world. The "truth," according to these official mentors, was that the Occupation was "doing fine." Thus there were no *ifs* or *buts* in the highly encouraging report published throughout America and Europe on January 24, 1946, to the effect that MacArthur had outlawed prostitution in Japan. The Japanese government had been ordered to annul all contracts binding women to bondage. General MacArthur acted, he said, under the Potsdam Declaration guaranteeing respect for fundamental rights.

An age-old scandal had been abolished. No longer would fathers be permitted to sell their daughters to the highest bidder. No longer would girls be bound by their debts to brothelkeepers.

The proprietors of brothels customarily took half of a girl's earnings for food, lodging, and overhead. She must then make payments against the cost of her purchase, and also she was expected to buy from the proprietor her cosmetics and other articles, including kimonos at three times their real worth. The result was that she went steadily more deeply into debt. Now by one stroke of the powerful MacArthur pen her debts were canceled and she was free to walk out and become a respectable citizen.

•

The intention was excellent as were all the intentions of this great humanitarian. But the public impression that the Yoshiwara had breathed its last was not well-founded. There is more prostitution in Japan today than at any time in history. The presence of womanless foreign troops, and the general breakdown of morals following the war, are contributing causes.

Another cause is the greater attractiveness of the profession now that a woman may go in business for herself rather than work for a rapacious landlord. One girl, when asked why she didn't quit the game now that she had the protection of the law, said, "Why should I? It has almost doubled my earning power."

There was no exodus from Tokyo's Yoshiwara. Said one resident: "With the terrible housing shortage we'd rather stay here." Of the 310 sumptuous and elaborate houses in this district before the war only nine had survived attack by the B-29's, but new houses were rapidly thrown up to accommodate the rush of foreign customers. Girls were readily recruited into the service.

A typical case was that of a girl who had been working in a teahouse on the Ginza. Her customers were Japanese and she complained that they were noisy and rude. She considered her status much improved when she was able to move to a good house in the Yoshiwara where she could earn many times more money by giving pleasure to polite Americans.

Innkeepers may no longer hold women in bondage. They must accomplish their purpose in a more indirect way. Therefore they offer accommodation, food, and clothing in return for 60 percent of the woman's takings. No contract is signed and the woman is theoretically free to leave at any time.

At the close of the war a great Tokyo munitions plant closed its doors and its owners faced bankruptcy. But presently they had an idea that proved to be their salvation. They reopened the plant as the world's largest brothel under the name of the International Palace. They rightly gauged the hunger of the occupying armies and the plant did such a tremendous business that Americans dubbed it Willow Run —because it processed its product on such a huge scale. Each woman "processed" fifteen GIs a day at $3.30 each. Half of this went to the management. Thus the two hundred and fifty women employed gave the International Palace a daily revenue of $6,002. The owners were satisfied. It was almost as good as making munitions.

A newspaper correspondent, Mark Gayn, visited the International Palace on May 10, 1946, more than three months after legal prostitution had "ended" in Japan. The place had by that time been put off limits for Allied troops and those who visited it must do so on the sly. He found that practically all the girls were deeply in debt to the company for clothes and cosmetics. He asked them if they had heard of the MacArthur directive canceling all such debts. They had not.

The correspondent, who stood on good terms with the Occupation authorities, did not risk their displeasure by sending this item to his home paper. But he jotted it down in his journal and later included it in his book, *Japan Diary.*

The girl market in Japan was chiefly in control of one man, Hitoshi Narikawa, who managed fifty thousand operators. He looked like Santa Claus and was known as Papa-san.

When the MacArthur directive was promulgated he promptly obeyed it. He notified the women in his six thousand houses throughout Japan that they were liberated. They were free to leave—but if they did they must not expect to be taken back.

Only five hundred of the fifty thousand accepted their liberty. The others said they'd rather stay.

"It wasn't that they loved their work," Papa-san explained.

"It was merely that they didn't want to be unemployed, homeless, and hungry. And anyhow, they liked the chance to meet an occasional kind American soldier."

So the girls stayed, but on a new basis. Papa-san merely charged them rental for the rooms.

The girls were not forced to pay their debt but if they insisted upon doing so, good. If they did not, it was all right. But they must not be surprised if they had an accident sometime at the hands of Papa-san's thugs.

The fact is that the sense of honor is so acute in Japan, even in the lowest stratum, that many girls felt bound to work out their debts in spite of a law that permitted them to abscond without payment.

Many girls were emancipated by compassionate GIs. A soft-hearted officer who had just bought out a sixteen-year-old girl for five thousand yen ($2.80) was asked why he did it.

"Just because she's young and beautiful," he said. "And she speaks English."

His friend replied, "Speaks English! The only words she knows are Mama, Papa, and Nice Boy."

"Yeah," acknowledged the officer, "but man, how she times them!"

•

Japanese villages in the vicinity of U.S. army bases complain of the influx of women to serve the needs of soldiers. In Nishitama village three miles from Yokota Air Base seventy houses are occupied by one hundred and twenty girls whose patrons are exclusively American military personnel. Their activities make a deep impression upon the children and young people of the village. When a teacher of the junior high school asked his 140 pupils to write themes on "Present-

Day Social Conditions" nearly a score of them wrote on this subject.

"Some described in detail," reported the *Nippon Times*, "and with youthful candidness, what they saw when they took a peek through paper-sliding doors. Some of the passages are quite unfit for print."

Parents and teachers in all such communities, silent and fearful during the Occupation, began expressing their resentment in no uncertain terms. Many American soldiers agreed with them wholeheartedly and one wrote the following letter to the paper.

> To the Editor:
> Much has been said and written about moral laxity in Japan. Yet we (the Security Forces) have been instrumental in bringing about this condition. Townsmen and villagers near the U.S. bases have tolerated us in silence mainly because we are the occupying force. I wonder what the reactions of our home towns would be if they were subjected to the same humiliation and shameful behavior by foreign soldiers. We are now planting the future outbreak of resentment against us. No nation will forget the moral humiliation it was subjected to. Unless army personnel is better controlled we will soon lose any semblance of respect.
> An officer, U.S.A.F.

Parents of impressionable young people did not like it when professional prostitutes set up housekeeping next door; but how much more painful it was when their own daughters were involved. The great majority of girls used by soldiers were amateurs. Professional women knew what to expect. It was the amateurs who really got hurt.

A girl was brought unconscious to a hospital in Hiroshima. She came to long enough to tell her story, then died. She had been raped by twenty Australian soldiers, then left lying in a wayside lot. The soldiers, when questioned, explained that they had just been out for a "bit of fun."

So many incidents of the sort occurred in Hiroshima that the Australian troops assigned to occupy that city came to be known as *yabanjin,* savages.

The methods of the Americans were less brutal and those of the British were almost refined. The latter depended upon blandishment and persuasion, and I came upon a group of British soldiers earnestly studying the chapter entitled "Phrases in Cupidland" in Sheba's valuable little handbook, *Japanese in Three Weeks.* They were learning to say, "I worship you," in Japanese: *"Anata wo suhai shimasu."* They pored over the Japanese equivalents for *I live for you only, My love for you is all my life, I love you long and I love you true, When you are gone darkness comes into my soul, My heart goes pit-a-pat when you kiss me, Each parting is a grief unspeakable, You are sweet as a demure violet, Dear heart you are mine alone.*

•

The use of such expressions is all in the day's fun for the soldier. He does not realize that they are nothing less than dynamite to the heart of a young girl who has never heard such terms of endearment from the lips of a Japanese. The girl wants to believe what she hears and serious misunderstandings are the result.

Little Tomiko, dragging a bashful GI after her, came into the office of a journalist, Miss Yoko Matsuoka, who had previously befriended her. The girl knew no English and the GI no Japanese, except a few love phrases. Tomiko announced jubilantly that her friend was going to marry her and take her to America.

Miss Matsuoka turned to the GI. "I understand you intend to marry Tomiko."

"No, I ain't promised anything like that. I'm going home in three months."

"What do you intend to do with her?"

He shrugged. His copybook Japanese had evidently won him what he wanted from the girl and he had no further interest in her. But he had some decency. And the journalist wrung a reluctant promise from him, then said to Tomiko:

"He has no intention of marrying you. He will support you until he leaves, but he will not take you to America. You misunderstood."

Two GIs, headed for the U.S., looked out of the window of the train about to pull out and bade a last farewell to two weeping Japanese girls. Evidently the girls knew no English, or not enough to understand the heartless wisecracks of their departing lovers. A sobbing question, "When you come back?" was answered with a laugh: "Come back? When you damn Japs bomb Pearl Harbor again, baby, I'll be back!"

•

We stayed a few days in the home of missionary I. L. Shaver in Oita. A pretty *moshi-moshi* girl (telephone operator) from the Oita Telephone Exchange came to consult the missionary. She wanted to find Jimmy Blank, a GI who had been like a husband to her but now didn't come to see her anymore. He had promised to take her to America. He had given her an auto tab of his car, his name on a piece of paper, and a snapshot of his sister.

She was in a highly emotional state. She could not eat or sleep, she was so lovesick. She was crazy about her GI, she said. She was wild to go to America. She was afraid he had been sent to Korea. He might be killed.

"If he dies I want to die too."

She couldn't get any information about him. Whenever she called up the camp and asked for Jimmy, every man who answered the phone said, "I'm Jimmy."

Mr. Shaver undertook to telephone for her. When he did,

he was told that Jimmy had leave until twelve that night. He wasn't using his leave to see her.

Whether the girl's hint of self-destruction was carried any further I do not know, but not a few of these international incidents ended in suicide. In a number of cases it was a double suicide when the soldier and his sweetheart could not see their way clear to wed and could not bear to part. An Air Force lieutenant, about to return to his fiancée in America, was poisoned in a geisha house by his Japanese friend who then took her own life. This is the only death on record of a soldier of the Occupation at the hands of a Japanese.

Usually the soldier is allowed to go and forget, and if there is any dying to be done, the girl does it. The suicide rate, always considerable in Japan, has risen sharply since the war.

The volcanoes are the favorite scenes for such acts of quiet desperation. Since the volcanoes are regarded as Shinto shrines it is an act of piety to give oneself, a living sacrifice, a burnt offering, to the gods. The smoking craters of Asama, Mihara, and Aso receive scores of the lovelorn every year.

Two GI's on the way down the slope of Mt. Aso met a weeping girl on the way up. When she sank to the ground they went to her assistance and somehow learned her story. She loved an American who had gone home. She had gowned herself in her best ceremonial kimono and had come by train all the way from Fukuoka to end her life here.

The GI's led her to a hotel at the base of the mountain, fortified her with a good meal, took her in their jeep to Kumamoto where they put her on the train for Fukuoka.

The number of GI babies is unknown. Any mention of the question in the press or on the radio was disapproved, and the Japanese radio announcer who referred to the birth of the first GI baby as "the first Occupation present" was fired.

Now the subject is freely and bitterly discussed. The government, as a matter of international courtesy, still refrains from making a census. The lowest unofficial estimate places the number of Madame Butterfly's children at twenty thousand. The great Tokyo newspaper *Yomiuri* declares that "international orphans with blue eyes or black faces who do not know their fathers or mothers now total two hundred thousand throughout Japan."

•

Of course there are more to come. Another Tokyo paper calls attention to the fact that "the number of half-breeds will be on the increase in view of the stationing of U.S. forces in Japan for a relatively prolonged period."

Every day press and public become more acid, and more obloquy is heaped upon the mothers of mixed bloods. The half-castes are becoming outcasts. They are considered morally unacceptable. Other children make fun of their light hair, or ridicule the kinky hair and black faces of children fathered by the Negro troops. Mothers dye fair hair black, but nothing much can be done with a black face.

Americans who suppose that their godlike attributes are the envy of the rest of the human race would be astonished at the Japanese antipathy for "faded hair, washed-out skins, beetling brows, big noses, and hairy chests." Particularly now that Japan has begun to swing away from her postwar adoration of western power, race prejudice is reasserting itself. The Japanese consider themselves racially purer than Americans—and with good reason. Japan is no melting pot. True, the race combines Mongolian and Polynesian strains, but the blending was completed more than a millennium ago. The Japanese are ethnically one of the most homogeneous peoples on the face of the earth.

This gives them no reason for pride, because a "pure" race is not necessarily better than a mixed race—in fact the odds are on the side of the mixed race. But people do not need good reason to be proud, and with the resurgence of nationalism in Japan anything alien is looked upon with increasing dislike and suspicion.

The *Yomiuri* suggests that all these unwanted half-breeds

be sent to the United States. "America is a melting pot of races, so these orphans would not be as forlorn over there as here in Japan." A few thousand have been sent to Brazil to be adopted by some of the three hundred thousand Japanese in that country. Brazil is even more of a melting pot than the U.S. and far more tolerant toward racial minorities.

But the great majority have no means of going abroad. They must stay in Japan and make the best of it.

There is agitation on the part of Ku Klux Klanlike elements in Japan against allowing Eurasians and Negrasians to attend the public schools. It is said that the presence of these "children of crime" would contaminate respectable children. Segregation is demanded. A government spokesman declares against discrimination. "So far we have made no racial distinction and we don't intend to."

In the meantime private institutions have been caring for GI babies. Missionary Egon Hessel, who has a hand in every sort of good work, took us through one of his kindergartens. Among the black-haired Japanese there was a single little brown-haired tot. Her GI father is with his family in America, but he sends forty dollars a month to support the child and its mother.

This is an exception. In most cases the fathers accept no responsibility for their Japan-born children. In many cases they do not even know that they exist.

A good-hearted Japanese woman, Miki Sawada, turned her father's farm in Oiso into a home for deserted half-breed babies. With contributions from Japanese and Americans she is caring for more than one hundred unwanted children whom she describes as "innocent victims of this age of war and violence." GIs connected with the Tokyo Army Hospital gave $4,000. Persons in Richmond, Virginia, contributed $300 a month.

The Pearl S. Buck Foundation has been a blessing to many abandoned Japanese-American children.

Our Lady of Lourdes Baby Home in Yokohama cares for

175 orphans. Sister Mary, chief nurse, raised funds to start a boys' school. "The poor things," she said. "The Japanese children will make them suffer if they go to public schools. Children can be very cruel, you know."

Other homes are being supported by American servicemen. "These are our responsibilities," was the slogan of the U.S. Naval Air Station at Atsugi in a drive that raised $2,200. A Battery in Yokohama donated $250 a month.

This spirit of goodwill needs to be applied for prevention as well as for cure. But the chance of this is slight so long as the ratio of American servicemen to American women in Japan is about 100 to 1. The men moreover are for the most part young, just at the age when they begin to look most insistently for female companionship. Armies since the beginning of time have been baffled by this problem.

Many servicemen, obeying a natural impulse but unwilling to indulge it to the injury of others, are marrying Japanese women. This need not be considered a comedown for the American soldier. In many cases he marries above himself, into a family of means, culture, and position. His bride may have the better of him in education and breeding. He deserves to be congratulated, not condemned for "going native."

Such marriages may help in the long run to solve the problem of half-caste children. With the increase in the number of legitimate Eurasians, the stigma attached to the illegitimate will fade. As Japan becomes racially more cosmopolitan, she should become less rabidly race conscious. That will make Japan a safer and better neighbor.

America too will be a safer and better neighbor if she chooses to receive cordially the Nipponese brides of returning servicemen. For them life in a strange country is a trying experience and may easily end in disaster for themselves, their husbands, and their children. In some cases Japanese wives in America have organized "War Brides Clubs" and travel long distances to get together once a month to discuss their problems of adjustment in this new land.

That is good, but it is still more important that these women, instead of isolating themselves, be drawn into community activities with their American neighbors and that their children should experience no discrimination in school or on the playground. The Japanese have rare qualities of culture and character to contribute to American life.

Whether on the whole the Japanese woman has been advanced or retarded by foreign intervention it would be hard to say. Perhaps her lot has been improved in spite of the Occupation, as well as because of it. The one really precious gift that has been conferred upon her is the suffrage. Probably she will keep it. So far as I am aware history records no instance of women being deprived of the suffrage once they have won it. With it the Japanese woman can, if she puts her mind to it, gradually free herself from a web of tyranny and humiliation twenty centuries old.

22

FROM WITCH TO M.D.

Only thirty-five years ago we found witches and sorcerers, ghosts and goblins, dominating the practice of medicine in Japan.

Not that there were no modern physicians, but back-country people placed more reliance upon the black arts.

Our friend the cooper who made bathtubs and set them out along the side of the road so that any passerby might scrouge down into them and try them for fit, complained of stomach aches.

"Perhaps you ate something that disagreed with you."

"No, no. This trouble has nothing to do with food."

"Then you know the cause of it?"

"Yes, I know. It's that Kato."

A neighbor, Kato, had died two months previously.

"But he's dead. How could he hurt you?"

The cooper smiled grimly. "It's his ghost."

"But what has his ghost against you?"

"Oh, Kato burned himself and blamed me for it. He

bought one of my bathtubs. He was careless about the stoveguard. It came loose and he got up against the stove."

The stove is an integral part of the Japanese bathtub and is separated from the bathing compartment only by a stoveguard or board.

"He wanted me to pay damages. Of course I refused. He said the day would come when he would get at my soul." He placed his hand over his stomach. He evidently thought of the seat of the soul as being the stomach or abdomen. This was once the common belief of much of Asia as far west as old Judea, where it appeared in such Biblical expressions as "bowels of compassion."

The weird conception at the bottom of all this fear of the deceased was that the dead had superhuman powers. They could do things that they never could have done while living. Alive, a man might be weak and of no importance in the community. Dead, he was a divine power, for good or evil.

This helps to explain something that mystified our fighting men, namely the apparent eagerness of some Japanese soldiers to commit suicide. One GI marveled, "They seem to think they are spiting us when they bop themselves off!"

The man committing *harakiri* was apt to hurl a savage cry at his enemies as if he were about to begin to fight, rather than about to quit.

He believed that once past the door of death he could emerge as a god with better weapons and supernatural strength. Then he would really begin to lay about him.

If you have a grudge against someone, commit suicide and wreak vengeance upon him from the vantage point of the spirit world. When the U.S. Congress passed the Exclusion Law, Japanese students killed themselves after writing notes explaining their intention of using their supernatural powers to make life miserable for American congressmen.

So the dead Kato was making it hot for the cooper.

"But have you seen a doctor about your stomach?"

"No. I went to the priest. He sold me something to put on my *kamidana*."

He took me inside the little house. On one wall, about six feet from the floor, was the *kamidana*, or god-shelf. On it was a miniature Shinto shrine (temple) made of beautifully grained wood. Inside it were tablets of white wood inscribed with the names of the cooper's ancestors. Before it stood small dishes containing offerings of water, salt, rice, fish, and vegetable.

"This is what the priest sold me," and the cooper indicated a small lamp in the form of a saucer containing rapeseed oil in which a burning wick floated. "I must keep it lighted all the time until I feel better. I think it has helped me some already."

This sort of thing came closer to home when our own maid complained of eye trouble. We offered to send her to an oculist in Tokyo and pay for glasses if they were needed. She was most appreciative but said she would have to think it over. Whenever the suggestion was repeated she gently put us off. Then one day she disappeared for a few hours and came back with a burned spot above each eye.

"Yes," she said when we remarked on it, "I am to have five treatments. The priest applied *moxa*"—a cone of mugwort which is placed on the skin and then set on fire—"there on my forehead, also here and here and here . . ." and she indicated the back of each forearm, the inside of each wrist, and the middle of the back. "And I must not eat eggs or fish the day before treatment."

The eye trouble, of course, was caused by evil spirits, possibly the spirits of certain relatives with whom she had never got along very well. The burning was supposed to make the spirits so uncomfortable that they would leave the body. The demonstration was very convincing, for the patient could tell by her own suffering just how much the fire was tormenting her unwelcome visitors.

After the five treatments she looked like the tattooed lady in the circus. The eyes continued bad. But she never went to the oculist.

Her husband, a fisherman, was one of the town fathers, had spent eight years in school, and read the *Asahi*. The wife could read too. They did not belong to any submerged class. They were quite typical inhabitants of the Japanese countryside.

One day the woman came in with her daughter's baby on her back and set before us two slim pink cakes. She explained that the baby had been crying, so she had taken it to the Nichiren priest on the hillside above us. He had performed a little rite of exorcism. He told her to contribute ten sen and make a prayer. Then he gave her these cakes as a sign that her prayer had been answered.

The cakes were *mochi*, rice paste, gummy and tasteless, but doubtless very high in spiritual value.

It was thought that the baby's crying was due to a certain insect that had managed to get into the body. You went to the priest to get the insect out.

Paper dolls, if properly blessed and paid for, were potent against disease. The village shrine called them *hitogata*. Cut out of paper, they came in two forms known as "man-shapes" and "woman-shapes."

The charcoal merchant suffering from a sudden headache could not use the woman-shape his wife had bought the week before. He must repair to the shrine and purchase a man-shape. The priest wrote his age and sex upon the *hitogata*. Then he took it home and proceeded to touch every part of his body with it while repeating a Shinto prayer that the offense he had committed against the gods for which this ailment was the punishment be pardoned.

Almost every house in the village, including the one we had rented, was plastered near the front door with papers bearing printed charms supposed to protect the household. Pilgrims made long and expensive trips to sacred mountains or famous shrines to obtain charms believed to be potent. Dragons, devils' heads, hairy monsters brandishing long swords, Kwannon of the thousand arms, all cooperated to repel evil.

•

One day a neighbor woman was showing my wife a drawerful of her small treasures. There were amulets and talismans sold to her by witch doctors. One made the eyes strong. Another warded off smallpox. Another was guaranteed to improve your handwriting. A few of the teeth of a deceased relative had been preserved. They had been picked out of the ashes after cremation. There were also some nail cuttings of various members of the family.

Among the articles was a small white package. It bore the woman's name. My wife expressed polite curiosity. The woman explained shyly that the package contained a portion of her umbilical cord.

It was saved by her mother at her birth and must be carefully kept until death when it would be buried with its owner. It insured rebirth. Reincarnation was impossible without it.

A woman was burned to death when she ran back into her blazing house to retrieve this vital link between the past and the future.

Fear of the bogeyman is nothing compared with the many terrors that could be used to control the behavior of the Japanese youngster. The *tengu* was a feathered monster with a human nose a yard long. The *oni* was an ogre with horns and a frightful reputation for eating bad children. A *nukekubi* was a head which during the day was securely anchored on the shoulders of some unpleasant person in the village but at night detached itself and went roaming about doing mischief.

The child who ate too much candy might expect a hideous

huge worm to visit him during the night. It would crawl under the covers, pry open his lips, and squirm down into his stomach where it would produce great pain.

Japanese children had a clear and terrible picture of the dragon. According to the famous Japanese author, Bakin, the dragon "has a deer's horns, a horse's head, eyes like those of a devil, a neck like that of a snake, a belly like that of a red worm, scales like those of a fish, claws like a hawk's, paws like a tiger's, and ears like a cow's."

A stream which ran through our village deepened into a pool which would have been a fine spot for swimming when the sea was too rough. But the boys never used it. I asked why.

"There's a *kappa* in it!"

It was a greenish creature with web-footed claws. It lived in deep pools. It reached up to clutch the feet of the unwary, dragged them down, and feasted upon their bodies.

And there were always ghosts, ghosts by the million. They floated through the air, their legs dwindling away to nothing, their necks drawn out to frightful length and twisted like a snake, their hands extended and fingers cramped as if about to clutch a throat. They were acutely uncomfortable and always seeking a chance to vent their spite upon the living.

Nor do the children escape the world of monsters when they die. On the bank of the Sai-no-Kawara (the Japanese Styx or river of death) they encounter the merciless she-devil, the hag Shozuka-no-Baba. She steals their clothing, then sets them to work in the broiling sun piling stones. They are told that if they make their piles high enough they may cross the river. But every night the hag and her devils pull down the little towers.

Even the educated were not quite free of such fancies. A college graduate drew me away from the edge of the pool where the *kappa* was supposed to lurk.

"Of course we don't believe in such things," he laughed. "But it's just as well to be prudent."

A strange complex was the dread of the fox, to our minds a harmless and sometimes handsome little beast, to the Japanese a demon. Not only the insane were supposed to be "foxed." The hospitals reported many cases of hysteria induced by the idea of the powers of a fox to enter the body and take control. In this demoniac possession the victim held conversation with the fox which replied in a high cracked voice.

It was a hypnotic phenomenon of great interest to psychiatrists. Often the doctor could do nothing—it was necessary to call in a witch who would argue with the fox and bribe it with cakes to leave the victim.

And this was not just the ignorant notion of some old women. Big department stores had fox shrines on the roof and many business buildings were similarly equipped.

"Some of our employees have objected because there is no fox shrine on our roof," Eric Sitzenstatter of the Tokyo branch of Eastman Kodak told me. "I tell them that this is an American firm. But they say an American oil refinery has a fox shrine and the annual convention of the employees is held there. The convention begins with prayer by a priest before the shrine. The fox is supposed to have a lot to do with luck, good or bad, in business."

The *soroban* doctor could tell you by manipulating the *soroban* or abacus what was the matter with you and what medicine you should have.

A *mamorifuda*, slip of paper bearing sacred characters, would be rolled up and swallowed for internal pains. Or it might be pasted on the head as a remedy for headache, or on the jaw for toothache.

As we walked through a village on the island of Kurahashi a woman opened her door and flung some rice into the street. Then, observing that she had barely escaped peppering us, she apologized.

"It's no matter," I said. "But why are you throwing away rice?"

"So the baby can sleep," she replied.

Since rice is not grown in the islands and must be brought from the mainland, it is costly. It is hardly something to be thrown away. What connection could there be between the waste of rice and a baby's sleep?

We questioned the woman until we had the story. It seems that there is an evil spirit that bothers babies. It comes in the form of a little man wearing a suit of armor and riding a horse. He can enter any room no matter how tightly it is closed. He prods babies with his sharp sword and makes them cry. But he dreads rice. It alone will keep him away.

"Once when I was nursing my baby," the woman said, "the door of the room slid open and ten little men came in. Each was as tall as my finger. They wore armor and rode small horses. They galloped toward us and my baby began to scream. But I always kept a dish of 'throwing rice' handy and I seized it and threw some rice at the little men. They vanished and a little smoke went up. The rice dish was stained with blood."

The woman obviously was not making this up. She really believed that it had happened. She believed it because people for a thousand years had believed it. Anything that had been believed that long must be true.

We were interested spectators at the building of a house. It seemed to us that it ought to face southwest because in that direction the view across the Inland Sea was superb.

"That wouldn't do," the carpenter said. "A gate on that side would be a *byomon*, sickness gate. Many diseases would enter by it. Yes, you have to know what you're about when you build a house. That's why it's wise to have an experienced builder. I've been building houses for thirty years. Now here's another thing you have to look out for—the well. It must be on the south side of the house. That's the prosperity side."

A Japanese who didn't know his directions would be in difficulty. Each point of the compass had its own significance.

For example, you must not sleep with your head to the north. That is only for the dead. If you are ill you must go in the correct direction to get your medicine, varying according to the disease. The local sorceress could help you, for she possessed a "disease compass." It was too bad for the local druggist when the medicine needle did not point in his direction. One druggist sought to solve this problem by spotting many small branch depots here and there through the countryside so that no matter where the needle came to rest it would point to his wares.

A kindly old lady heard me complain of a nightmare induced by a too-hearty meal of *tempura*, prawns fried in batter.

"You should have a *baku*," she said. "Then you may eat whatever you please and you will have no bad dreams. Wait—I will get one for you."

She retired into her house and in a moment brought out a sheet of paper bearing a picture of an extraordinary animal with a pointed head, rhinoceros eyes, a nose like an elephant's but shorter, a tiger's legs, and a cow's tail. Altogether it looked more like a tapir than anything else.

"You put it under your pillow," she said. "It will eat all your dreams and you will have perfect sleep."

The tradition of the *baku* or dream-eater came from China, probably in the eighth century. The legendary beast was supposed to be able to eat anything, including rocks and iron blocks, and it especially enjoyed feeding upon nightmares.

If the members of a family could not resolve a family problem they consulted a dead father or grandfather through an *ichiko* or medium. The spirit of the dead entered the body of the *ichiko* and spoke through his mouth.

In the household shrine were the *ihai* or mortuary tablets of the family dead. An *ihai* was regarded as something almost alive, or something that might become alive if the dead person it represented needed to return to earth. Then it became flesh and blood. If a sick child cried for its dead mother, she might thus return to suckle it. A wife might come back to comfort her bereaved husband or even to bear him a child. A servant could come back to aid his former master. An enemy could return to take revenge. After the errand of vengeance or mercy was performed, the living dead became once more only a tablet.

The older folk of the islands still believe in reincarnation. Children are warned that if they are not good they will come into the next life as hideous animals or insects. An old widow lavished great attention upon her cat. The neighbors speculated that the cat was really her departed husband in his new incarnation.

Names were lucky or unlucky according to the number of strokes and dots in the ideographs forming the name. One who was ill could be cured by a change of name. You could have a serious accident if your ideograph had too many dots and too few strokes.

In a medicine shop on the Ginza we found dried and pickled snakes, snake blood, cremated spiders, toads, centipedes, moles, bats, owls, sparrows' claws, rats, angleworm liniment, skunk gas pills ("an infallible remedy for everything from a red face to a bed sore"), monkey skulls, viper powder (for women's complaints), rhinoceros pills ("a certain cure for tightness of the chest, pain, gnashing of the teeth, depression of the spirits, and in fact every other disease under the sun").

On a country road we came up with a boy leading a pony loaded with brush topped with two large skinned snakes which he was taking home to eat. He explained that they were good for pleurisy.

In Tokyo sixty-five licensed snake dealers sold five million snakes annually. They were a panacea for all diseases. Since they were guaranteed to make one strong, they were particularly favored by athletes.

The woman who worshiped before a stone phallus would be fertile. A child if passed through the hole in the "Measles Stone" in Yutenji temple cemetery, Tokyo, would be promptly cured of measles. From February to May when measles were prevalent, long lines of parents with their children waited their turn at the stone. Those who could not wait bought an antimeasle charm from the temple priests. It was good business for the temple which sold over a million such charms every year.

A medical catalogue advertised: "Women's Happy Medicine. If try a lady who does not feel better when unite with a man use this then happiness will recover as her young age it was."

•

Today there are still a few who depend for health and happiness upon the sorcerer, the astrologer, the palmist, the spiritualist, the priestly vendor of charms and talismans, the commercial dealer in powdered bugs and beasts.

But scientific medicine has made gigantic strides.

It is not generally known that Dr. Umetaro Suzuki discovered Vitamin B; that it was Dr. Hosoya who first isolated reticulin, tricomycin, and two other antibiotic drugs; that Dr. Takamine first produced the constituent now used everywhere in starch factories, and first found a way to produce adrenalin; that Professor Yoshida of Tokyo University identified the cancer that the medical world now calls "Yoshida Sarcoma"; that the late Dr. Hantaro Nagaoka pioneered atomic theory; that a Dr. Kakizaki discovered the vaccine for rinderpest.

Medical breakthroughs in Japan include the first successful attempt to destroy a brain tumor by irradiation with neutron rays.

Treatment by laser beam, still unfamiliar in America and Europe, is practiced in Japanese hospitals.

The monthly Japanese production of penicillin exceeds one trillion units, second only to the United States.

Bacteriological examinations can be made in any part of Japan.

Japan is the only Asian country to have eliminated cholera

and typhus. Typhoid and paratyphoid have been reduced 90 percent. Dysentery, once common, is extremely rare.

In prewar times, every other student had tuberculosis, the greatest killer in Japan. The percentage of deaths from this disease has dropped from 13.5 in 1950 to 3 in 1970.

Life expectancy, now seventy-one years, was fifty thirty years ago.

Infant mortality has dropped from twenty-five per thousand births to fifteen.

Children are much taller, bigger, healthier than before the war. School desks have had to be enlarged twice during that period. Low ceilings have been lifted, doorways have been cut higher. The average height of eleven-year-old boys has increased by five inches; of girls, by five and a half.

Weight of boys has gone up fourteen pounds; of girls, nineteen pounds.

"Today," a ministry survey reports, "it is common for fourteen-year-old children to be taller than their parents."

The reasons: improved medical care, and better diet. The per capita intake of animal protein was fourteen grams in 1949, twenty-nine grams in 1966. Fat intake during the same period increased by twenty-four grams.

The Japanese are drinking twenty times as much milk as twenty years ago.

They took fifty milligrams of calcium a day in 1966, compared with only two milligrams in 1949. Calcium is an important nutrient for human bones.

"It may be that in the not-so-distant future the Japanese will surpass the Americans in their physical measurements," says Dr. Shinkichi Nagamine of the Ministry of Health and Welfare.

American doctors go to Japan for the express purpose of studying the laboratories which are considered superior in some respects to those in the West.

What part the Nipponese gods had in all this is not clear. A Japanese author in 1811 wrote: "The art of medicine, though introduced to Japan from abroad, appears originally to have been taught to foreign countries by our own great gods."

However that may be, not a few of the arts of medicine are today being taught to foreign countries by Japan.

23

BIRTH CONTROL

On every island we visited in the Inland Sea, the inhabitants (if there were any) immediately set to work to show us the local sights.

These were usually the temples, shrines, gardens, groves, views from the hills—to satisfy our hosts we must climb to the very peak of every one—and the island industries.

Having become used to this routine, it was a surprise at one landing to be whisked promptly to the island's proudest institution, the birth control clinic.

We were in it before I realized its nature. Then I tried to retire but soon found out that if I did so official feelings would be hurt.

"This is a very important office," I was told.

"I am sure it is important," I replied, "but do I belong here?" I glanced around the outer room where pregnant women silently waited while from behind a closed door came the sound of discussion.

"Why not?" said my guide. "All members of the committee are men."

The closed door was opened and we were ushered into a room where a terrified little woman sat before a long table behind which four owllike judges studied her papers.

They at once rose, bowed, and drew breath. We were introduced. They were honored, they said, that their work should interest visitors. They were the members of the local Eugenic Protection Investigation Committee. We sat down, and of course tea was brought in.

I stole a look at the woman, expecting to find her painfully embarrassed by so much masculine scrutiny of her private affairs. But she had brightened up considerably and was chatting amiably with our official. No women are more modest than the Japanese, but they are modest by rule and rote. A woman who would not uncover the back of her neck on the street will walk nude into a bathroom. The one is improper, the other is proper. The new law had given this woman the right to plead her case before this committee, therefore she felt no embarrassment. But she was worried for fear her application would not be granted.

"We are very poor," she said when the committee chairman asked her reasons for application. "We cannot feed the children we already have. It would not be wise for us to have another."

The chairman fixed his disapproving eye upon her. "Was it wise for you to allow yourself to become pregnant in the first place?"

The woman bowed before she answered. "I assure you we made every effort to prevent it."

"You mean you used a contraceptive device?"

"We did. But it failed."

"So you ask authorization for interruption of pregnancy?"

The woman bowed.

"For economic reasons?"

"For economic reasons."

"The case will be investigated. You may go now."

The woman rose, bowed in turn to every person in the room, and left.

A name was called and another woman in like condition came in. It was hard to convince myself that our presence was not an added trial to the applicants and I suggested to our companion that we would like to see more of his fair city. We retired, the women in the outer room raising their heads dully as we passed.

The term "interruption of pregnancy" as used in the birth control clinics is a polite substitution for the harsher word "abortion." Abortion was made legal in Japan by the Eugenic Protection Law of July, 1948. It may be resorted to if childbirth would endanger a woman's health, if the family is unable to support another child, or if the woman has been made pregnant against her will.

Abortions have always been numerous in Japan, though illegal before passage of this law. For three centuries before the arrival of Commodore Perry in 1853 the population of Japan was stationary at about twenty-six million. It was held stationary by the practice of infanticide.

Now abortion has official sanction and any woman who can meet the conditions prescribed by the law may have an abortion for ten dollars (as against $700 to $1,500 in the U.S.). Some doctors, alarmed at the number of legal abortions (a million a year), objected to the law on moral grounds. Many believed that emphasis should be placed upon the prevention of pregnancy rather than its interruption once it had begun. This opinion was echoed in the press. Said the *Mainichi* in 1951:

> A characteristic feature of birth control this year was that the couples concerned took recourse to abortion rather than to contraception. This drastic measure was taken mainly on account of the fact that (1) organized institutions for dissemination of knowledge concerning contraception are not enough in numbers as

well as in their established facilities and (2) trustworthy drugs and devices are not available ... Of the thirty-five different kinds of drugs for contraception which were permitted to be sold, there was only one that passed the examination as to the effectiveness thereof when such an examination was recently conducted by the Ministry of Welfare.

Contraceptives are sold to the tune of fifteen million a month. The law requires every prefecture to maintain at least one office where free instruction in contraception may be given. Some two hundred of these offices are now functioning. Newspapers and magazines treat the subject quite frankly, illustrating their discussions with anatomical drawings.

That the birth rate needs to be controlled is now recognized by all Japanese except those who still cherish the dream of Japanese domination over Asia. At first little was done about it. In spite of the legalizing of abortion and the talk of contraception, each family seemed to consider family limitation as the problem of the folks next door. In a land where the veneration of ancestors is considered important, a man must have children to venerate him when he becomes an ancestor. Male children are needed to carry on the family name. Children can help on the farm. Female children are a financial asset, for in times of stress they may be hired out to the cotton mills or sold to a geisha house. If wedded they may bring a good dowry.

Besides, for a solid century now, the Japanese have been taught by their government that they should have plenty of children in order to compete with the West. Commodore Perry started it. When his black ships sailed into Uraga Harbor in 1853 Japan began her struggle to match power with the West. The population grew rapidly. By 1925 it had doubled. For three centuries before Perry Japan had avoided foreign wars. Her new ambition to become one of the world powers made it necessary for her to have more sons to fight

Russia, to take over Korea, Formosa, and the isles of Micronesia, and to prosecute the "China Incident."

It was patriotic to have many children. The fever of propagation rose to its greatest height just before the attack upon Pearl Harbor, and government posters appeared carrying the slogan: "Bear more children and increase the population." A law effective in 1941 offered subsidies to big families, subsidies to men who married before the age of twenty-five and to women who were married at twenty-one when, according to the document, they should have a procreative period of about twenty years. The law declared as its objective an average of five children to each family and the increase of the population of Japan to one hundred million by 1951.

And so the baby mill went into high gear and in 1947 the birth rate reached a peak of 34.8 per thousand—the highest ever recorded in Japan.

By this time the rabid nationalists who had dreamed of overwhelming the world by sheer force of Japanese numbers had been discredited. They were purged, exiled from public office. But they could look on with sly satisfaction as their work was continued by those who had purged them. The Allied Occupation unintentionally contributed more to the overcrowding of Japan than the Japanese militarists had ever been able to do in the same period of time.

Population growth is stimulated by either raising the birth rate or reducing the death rate. The Public Health and Welfare Section of SCAP, under the inspired direction of Brigadier-General C. F. Sams, launched drastic medical reforms that so improved Japanese health that the death rate was reduced from 29.2 per thousand in 1945 to 10.3 in 1951.

By measures of sanitation and a concerted attack upon endemic diseases the average life span of the Japanese was prolonged by thirteen years as compared with that in 1935. Millions of babies who would have succumbed during the first ten years were kept alive to become adult and claim a place in the crowded sun.

The achievements of Sams and his devoted assistants deserve nothing but the highest praise.

He recognized Japanese medical schools, and opened the first nursing schools. He persuaded the Diet to pass a medical service law stipulating minimum standards in hospitals. A child-welfare law was enacted. Narcotics were placed under strict regulation. By encouragement of new branches of agriculture, nutrition was improved.

It was a glorious story of unselfish service, though not a new one. The same humanitarian spirit was shown long ago by the British in improving the health of India, by many European nations in their colonies, by America in the Philippines, by the Japanese themselves in the Micronesian islands. But perhaps nowhere and at no time has there been such an outpouring of practical goodwill from the victors to a defeated enemy.

Perhaps "practical" is not precisely the word since it was hardly practical to take measures that would drastically reduce the death rate in an already overpopulated country without at the same time paying attention to the need of reducing the birth rate. General Sams was aware of this problem but was not free to do anything about it. He did not determine Occupation policy. That policy, as demonstrated by General MacArthur, was to promote the health and longevity of the Japanese without assuming any responsibility for the overpopulation resulting from such measures.

That SCAP was unwilling to come to grips with Japan's greatest problem, that of population, was proved when Professor Ackerman was trimmed down to size. At the request of SCAP Dr. Edward Ackerman of the University of Chicago came to Japan and spent two years on a detailed study of Japan's natural resources.

The outcome was a two-volume analysis of Japan's economic condition. Dr. Ackerman's conclusion was that overpopulation was Japan's main economic problem. He stated that only by holding population at the present level could the

Japanese have any hope for a balanced economy. If Japan did not limit her population the consequence would be a starvation living standard, and increasing reliance upon aid from America or elsewhere.

Some of the first copies of the Ackerman report fell into the hands of American religious workers. A few Protestant opponents of birth control protested to General MacArthur. The American Catholic Women's clubs of the Tokyo–Yokohama area challenged him to disavow advocacy of family limitation.

He promptly did so by suppressing the report. Only fifty-seven copies had been distributed. The remaining 2,443 copies were locked in a Tokyo vault. The chief of the Natural Resources Section, which had published the report, got a sharp reprimand for having "embarrassed" the Supreme Commander. He was ordered to tear out the offending pages, including his foreword which contained the sentence: "Japan is a nation of too many people on too little land, and its most serious economic and social problems stem directly from this condition." All charts and figures representing the need for family limitation were ordered out.

Why this sudden withdrawal of the Supreme Commander's support from a conclusion which he had previously endorsed by releasing it for publication? One of his civilian aides gave me what he believed to be the reason: "Mac didn't want to be caught in the middle." In other words, his rejection of his economic expert's findings was due not to any doubt as to their accuracy but to fear of criticism both from American groups and from militaristic factions in Japan.

For the same reason he refused an entry permit to Dr. Margaret Sanger, birth control advocate, when she was invited to give a series of lectures in Japan under the auspices of Japanese organizations seriously concerned over postwar population increase. She had to wait until after the Occupation. In 1952 she filled her engagement.

MacArthur justified his action on the grounds that population limitation was something for the Japanese to decide for themselves. This excuse had considerable merit. Many of the questions decided by SCAP might better have been left to the Japanese. If they had been, there would not later have been such widespread rejection of SCAP reforms.

But just why it was proper to impose the will of SCAP upon the Japanese in hundreds of smaller matters, but improper even to give advice on Japan's most pressing problem, is not clear.

MacArthur also excused his position with the familiar theory that as a nation industrializes, its population growth slows down. Certainly that has happened in the case of some western nations. But it takes a century or two when it works, and often it does not work. To trust to this chance rather than to active measures would be like waiting for lightning to do what ought to be done by electricity.

The shakiness of the theory may be illustrated with a single example: The population of China, an unindustrialized nation, remained practically stationary while Japan, which had been highly industrialized for half a century, had a more rapid population increase than any other nation in Asia.

How could Japan afford to wait a hundred years on the bare chance that urbanization might slow her growth, when in only thirty-three years her population would double at the then rate—a rate more than twice as fast as the increase of the world as a whole! Japan was becoming less self-sufficient daily as the number of her people grew. She produced food for about sixty-five million people. She had eighty-six million people crowded into an area no larger than the state of Montana. Only 15 percent of this land was arable.

"No country," wrote Professor (later Ambassador) Edwin Reischauer in *The United States and Japan*, "not even the teeming lands of India, China or Java, can equal Japan's record of almost nineteen hundred members of the purely agricultural population to each square mile of cultivated land. The average Japanese farmer has less than one-fifth as much land to cultivate as the average farmer in Belgium, the West's most densely populated country. Include Japan's huge cities, and she has more than thirty-four hundred people per square mile of cultivable land, putting her far above all competitors as the world's most crowded land. She has more than twelve times as many people to feed per square mile of farm land as the United States and approximately one-third more people to feed per acre than a thoroughly industrialized and urbanized land like Great Britain."

Emigration was no adequate answer. The Japanese do not want to leave home. While Japan controlled the great fertile expanses of Manchuria, few Japanese could be persuaded to settle in that rich land. They didn't like to leave their friends, they didn't like the Manchurian winters, they couldn't compete with the Chinese peasants already settled in Manchuria. Comparatively few Japanese ever went to Formosa and only a handful to the Japanese Mandated Islands. Since the loss of these territories, their settlers have returned to Japan.

Countries not controlled by Japan did not have a very large welcome mat out for the Japanese. It once looked as if they would gain entry to New Guinea, the Philippines, and other parts of Southeast Asia. But their war upon these lands made them feared and distrusted. Australia, the emptiest land on the Asiatic side of the world, barred Asiatics. The United States, where Japanese farmers willing to work sixteen hours a day were a serious embarrassment to American farmers who preferred to go at an easier pace, had all but closed the doors.

Japan was delighted when in 1951 Brazil extended an invitation to Japanese emigrants to grow jute in the Amazon valley. Japanese enthusiasm cooled when it was learned how many emigrants were wanted—only five thousand. There were more than five thousand babies born in Japan in a single day.

And even if all doors were open, which they were not, and if the Japanese were willing to break home ties and move to strange lands, which they were not, it was incredible that emigration could be organized on such a scale as to offset Japan's population growth of two million a year.

"I shudder to think of the explosiveness of this population growth," said a sober-minded Occupation official in Japan. Intelligent Japanese were keenly alive to the danger. Dr. Kageyas W. Amano, a prominent Japanese physician, said, "The rising birth rate will make our country increasingly vulnerable to the communists or militarists."

No nation has a moral right to allow reckless increase that will lead either to the poverty and privation of its people or to seizure of the lands of its neighbors. Expansion leads to aggression, and aggression, as the Japanese well know, leads to disaster.

MacArthur's word was law in Japan. When he threw a wet blanket upon proposals of family limitation and discredited those who had made them, the several Japanese movements on behalf of regulation collapsed. For a time no one dared advocate control.

With the passing of the Occupation, the heretics began to come out of hiding, their doctrine was more widely accepted and "marriage consultation offices" were established by the government. The great newspaper *Mainichi* published and heartily endorsed the statement by Warren Thompson, scholar of population:

"An intelligent and persistent effort to educate the Japanese people in the need to keep their families small will do more to increase the nation's welfare, to raise the general level of living, and to rehabilitate Japan's economy than any other single program that can be undertaken."

Today, Japan has done what other nations are only talking about doing. Her population, which at the former rate would now be 120 million, has been held down to a shade above 100 million.

Just after the war the birth rate was thirty-five per thousand. By 1963 it had dropped to 17.4—below that of Britain, 18.5; France, 18.2; the United States, 21.6.

In 1970, Japan's record was 17.3, and still decreasing.

Japan's overall rate of population increase, counting both birth rate and death rate, fell from 24.4 per thousand in 1947 to 8.4 twelve years later!

It is still dropping, but more slowly. The annual growth which was two million is still half a million—largely because old folks live longer. Prewar Japan used to say, "Life is fifty years long." The western world's three-score-and-ten seemed unattainable. Now it is commonplace.

Japan is fortunate in that her two great religions, Shinto and Buddhism, raise no objection to population control. On the contrary, the Buddhists organize clinics to give information and supply contraceptives. The Japanese have not reached their goal—stabilization—but appear to be closer to it than any other nation.

24

GREEK JAPAN

Theodore Roosevelt wrote "I agree" opposite this paragraph in Dickinson's *The Greek Way of Life:*

> Japan is the only country I have visited which reminds me of ancient Greece. There is a universal prevalence of art. Every common thing is beautiful, the cups, the teapots, even the toys. Never since the Greeks has art so pervaded the life of a people. Every war has interrupted its development, but with each restoration of peace art has revived with amazing swiftness and vigor.

It is true, as demonstrated again by the swift revival of art since World War II. Now Japan not only creates beauty for her own satisfaction—but exports it.

Consider the pearl. Japanese pearls have migrated all over the world. They come from Toba on Japan's Pacific coast. There, millions of dollars in pearls lie beneath the quiet surface of the bay.

Bringing them up is not easy. I tried it. A comely mermaid

lent me her diving helmet. A rope was fastened to my waist, the other end attached to a tub which floated on the water. I was to dive to the bottom, fill my hands with oysters, rise and put them in the tub, and repeat the round trip until the tub was full.

"Why am I tied to the tub?"

"So that you will find it easily when you come up," the girl answered.

"And so we can find you if you don't come up," one of my friends remarked. I ignored this.

A cynical audience made up of my wife, other visitors, and employees of the pearl farm, watched from the nearby pier as I dived from the launch used by the divers as headquarters.

Struggling against water pressure, I swam down, my feet tangling in the rope. Here and there I could see white flashes of arm and leg as the diving girls went about their work.

The bottom was visible, but distressingly far away. The swimming became harder every second. It seemed impossible that the body should be so corklike, so determined to bob to the surface. The exertion winded me.

At about nine feet, with the bottom still several feet away, I gave up. I shot to the surface, gasping for air, and with no oysters to put into the tub.

My audience on the pier was amused.

When my breathing grew easier, I up-ended and went down again. This time it was even harder, since I hadn't the momentum of the dive from the launch to help me.

At a depth of perhaps seven or eight feet I was about to quit when a white something flashed up to me and oysters were pressed into both of my hands.

Up I came, and, to the astonishment of all spectators, poured two good handfuls of fine oysters into the little tub.

Scarcely had the murmurs of admiration died away before I was down again for another rendezvous with my fair collaborator. She did not fail me, and the trips were repeated until the tub was full.

My wife professed she had known all along that I could do it, and she was rewarded for her unswerving faith by a dish of fried oysters for lunch, every one of them containing a pearl.

•

One of the most amazing ingenuities of the Japanese is the cultured pearl. This is not an "imitation pearl." It is in every sense a real and genuine pearl. But it is planned, not accidental. And its cost is, because of the planning, only a fraction of the cost of an accidental pearl.

Ordinarily, only one oyster in many hundreds of thousands develops a pearl. It is much easier to find a needle in a haystack than a pearl in an oyster bed. Therefore when one is found it is worth a great deal. But if every oyster contained a pearl, the price would drop to a trifle.

This was the dream of a young noodle maker named Mikimoto. He left his wife in charge of the noodle shop and went to the seashore. He began tinkering with oysters. He knew that when a grain of sand gets inside an oyster's shell, it annoys the oyster, which proceeds to coat the irritating particle with a secretion, which hardens, thus gradually building up a pearl. If he could put sand in every oyster . . .

He went bankrupt three times before he made it work. Then he became many times a millionaire and his pearls covered the world.

A visit to one of his pearl farms is an interesting experience. You see girl divers plunge to the bottom some twenty feet down to bring up oysters which are then taken to the laboratory for their operation. Each shell is opened and a bit of mother-of-pearl inserted. The oyster is put back in the bay and left there for five years. It takes time, even for an educated oyster, to make a pearl.

We saw oysters that had been working for five years to

cover their troubles with beauty removed and opened. Some of the pearls were useless. Seven out of ten were excellent.

Here modern science and ancient superstition are curiously linked. We ascended to the top of a nearby hill and looked upon a shrine built by Mikimoto and consecrated to the oyster. Since Buddhism forbids the taking of life, and Mikimoto took many lives, he sought absolution by having a Buddhist priest come once every year to conduct ceremonies of penance before this shrine and offer prayers for the souls of departed oysters.

On another hill the penitent inventor raised a monument, the base of which is a coffin with concrete walls so thick as to defy thieves. Within the coffin are a million pearls.

They are a peace offering to the god of oysters.

Thanks to the genius of the old noodle maker, women everywhere may enjoy the lustrous beauty of real pearls.

•

Lacquer. The name has been loosely applied to ware made in America and Europe from the gummy deposit of an insect. Using this method, a plate, platter, or bowl can be turned out in a day and may last five years or so, then crack and peel.

The lacquer of the Far East is quite different. It comes from the sap of the lacquer tree *(Rhus vernicifera)* and this tree finds its most congenial climate in Japan. Japanese lacquerware cannot be turned out in a day and, properly made, will last for a century.

One piece of gold lacquer may require ten years to make and should endure for a hundred. Kyoto is the lacquer center of the globe. On one of our earlier visits to Japan we bought lacquer aged eighty years, not being able to afford the century-old treasures. But that was twenty years ago, so these pieces have now passed the century mark, and still look brand new.

The making of lacquer is a test of patience. The basic wood is cypress because it is least likely to warp or contract. Two days are required to lay just one coat of lacquer. Then the article is put aside to rest. After a few weeks or months, another coat goes on. It is polished with magnolia charcoal. Now it is put aside again to dry for several months. With a brush made of human hair, this painting and waiting is repeated ten times. After each coat, the object must be placed in a *damp* room to dry slowly, then polished with charcoal, and polished again with calcined deer horn. A final strong coat and polishing give the piece an enduring luster. Again it goes into a dark damp room to dry.

I have sketched the process only briefly—there are many more operations necessary. The final product may be used to hold boiling soups, alcoholic drinks, even burning cigar ash. After all is done, the maker has lived so long and so intimately with his creation that to him it is almost sacred and he may refuse to sell it.

•

Cloissoné was not created by Japan, but by the Egyptians some four thousand years ago. The Japanese, with their talent for adopting from others and adapting to make it better, are now the masters of the art. On a metal base of gold, silver, or copper, a design is applied which is then traced by thin wires of gold or silver. The spaces between the wires are filled in with enamel pastes of the required colors to bring the design to life. This mosaic is baked twelve times, and the result is a vase or other object of enduring beauty—and high cost.

•

Damascene, originating in Damascus, found its way to Korea, and thence migrated to Japan two thousand years ago. There it was, like so many other arts, improved and refined until it bore little resemblance to its Damascene ancestor.

More than half of the Japanese production is exported. Steel is usually the foundation. A design is drawn on tissue which is placed over the steel and traced into the metal with a fine chisel. Into these minute grooves, gold or silver threads are hammered. The object is then baked from fifty to a hundred times.

The next step is to coat the surface with powdered charcoal and oil. Bake ten to twenty times, adding more charcoal and oil each time. It may take a month to turn out one piece. In some other lands a piece of so-called damascene can be turned out in a day.

•

Satsuma, that beautifully decorated crackled porcelain, soft, warm, adorned with a wealth of gold, red, green, and blue enamel, is named after the general who brought Korean potters to Japan in 1598 after failing to conquer Korea. But, at least, the acquisition of this art was a victory. The potters, who had known no honor in their native land, were promptly made two-sword samurai before whom all commoners must bow. They were subsidized by the government so that they need not think of making a living, but only of making beauty. The skills were rapidly picked up by the teachable Japanese, and within a few decades there were no Korean potters but plenty of magnificent Satsuma-ware. Today, of course, it is known to the whole artistic world.

•

Embroidery, with its wealth of detail and color, its forest scenes, gorgeous golden pheasants, flowers, landscapes, was not an imported skill, but a purely Japanese creation dating back to A.D. 794. As then, it is still done by hand, never on a loom. Five or six years are sometimes necessary to finish an important piece. Japanese embroideries hang on the walls of the Hague Tribunal, are displayed in museums and art galleries from London to San Francisco, and have been featured in nearly every world fair since Austria's International Exhibition in 1874. Eighty percent of the production is sold abroad.

•

Painting has had a checkered career in Japan. While it remained Japanese, it was exquisite. When it tried to copy the West, it launched out upon troubled waters.

We strolled through the Imperial Art Gallery during a special showing of "Japanese art." It was all Japanese in the sense that it was all the work of Japanese artists. But in effect, it was half Japanese and half barbarian.

The pictures were housed in two enormous rooms. One was devoted to traditional Japanese water colors, the other to foreign-inspired oils.

The water colors were thrilling evidence of the art contribution Japan has to make to the world. Delicacy was their hallmark. Everything seemed to float. Even stone lanterns took wings. There was an evanescence, a dreamlike quality, a veil lightly covering landscapes, cliffs, waterfalls, rivers, temples, teahouses, stepping stones, reflecting pools, arched bridges, trees, shrubs, flowers, birds, and half-sketched humans. There were no shadows. The colors were light colors, translucent, pastel, apparently intended to be looked through, not at. Wisps of cloud were too diaphanous to hide the mountains. The whole effect was decorative, not realistic. Yet you were left in no doubt as to the identity of every object. That tree, though etherealized, was still a tree, not a nameless smudge. There was nothing that could have been done by a donkey's tail. In all, there was a reverence for the perfect line, and an unashamed love of nature.

But what a chamber of horrors in the other room! Heavy, dark, muddy oils predominated. Many of the subjects were frankly ugly. Frightful, bulbous, villainous or stupid-looking nudes reflected life "as it is"—at its worst. Shadows were opaque, dreary, depressing. The oriental lightness of touch was gone.

One has the feeling that if the Japanese would only stick to their own art, they could lead the world. The western artist who wants to do something new should study one of the oldest art styles in the civilized world. Ancient Japanese and Chinese painting might well be the ideal toward which western modernistic art is struggling with so much pain and frustration.

France did take advantage of the Japanese example. When Japanese art came to France it was seized upon with avidity, and the result was impressionism. This was in turn exported to the New World but apparently suffered a sea-change on the way. Having already been modified, it was further muddlefied in America. To recapture the original inspiration, American artists should go directly to the source.

•

Poetry has languished in the West because it has adopted so recondite a form that it means nothing to the average reader. There was a time when words were used to convey thought. But today's poets, with a few brilliant exceptions, use words to conceal thoughts. Clarity is despised as naive and simplistic. So poetry has disappeared from the pages of major magazines and newspapers, and few books of poems are to be found in bookstores. The writer who depends upon the sale of esoteric poems for support will starve.

The Japanese are not yet so sophisticated as to believe that a poem must be a Chinese puzzle. Innumerable poetry magazines are published. It seems that everybody, from the emperor down, writes poetry. The annual Imperial New Year's Poetry Contest draws some fifty thousand entries, one of which is always the emperor's.

There are three prescribed forms of Japanese poetry—the *naga-uta*, or long poem; the *tanka*, which must be confined to exactly thirty-one syllables; and the *haiku*, most difficult of all, since it must tell its story in seventeen syllables.

Anyone, from emperor to outcast, is expected to be able to turn out a poem on a moment's notice.

A breathless policeman accosted us in Miyajima. "I've been chasing you for a week," he said. We racked our brains—how and where had we broken the law?

He produced a scroll a foot long. Was it a warrant for our arrest? But when he presented it to us we saw it was blank.

"Write me a poem," he demanded.

•

Japanese culture shows itself in many forms—flower arrangement; landscaped gardens; *bonkei* or miniature garden in a tray; *bonsai* or dwarf tree grown in a pot and reaching the age of a hundred to five hundred years, yet never growing more than a foot or so high; the tea ceremony; the yearly admiration of the cherry blossoms in the spring and maple leaves in autumn; the ancient dramas of *kabuki* and *noh*; motion pictures, more produced annually than in any other land; 25,000 books a year, twice the number per capita published in the United States; newspapers, more than in any other country except Britain and Sweden; four hundred radio and three hundred television stations; music, not only oriental but western—Tokyo alone has five symphony orchestras, and bars will entertain you with anything from Beethoven to "rockabilly" (a blend of rock and hillbilly).

•

The Japanese bath is an excellent barometer of culture.

In our Japanese house the bath consisted of a wooden tub four feet in diameter and three and a half feet high. Kneeling in it, the bather was immersed up to the chin and no part of him was visible except his head above the edge of the tub.

After we returned to the States I sent to *National Geographic* an article and photographs, one of which showed our Japanese tub and my wife, or rather only her head, the rest completely out of sight. In the caption I did not mention that the bodyless head was Mary's, but wrote only "An American lady enjoys the Japanese bath."

But the editor recognized the lady and wired me, "May we identify lady in bathtub as Mrs. Price?"

We had just moved into our new house in a village adjoining Palm Springs and the telephone had not yet been installed. Therefore Western Union in Palm Springs telephoned the message to our local hardware store—which in turn phoned it to the library—which relayed it to the grocer—whose boy brought it to us.

By this time, of course, the story was all over town—some sort of scandal about Mary Price in a bathtub, and there was a sudden rush to subscribe to the *Geographic*. Of course our neighbors visualized the tub as similar to their own, and were keenly disappointed when the article appeared, revealing nothing but a head. Two of the new subscribers angrily wrote the magazine demanding their money back.

The one institution that wins unanimous approval of foreign residents is the bath. No one can live long in Japan and fail to surrender to it. Eight inches of water in an American tub will always seem inadequate and ridiculous after experiencing the delicious embrace of a hot bath three feet deep.

If Japan has any claim to be recognized as a civilized nation it should be based, not upon her ability in war, but upon her invention of the planet's best bath. Here is one thing she did not copy from China or the West.

This at least Shinto has done for the Japanese. While Shinto is entirely without ethical content and makes no demand for the purity of the heart, it does insist upon physical cleanliness.

The Japanese are clean, on the outside. Not that bathing is indulged in merely for the sake of cleanliness. It is enjoyable for its own sake, and it is a way to keep warm in a land that has hardly heard of central heating.

It seemed to me that every time I called at a certain farmhouse I found the whole family in the tub. It was a large tub and a hot spring kept the water continually at $120°$. I would be invited into the bathroom to chat with them while they soaked.

"How often do you bathe?"

"Whenever we get cold. Four or five times a day."

"And in summer?"

"Oh, we are too busy then. Only once a day in summer."

The usual home, without hot spring facilities, has a tub large enough for only one person. The master bathes first, then his wife, and so on down, the servants last. The same water is used but does not get dirty—because the real cleansing is done with soap and small buckets of water before entering the tub. Thoroughly scoured and rinsed, you step into the tub and crouch in it up to your chin for the thorough heating and relaxation it affords.

Rheumatic ills are dispelled by the very hot water. But you must not compromise. If the bath is made lukewarm by adding cold water, the aftermath may be kinks and cramps—whereas a bath that is hot enough to leave the body as red as a boiled lobster leaves a rich store of heat within the body. In back-country villages men and women may be seen walking home stark naked from the public bathhouse even in the chill winds of midwinter.

Sometimes a small shopkeeper will keep a tub under the counter and step into it when he or she becomes cold. Business goes on as usual, the occupant occasionally stepping drippingly out to pluck goods from the shelves.

In public bathhouses, mixed bathing is now contrary to law. Some have separate rooms for the sexes. Some merely have separate entrances marked "Men" and "Women," but once inside you are in a common bath. Sometimes the two sections of the bath are divided only by a bamboo pole, or by a string, or a panel of glass.

I was disconcerted to find upon entering a huge public bath in Atami that the great thirty-foot pool was not divided even by a string. Some two dozen men bathers were obviously enjoying the water antics of about as many of Atami's famous geisha. Ordinarily, however, the two sexes pay absolutely no attention to each other.

In the inns, no law applies, and there is but one bath for male and female. If you are squeamish, the proprietor can arrange that you will be undisturbed.

However, a newcomer will not interfere with you in any way except perhaps to say *Gomen nasai*, Pardon me, before stepping down into the water. This apology is made, not because of any sense of impropriety in sharing the bath with you, but because the entry of another person makes a movement in the extremely hot water, thus causing discomfort to the one already in the bath.

According to Japanese ideas, any exposure required by one's work or incidental to health and cleanliness is proper; exposure done merely "to show off a pretty figure," even if it be the slight revealing of the neck or a shapely ankle, is improper.

Education, the chief hallmark of culture, is more advanced in Japan than in any other Asiatic country. It is the main force behind Japan's rapid growth.

According to official figures, practically all Japanese students go through junior high school. Before the war two out of every ten went on through senior high—now six of every ten. The figure for Britain is four. Sixteen percent complete college as against 8 percent in Britain.

Japan's most desperate educational problem is the Japanese language. Written Japanese is probably the most difficult language in common use today. It is more difficult than Chinese, from which it was derived, because many new hurdles have been added to it since it was imported from China in the fourth century.

"Japan in its two millenniums of history has copied many things from the cultures of many nations," says a professor of comparative education at Columbia University. "It is quite possible that this was the most disastrous of all its importations. To the occidental student of western languages, all written in some variant of a phonetic system, it may be difficult to appreciate fully the monstrous handicap which the Japanese writing system has imposed upon that people."

Japanese is a system of ideographs, picture symbols, comparable to the hieroglyphs of ancient Egypt but far more complex. It is impossible to tell by looking at an ideograph how it is supposed to be pronounced. It is not even possible to be sure of the meaning since a single character may have a dozen different meanings, depending upon the context. There are ninety-three Japanese equivalents of the simple English pronoun "I," each with a different connotation.

The Japanese do have a simplified phonetic system called *kana* in which each syllable is represented by a mark. However, this system is scorned as being too easy, and as failing to bring out all the nuances of Japanese thought.

More than 40 percent of an elementary student's time is spent in learning to read and write. Even with this great expenditure of time, he learns very little. It has been found that the average graduate of the six-year elementary course has acquired about six hundred characters. Newspapers, even those which make a deliberate effort to limit the number of characters, use 3,500. Approximately nine thousand characters must be understood if university reference books are to be read. A scholar needs from twenty thousand to thirty thousand.

Speaking of the stumbling blocks of Japanese education, Dr. Inazo Nitobe once said:

> The use of Chinese ideographs is the root of all evil in this respect. A large part of the school life is spent in mastering some four thousand ideograms, most of which are pronounced in three or four ways and written in at least three ways. The waste of energy thereby incurred is worthy of the most serious consideration and can be prevented only by the adoption of transliteration, that is, the use of the Roman alphabet instead of Chinese ideograms.

A Japanese typewriter carries a total of nearly three thousand characters. Under such a handicap speed is impossible.

Linotype machines cannot be used in printing plants. All type must be set by hand. Instead of twenty-six letters, the Japanese compositor must wrestle with a minimum of 3,500 characters.

A Japanese index is a sour joke. There is of course no alphabetical clue, and I have seen a Japanese student search twenty minutes for a word that would be turned up in ten seconds in an alphabetical dictionary.

Blind persons may be better educated than those who can see because they do not have to spend 40 percent of their school time in learning ideographs. Japanese Braille is phonetic.

Pedantry blocks reform. Scholars take pride in their hard-earned knowledge and oppose a simplification of language that would place the common man on their level. Pundits frequently write material which they know cannot be understood by those to whom it is addressed.

"I hate to write to my uncle," said Chigoro Sugiyama, a law student in Tokyo University who was helping us with our Japanese, "because the letter must be written in the literary language and it takes me all day to write it."

When SCAP proposed that the new teachers' manual be written in simple, understandable Japanese, a Japanese professor, former minister of education, objected on the grounds that if the Japanese teachers could read it without difficulty they would be "insulted."

To study Japan's educational needs SCAP brought to Japan an Education Mission made up of twenty-seven distinguished American educators. After detailed study in conjunction with Japanese educators, the Education Mission recommended "a drastic reform of the Japanese written language." The mission advised that the use of Chinese ideographs should be abandoned in the popular written language and that a phonetic system should be adopted using the Roman alphabet.

Could so radical a change be made? Attention was called to the experience of Turkey. There the vigorous Mustafa Kemal abolished practically overnight the complicated Turkish writing system and replaced it with a twenty-eight letter Romanization. No such sudden change was recommended for Japan.

Many liberal Japanese educators support the plan. Curiously enough, opposition to it developed mainly within SCAP itself. The Education Division of the Occupation was against it. The project died before it was born.

If the Japanese language is difficult for the Japanese it is doubly so for the foreigner. Our maid spoke no English, and was highly entertained by our attempts to speak Japanese.

One day I heard my wife say: *"Ima neko tabemasho, ga yasai sukoshi mo."* It was a very slight error, the use of *neko*, cat, instead of *niku*, meat, but it made the general effect rather astounding.

"We'll eat the cat now, but give the vegetables a little more time."

And as for me, there was that rhapsody in honor of the smell of *sakana*, fish, when I meant to praise the *sakura*, cherry blossom.

Being accosted by a lady on the street and not quite sure of her identity, I politely inquired, "Are you the wife of the big white radish?" She as politely replied, "Yes, I am." She understood my slight error—the use of *daikon*, big white radish, instead of *daiku*, carpenter.

But if the Japanese language is difficult for the foreigner, English is equally difficult for the Japanese. The menu in the coffee shop of the Osaka airport was obligingly printed in "English." It featured spagelt meit boll, toriple sfew a la maison, pork chep a la derabi, steek, chetai briaot, bitak a la russe, speciol rif steek, grelled haey chicken, and tish and cliyps.

The Japanese find it particularly hard to pronounce English names. Because *kana* is based upon a syllabary rather than an alphabet, my name came out U-i-ra-do Pu-ra-i-su. Mail intended for a Mr. Braith came to me and mine to him. It would seem impossible to confuse Price and Braith, but in *kana* the two were almost identical—Pu-ra-i-su and Bu-ra-i-su.

As the Japanese student moves up the scale from elementary to secondary to university to postgraduate to professional, he is expected to learn five Japanese modes of expression—common, epistolary, Chino–Japanese, classical, and archaic. If he uses any of the last four in addressing a commoner, he cannot be understood.

With all these hurdles, it is amazing that anyone emerges from the educational mill with a rounded education. But so intense is the Japanese student's application to the business of learning that he comes out prepared to take his place in industry, commerce, the professions, or government. It is the outcome of the almost fanatical Japanese worship for the mind. This worship is evident in many Japanese maxims:

"Treasures that are laid up in a garner, decay; treasures that are laid up in the mind, decay not."

"Though thou shouldst heap up a thousand pieces of gold, they would not be so precious as one day of study."

"If thou be born in the poor man's hovel, but acquire wisdom: then shalt thou be like the lotus-flower growing out of the mud."

Even the Greeks had no more reverence for wisdom.

25

NIPPONESE BABYLON

Tokyo, world's largest city, houses twelve million people—50 percent more than its closest rivals, London and New York, each eight million strong.

It is a nation-size city, as populous as all Austria, or Hungary, or the Netherlands, or Portugal, or Australia, twice to five times as large as threescore other countries.

It covers 792 square miles as against New York's 320. Yet, with all this spread, it is incredibly congested. Outside stairways are steep, to save room. Houses are small. Gardens are minuscule. Open spaces are few—7 square feet of park to each person as against 128 in New York.

In addition to its dozen million residents, it must accommodate two million nonresidents who pour into it every morning and pour out every night.

Commuter trains are jammed to suffocation. Staunch "pushers" squeeze people into cars. Passengers have shoes torn off or sleeves ripped away and in a few cases are even disrobed down to their long underwear.

Street traffic is horrendous. At some intersections, if you are bold enough to cross the street, you pluck a yellow flag from a rack, carry it high above your head like a flag of truce, and deposit it in a rack on the other side.

World's first in so many lines, Tokyo has also the dubious honor of being the world's first, and worst, in smog. The fallout of dirt, dust, and smoke particles is estimated at seventeen tons per square mile per month. Doctors blame "Tokyo asthma" on the contaminated air. On one street where a sudden dip in the road causes smog to accumulate, oxygen tanks are provided for elderly pedestrians and children. The policeman at this point must be relieved every two hours, even though he has inhaled oxygen before going on duty. At the busiest junctions a glass case like a phone booth, but airtight, stands in midstream and within it the officer directs traffic in relative safety.

At some major intersections devices with lighted numbers register the decibel count of the noise. If the horns of impatient motorists exceed the prescribed maximum, arrests are made. The shouts of close-packed pedestrians and the clatter of their *geta*, wooden clogs, tax the capacity of the decibel counters.

Voices rise in a confusion of tongues greater than Babel ever knew. Tokyo is not a Japanese city *per se*, but a cosmopolitan megalopolis overflowing with non-Japanese visitors, Americans, Europeans, Koreans, Filipinos, Vietnamese who have had enough of Vietnam, Hong Kong Chinese, Taiwan Chinese, Japanese predominantly in western dress but enough still in kimono to remind one that this is not exactly New York, though close to it.

The city boasts 27,000 taxis, 125,000 drunks, 97 universities, 93 newspapers (five of them in English), land worth up to $3,000 a foot, 97,000 restaurants, and the highest prices on this side of the Pacific. Roast beef may cost $12.00, oranges $2.00 a dozen, and dinner may run all the way from $1.00 to $50.00 a person, depending upon the class of the dinery.

With all these counts against it, should visitors avoid Tokyo? Not at all. It abounds in survivals of a rich past, the temples of the shoguns, moats, castles, pine-crested embankments surrounding the imperial palace, charming oriental landscaping around the great hotels, parks and gardens which, though limited, have an exotic charm, a riot of cherry blossoms in spring, lotus in summer, maples in autumn. And at night it becomes an entrancing Babylon of light and color, movement and mystery.

Nevertheless, the prevailing mood of Tokyo is ultramodern. Strolling down the Ginza, you pass great department stores, boutiques, bookshops, coffee shops, windows full of newer-than-new cameras, color TVs better than those in the West, electronic calculators, computers, tapes of the Beatles and Baez, and come at last to the Tokyo Tower (fifty feet higher than the Eiffel) in which three floors are devoted to a "Modern Science Museum" full of amazing Japanese inventions.

Under Tokyo is another city. So far it has fifteen giant shopping centers and forty-three streets. And it has only begun to grow. One of the rewards of going underground is that you breathe clean filtered air, escape the danger of traffic accidents, noise, and smell, and have the convenience of a subway line more beautiful than any in the West except in Buenos Aires.

In this city beneath the city are banks, art galleries, medical and dental clinics, a shopping promenade the size of three football fields accommodating 350 stores, restaurants and bars of all kinds, tailor shops, jewelry shops, furriers, florists, another science museum, and a parking lot for a thousand cars. Before it is done it will be twice as big and the target date for completion is December, 1971. When finished, the underworld will be four levels deep.

The megalopolis is going not only down, but out. Riding the 125-miles-per-hour train following the ancient Tokaido Road 300 miles from Tokyo to Osaka, you see little but city all the way.

Osaka is the second largest city of Japan and even more modern and industrial. Its Expo 70 was the greatest exposition yet on the planet, and practically all of its Japanese pavilions were devoted not to Japanese art and poetry and tradition, but to the business of the day after tomorrow. That made it fascinating to the Japanese—perhaps not so fascinating to visitors who had come to Japan to see Japan.

Within ten years one great metropolis will reach 300 miles from Tokyo to Osaka. Whether it will be called by one name or by several names does not make much difference. It already has a name, not very complimentary, bestowed upon it by foreigners who dub it the "Tokaido Slurb."

26

OLD JAPAN ENDURES

Prosperity can be too rich a diet. It has destroyed nations and could destroy Japan—were it not for the fact that Japan has the unique talent of preserving the old while absorbing the new.

From Tokyo, city of the future, the business man comes home to shed his western suit, take a hot bath, don a loose, comfortable *yukata*, sit on the floor to eat dinner or look at TV. His wife, smartly dressed in mini, midi, or pants during the day, will return from her secretarial job and put on a kimono that almost touches the floor.

If the house is in the upper brackets it will have a carpeted parlor full of American-style overstuffed chairs in which to entertain foreigners. But when there are no such guests, the room will get musty and stuffy because hermetically closed, and all living will be done on the *tatami*.

There are, of course, exceptions. In one home we found the lady of the house so thoroughly Americanized that when we persuaded her to wear a kimono for a picture she had to call in a neighbor to show her how to tie the obi.

But on the whole, the kimono has persisted, unchanged. Where in the West do people still wear eighteenth-century clothing? That, of course, is what the kimono is.

Go a mile or so outside the city limits and you will find the traditional straw-thatched home with paper walls; sacred alcove; god-shelf bearing a miniature Shinto shrine and wooden tablets inscribed with the names of the ancestors; *kotatsu*, or hole in the floor in which you can hang your cold feet over a charcoal fire; or, in a more sophisticated house, a charcoal-burning pot called a *hibachi*. The ceiling and posts will be of sweet-smelling unpainted wood.

For five years we lived in such a house. It was simple in the extreme. Sliding paper doors walled it in. When they were slid back the house was an open pavilion. House and garden became one. Butterflies drifted in, and the scent of the *yamayuri* (mountain lilies) joined with the fragrance of the natural woods used in the house.

The floors were of *tatami*, which in English are sometimes called mats. But they are not mats in the ordinary sense. They are slabs of straw three feet wide, six feet long and two inches thick. They are fitted together closely so that they cover the entire floor without a break. This surface is kept spotlessly clean. It feels pleasantly resilient under stockinged feet—shoes are left in the vestibule.

A Japanese house is lovely for the lazy. Prate not to me about the couches of the ancient Romans! In a Japanese room you may recline on the bed all the time. The Japanese word *toko* means both floor and bed—because the floor is a bed, a strong, springy, two-inch-thick, straw mattress. Its reed surface is so light in color that any dirt could be instantly detected. No dirt is ever tracked in upon it, therefore it is as clean as a bed—cleaner than most. The whole room gives one a sense of clean comfort. One would feel guilty about loafing on an ordinary bed during broad daylight; but here there is no guilty feeling because there is no place *but* bed. Sitting on the heels gets uncomfortable, even for the Japanese (who partially lose the habit during their years in school when they sit on foreign benches). But reclining on the floor is quite Japanese and luxurious—or sitting with the legs spread out before you and your back against the wall.

There is not much furniture, and what there is is diminutive. One of the charms of this country is the smallness of everything. You feel like a Gulliver among the Lilliputians. Everything in the house is child-size, if not doll-size.

The table is ankle-high. The dishes are tiny. Each contains only a trifle. Slender chopsticks take the place of large and heavy silverware. Strawberries are eaten with a toothpick, not with a spoon. The brass *hibachi* or brazier is not much higher than the "table." The "chairs" are silk cushions resting on the floor. The dresser (sometimes there is one) seems to belong in a child's furniture set. One must kneel before its mirror to shave. The wastebasket (we would call it a desk-wastebasket at home), is big enough to hold just one good scrap. The bamboo spittoon is as small as a cup.

On the doors of the low cupboard, gaily colored samurai knights on horseback look, for all the world, like nursery decorations. The paper windowpanes in the *shoji* are half as big as a lady's handkerchief. The ceilings, particularly in the doorways and above stairways, are so low that after getting an assortment of bumps one learns to skulk.

Outdoors, across a veranda as narrow as a gangplank, you may feast your eyes for hours upon a tiny garden, which we might consider large enough for one tree, but in which Japanese artistry has arranged a dozen varieties—dwarf pine, azalea, cherry, cedar, and what not—a gnome's forest, surrounding a pool so small that a large pebble on the bank looks like a boulder and a tiny crimson span a foot long seems as eye-filling as the red bridge of Nikko.

We were awakened at five in the morning by the bugles of the palace guard. That was the emperor's rising time and the village followed suit. At five-thirty the drum began. It was played by a Buddhist priest in a small shrine halfway up the mountainside behind us.

He played from five-thirty in the morning to nine at night. Thus he hoped to shut out all thoughts of the world and numb his soul into complete submission. He numbed the souls of his listeners as well. We found ourselves making rhythmic movements of hands, feet, tongue, eyes, in time with the drumming.

An early arrival was Moria, our servant. She was any one of three persons, or she might be all three. They were a fisherman's wife and two grown daughters, and all preferred to use the family name, Moria. We paid the family as a family, and the maids came one, two, or three strong according to the amount of work on hand.

The first task of the morning was to make the beds. Since the beds consisted merely of padded quilts, *futon*, laid on the floor, all that a Moria needed to do was fold them neatly and put them in cupboards. Thus the bedroom became a living room; and presently turned into a dining room as breakfast was served on the ankle-high table.

Every Japanese meal is an adventure, except for the visitor who limits himself to the western hotels where he will dine exactly as at home.

Since Japan is a group of islands entirely surrounded by fish, it should not be surprising to discover fish in almost every dish.

And yet it is a distinct shock to take the lid from a lacquer bowl and see the twisted tentacles of a young octopus. You pick at it gingerly with the chopsticks. There are eight tentacles all attached to a mouth from which the body has been cut away. They droop and curl as though they were still alive.

You raise the weird tangle before your face and nibble one tentacle. It is not bad. Presently you devour everything except the mouth. You even become accustomed to the tongue-tickling of the small projections along the inside of each tentacle, like the feet on a caterpillar.

Raw fish, *sashimi*, is found to be quite palatable when dipped in soy sauce. It is not so hard to eat when one recollects how many times one has eaten raw oysters without aversion. Raw fish, curiously enough, is the only sort that does not taste fishy. In fact, it is almost neutral in flavor, and acquires taste from the bean sauce in which it is bathed.

Your chopsticks explore the mysteries of a dozen bowls. In one is an omelette as light as sea foam; in another a delicious baked fish; in another fried fish; in another boiled fish. Another bowl offers *tofu*, little cubes of juicy bean curd. Another contains seaweed. Here are succulent mushrooms, there is dark, purple *nasu* or eggplant, and yonder are bamboo shoots.

The system is to take a mouthful of rice, then dip into some dish for a flavorful morsel to go with it; then more rice and a bit from another dish, and so on until you have made the round of all the dishes. Thus each mouthful has a different flavor. Then begin again. Keep going until all the bowls are empty.

Eels and rice is a favorite dish. In some restaurants the eels swim about in a tank, and you may pick the one that you wish to have broiled.

Lotus, the gorgeous flower of the Orient, has a root a yard long. When sliced and boiled in soy sauce it is very satisfactory.

Bamboo, when it first sprouts from the ground, grows at the rate of a foot a day. When cut before it gets tall and tough, it makes a good food.

If you enjoy chewing a raincoat you will like *yuba*, the skin of bean curd. It is yellow and slippery, almost tasteless.

Then there is *kamonamban*, meaning "duck of the southern barbarians." This dish of duck and macaroni was brought to the country by the early Spanish sailors.

Very little meat is eaten. Buddhism forbids it; but there is a better reason. There is not enough room to raise cows, sheep, and pigs. The average farm is only two acres, and every inch is used for grains and vegetables.

Why not use one acre thus and the other acre as pasture for animals? Because if you eat the produce of the earth direct you get five times as much food value as when you let the animals eat it and then eat the animals. Therefore badly crowded countries cannot afford to waste farm land in raising meat.

Fortunately meat does not appear to be necessary to the health of the Japanese. No more tough and hardy race exists. The strength of their farmers, who must do with their own hands all the heavy work that is done by horses, mules, and tractors in western lands, the prowess of Japanese athletes in international sporting events, are fairly convincing testimonials to the virtues of a diet of vegetables, rice, and fish.

•

The short-time visitor in Japan will not rent a house, and could not if he wished. In Tokyo he will find it hard to escape the fine western-style hotels, Imperial, Okura, New Japan, New Otani and the rest, where he will live exactly as if he were holidaying in New York or Miami instead of Japan.

But in the country he will put up in a traditional Japanese inn *(ryokan)*. The inns have scarcely changed in five hundred years—and it is to be hoped they will not change in another five hundred.

The guest will be received by bowing maids. He will remove his shoes in the vestibule, put on soft slippers, and be led through shining corridors to an artistic room carpeted with *tatami*. The chief feature of the room is the *tokonoma* or sacred alcove occupied by a beautifully designed hanging scroll and a flower arrangement. You sit on a floor-cushion *(zabuton)*. Meals are served in the room at an ankle-high table. There is no public dining room in a Japanese inn.

But before dinner you must bathe, whether you want to or not. To come to dinner without having bathed would be as serious a breach of etiquette as to place one's feet on the table in the Waldorf Astoria.

Usually the innkeeper, aware of the peculiar notions of his foreign guests, will see that they have the bath to themselves. However he does not consider that he will offend you if he sends in a man or girl to wash your back.

The first time this happened to me I peevishly ordered the girl out, informing her that I would wash my own back. In a few minutes the proprietor came with another girl.

"You like her better?" he inquired. "*She* will wash your back."

I tried to explain my point of view but it sounded prudish even to me and was quite incomprehensible to the proprietor and the girl. He was visibly distressed and she began to weep.

"Oh well," I relented. "Come on. Wash my back."

Occasionally another guest, not forewarned, would stray in. Once a lovely young woman who found me alone propositioned me.

"I'll scrub your back if you'll scrub mine."

Being constitutionally a knight errant I could not refuse a lady in distress. I soaped, pummeled, and rinsed her back. Then she went to work on me. In the midst of the process, my wife entered.

"Pardon *me!*" she exclaimed. "I guess I'm not wanted here!" and she started to back out.

But my scrubber was after her immediately. "Come. I will wash your back too." And she did.

We thought we had acquired a friend but when we encountered the same girl on the street she passed us without a sign of recognition. This is part of the etiquette of the Japanese bath. Acquaintanceships made in the bathroom are without sanction outside of it. And a lady who would reveal herself completely in the bath without thought of impropriety would, when dressed, be mortified if her kimono should part far enough to show her knee.

After the bath you don your *yukata* (summer-weight

kimono supplied by the house) and return to your room. A wonderful sense of well-being suffuses you as you seat yourself on a cushion placed on the floor before the low table. The maid brings in your meal on trays and stays to see that you eat it.

Thanks to a moderate use of sugar and carbohydrates, Japanese food generates little acid and is acceptable to weak stomachs. It even becomes acceptable to the taste although after a few unremitting weeks of it one longs for a hearty beefsteak or a plate of ham and eggs by way of change.

Japanese food is to be preferred to Japanese versions of western food. You may have beefsteak if you ask for it but it is apt to be overcooked and smothered in a flavor-destroying sauce. Fried eggs are burned and crimped on the bottom until they look like browned crepe paper and taste like rubber. Bread, if you must have it, comes in slices as thick as books. The butter appears to have had a long hard trip—and so it has, all the way from Australia, in tins.

Of course in the large western-style tourist hotels or on Japanese cruise ships western dishes are competently prepared. It is only natural that a small inn that doesn't have more than one or two foreign guests a year should be no more proficient in cooking western style than would be the commercial hotel in Oshkosh if it should attempt to serve Japanese guests with the dishes of their own country.

Later, the maid returns to convert our living room–dining room into a bedroom. She draws heavily padded quilts from a closet and spreads them on the matted floor. The resultant couch is a good ten feet wide.

Two cylindrical sacks of oats are the pillows. A paper-walled lamp *(andon)* is placed at the head of the bed. Near it is put a carafe of water with a glass, and a tobacco box. The tobacco box contains a small *hibachi* from which you may, if you smoke, light your cigarette. Also there is the miniature bamboo spittoon.

If you were dressed the maid might then politely inquire,

"Shall I undress you or do you prefer to undress yourselves?" But you are already in sleeping attire and have been since the bath hour. The *yukata*, a light cotton kimono usually figured in blue and white, serves not only as bathrobe but is entirely proper as dinner gown, evening gown, and nightgown. Being loose and free, it is the ideal costume for floor dwelling. It is even acceptable for street strolling on a warm evening when a suit would be tight and sticky.

The maid shuts the *amado*, sliding wooden doors, facing the garden. It will be of no use to tell her that you wish to breathe the night air. She would be horrified. Night air is thought to be dangerous, full of miasmas and unnameable diseases. So you wait until she has left the room, then open the *amado*.

This makes it a simple matter for a burglar to step into the room. But a Japanese room is always open to thieves, day or night. You are never given a key to your room, for there is no lock to put it in. A New York hotel room without a lock would be inconceivable—no guest would accept it. He would not dream of going out for the day and leaving his unlocked baggage in an unlocked room. Yet you do that as a matter of course in Japan. I don't mean to draw an invidious comparison between the honesty of New Yorkers and the honesty of Japanese. Perhaps it is just a difference of habit. It may relate to the Japanese respect for each other's persons and belongings made necessary by overcrowding. Whatever the reason, you may leave jewelry, watches, cameras, or other valuables lying about the room during your absence without fear that they will be touched. Visiting several hundred inns during our years in Japan before the war and five months after it, we missed only one item—a comb. Since the maid had admired it we half suspected that she had taken it. A month later we found it where it had slipped behind the lining of a bag.

The night air rolls in, sweet and cool. You crawl in between the *futons* and turn out the light in the *andon*.

It is quite idyllic—until the *futon* above you, as thick as a mattress, begins to feel too warm. You lay it aside, and you are too cool. Later as the night grows colder you put it on again. But it is too short; your feet stick out. And it is too bulky to tuck in around the neck. The sack of oats grows hard and you substitute a doubled-up *zabuton*. The bed beneath you is as firm as an orthopedic mattress and you try to keep in mind that this is good for you.

But on the second night you circumvent these difficulties. You ask for an extra futon beneath, and two light futons on top instead of a single heavy one. You get also an auxiliary quilt to lay over the feet. With these modifications you should sleep perfectly.

The greatest charm of the *ryokan* is the warmth of the personal attention you receive from everyone on the staff, from smiling proprietor to pretty maid to boot-boy. You try in vain to give tips—but a little present is happily accepted and you receive one in exchange! The atmosphere is completely different from that of impersonal western hotels where you may be regarded more as a pest than a guest.

The less contact the countryfolk have had with the brusque foreigner, the greater the courtesy. This courtesy sometimes infringes upon privacy. During our journey by junk down the Inland Sea we would anchor for the night well away from the shore. Side curtains would be let down, dinner cooked on the charcoal-burning *shicherin*, and eaten. Presently a smiling face would come poking in under the canvas, then another, and another. Small boats plied back and forth between shore and ship and presently we had several score guests aboard. They let themselves in under the canvas until there was no more room and the rest stood outside on the deck and peered in through the cracks. They had a hundred polite but intimate questions to ask about our way of eating, sleeping, dressing, and undressing. "We want to wait and see you go to bed," said one. An old man apologetically explained that we were the first foreign visitors the village had seen in twenty years, it being quite off the path of tourism.

Courtesy took a very practical form when our miller in Hayama undertook to save us money.

We had ordered some quarter-ground rice. The Japanese contract beri-beri and other deficiency diseases because they prefer their rice fully ground with all the hull and germ removed. The partially polished or "brown" rice is thought fit only for chickens. We, being vitamin-conscious, wished to share the proverbial good health of Japanese poultry, hence our request for quarter-polished rice.

The rice was delivered at our door by the miller himself. It had been polished to a gleaming white.

"But we asked for the quarter-ground."

The miller beamed and bowed. "You ordered the brown because it costs less than the white," he surmised. "You will pay me only for quarter-ground. But you will accept the white with my compliments."

Our fellow-villagers were as honest as they were thoughtful. We never locked our doors. In fact we left the sliding doors open at night to admit air. It is true that Mary one night became apprehensive and placed a pile of pans just inside the opening so that no marauder could enter without making a clatter. I was roused in the middle of the night by a cascade of pans.

"Who is it?" I demanded fiercely.

The only answer was a suppressed laugh and then Mary's voice, "I forgot they were there."

By mistake I left two one-hundred-yen notes in the pocket of a pair of trousers sent to be pressed. When the garment came back the notes were still there. There was no crease in the cloth surrounding the wad, thus indicating clearly that the money had been removed, the suit pressed, and the money replaced. The garment was returned to me without comment ... no suggestion of "See how honest we are."

In thirty years of visits and residence in Japan I have never had so much as a toothpick stolen. One writer asked his inn proprietor to keep his expensive watch and a considerable sum of money in the hotel safe while he was away on a rough country tour. The proprietor, explaining that he had no safe, brought a tray, placed the valuables in it, and left it on the low table in the guest's room. He assured the guest that his belongings would be quite safe. The American came back at the end of a week to find that, although the room had twice been used by other guests, and servants had been in and out of it repeatedly, his valuables were exactly as he had left them.

Such trust is highly to be commended, but not recommended. Thefts do occur, even in Japan. But in general, *things* do not excite in Japan the cupidity that they seem to arouse in the West.

One reason may be—and this leads us to another good trait characterizing the old Japan—simplicity. The wants of a Japanese are few. He has learned how to get along with little. In thrift he is surpassed only by the Chinese.

He applies thrift even to his artistic interests. He draws a picture with only a few lines. He paints a watercolor scroll with astonishing taste and simplicity. He is the world's best watercolor artist, the world's worst in oils. They are too rich and sumptuous for him.

He likes to give an impression of a thing without picturing the whole of it. He loves little things. It has been said that Japanese art is great in small things and small in great. The artist leaves noble masterpieces to the European and contents himself with helping us see the beauty in a fish or a spray of bamboo.

The artistic ability of the Japanese is a rich heritage for all peoples everywhere. In painting, pottery, damascene, ivory, cloisonné, and lacquer, Japanese creations are an immediate and lasting delight. Even household objects are designed with taste. The dress-goods department of a Tokyo department store is a museum of lovely textiles, and the *obi*, the twelve-foot sash in which a woman winds herself, is often a superb work of art.

As for the other many fine qualities of old Japan that still

survive, they may be glimpsed in the following native epigrams—for a people is known by its proverbs:
Breeding rather than birth.
Proof rather than argument.
A sorrow is an itching place that is made worse by scratching.
The second word makes the fray.
It's no use cutting a stick when the fight is over.
Make sure of a thrifty wife even if you have to wear your shoes out looking for her.
Cows herd with cows, horses with horses.
Better to wash an old kimono than borrow a new one.
A good drum does not require hard striking.
One can see the heavens through a needle's eye.
A man's good name is as precious to him as its skin is to a tiger.
No standing in the world without stooping.
One good word can warm three winter months.

Struggling by taxi through the traffic jams of Tokyo we never heard the driver rail, no matter how needlessly or stupidly the car was blocked by bicycles, wagons, *fu* carts, or stubborn pedestrians. If someone had carelessly left his cart blocking the road, our driver would dismount, go into one shop after another until he found him, get him to move his cart, then beg his pardon for putting him to so much trouble. *"Sumimasen,"* he would say, "I humbly apologize." The other would also apologize and there would be an exchange of bows before we could proceed.

It was all a part of the Japanese pattern. During five months in Japan I did not hear one harsh or impatient word spoken by anyone—except perhaps by me when I became impatient of the patience of our Japanese companions.

Japanese young people respect their elders—not so much as formerly, but more than their contemporaries in America.

Our visit to one village happened to coincide with Old

Folks' Day appointed by the mayor in honor of the aged. A special feature, free to citizens over seventy years of age, was a theater party. It drew 830 old-timers to the city's finest theater where a stock company played an old-fashioned samurai melodrama. Upon filing out, each guest received a gift from the hands of the mayor.

I did not remember that an Old Folks' Day had been celebrated in Japan before the war and said as much to the mayor.

"We didn't need it then," he said. "Everybody respected the aged as a matter of course. There was a change after the war. Our young people went too far in adopting western ideas of individualism. They rebelled against the discipline of their elders. They thought democracy meant they could order their own lives without any advice from older people. It was just a part of the general postwar excitement. Now they are coming back to their senses. Occasions like this help to remind them of the debt they owe to parents and grandparents."

Dislocations in Japanese thinking rarely last. Instinctively, and from long habit, the Japanese come back to "the cake of custom."

Many such virtues in western lands are ascribed to Christianity. This faith has never taken deep root in Japan. The virtues existed before the first Christian missionary stepped ashore. Francis Xavier wrote:

"Of all the lands I have seen in my life, whether those of Christians or of heathens, never yet did I see a people so honest."

Which was a good deal for a missionary to admit.

The Japanese are honest—yet they are the world's best liars.

They lie to please you. They honestly wish to give you pleasure. They give you the answer you want.

Westerners who try to do business with them find they cannot be direct—they must go roundabout. Indirection is expected of the foreigner, because the Japanese himself is indirect. He is bewildered by directness. A Tokyo judge in whose court Englishmen had appeared as witnesses complained,

"Foreigners deceive by telling the truth."

A Kagoshima surgeon, graduate of an American university, lamented,

"If a Japanese has been educated in America he fails in Japan—and the reason is, America has made him too direct."

Whether you are trying to rent a house or sell a shipment of goods it is difficult to extract from a Japanese a clear, unequivocal statement. He may do much better than he seems to promise—or worse.

If the contract is put in writing you are little better off. For the Japanese language is so vague and slippery that it would be hard to set down a declaration that could not be interpreted in three or four different ways.

Lafcadio Hearn, staunch friend of Japan, admitted that to think like a Japanese it is necessary "to think backwards, to think upside down and inside-out, to think in directions totally foreign to Aryan habit. Experience in the acquisition of European languages can help you to learn Japanese about as much as it could help you to acquire the language spoken by the inhabitants of Mars. To be able to use the Japanese tongue as a Japanese uses it, one would need to be born again, and to have one's mind completely reconstructed, from the foundation upwards."

The Japanese are adept in seeing what is not there, and in not seeing what is there. Walk in upon a Japanese when he is not properly dressed to receive you and he will rise and leave the room without a word. When presentable, he will come in and greet you as if he had not seen you before.

A man who has been your traveling companion for weeks may not seem to know you from Adam when you encounter him in shirt sleeves in the washroom of the Japanese inn.

As you soak in the inn's tile bath a Japanese lady may enter stark naked, soap and rinse herself, then step into the stove-heated tub with you without appearing to distinguish you from the stovepipe.

Even the solemnity of the hour of death may not deter the family who pray and weep beside the coffin from pulling a fast one. Should the deceased be an official it may be profitable to move the date of his death forward a few days. If the government can be persuaded to grant him a promotion, a larger pension will accrue to the family. But since he cannot be promoted after death, he is fictionally kept alive. Everyone may be quite well aware that he died on Sunday, but the newspapers have him giving orders on Monday, making a speech on Tuesday, being promoted on Wednesday, and finally dying at such and such an hour and minute on Thursday. The family, the government, the press, and the public all share cheerfully in the hoax.

Your companion will pretend to understand you when he does not. A certain Shimada-san replied "I think so" to every statement until I became suspicious that he had no idea what I was saying. In a pleasant tone I remarked,

"You are a double-dealing, poker-faced son of perdition."

Shimada smiled and nodded. "I think so," he said.

My friend John Patric was gratified to have a most attractive listener whose stock reply was "I see." Finally a gnawing fear that his eloquence was being wasted prompted Patric to test his audience with the rigmarole of Lewis Carroll:

> 'Twas brillig and the slithy toves
>   Did gyre and gimble in the wabe;
> All mimsy were the borogoves
>   And the mome raths outgrabe.

"I see," said his companion promptly.

Even after MacArthur forced the emperor to disavow his divinity, General Hayashi said to a foreign reporter, "We still regard our emperor as a living God. For us it is not a question of historical or scientific accuracy. It is an article of national faith."

This admission that there may be no accuracy in the emperor myth reveals the remarkable Japanese capacity for indirection.

"It is my duty to believe it," was the excuse of a student when ribbed for supporting the god-emperor theory.

"We don't talk about such things," said another. And a common evasion is "Only a Japanese can understand such things."

The Japanese are so familiar with this art of deceiving both themselves and others that they have a name for it. It is *naibun*. It means feigning ignorance of what everybody knows. They easily carry over this kind of double-dealing into their higher intellectual life. *Naibun*, pretense, has become a Japanese thought-pattern.

Self-hypnosis has made officials themselves believe what they preach. It is easy to believe what it is to your interest to believe. When precious careers are dependent upon the blindness of the people, convenient fairy tales become eternal verities.

I probed an official in the Foreign Office on this subject. He had traveled the world and knew several languages.

"But," he said, "I spent my formative years in school here in Japan. I suppose what you absorb between the ages of two and twenty you never lose. It seems that I reject these things with a part of my mind and accept them with another part."

But the full duplicity of the Japanese mentality came out in the bland statement of a member of the Imperial Diet when asked about Japan's national god-king theory.

"Oh, we know it's not true," he said, "but we believe it!"

It is only another instance of the tenacity with which modern Japan clings to the past. The Japanese mind races ahead, but the heart lingers in the Dark Ages.

•

The love of nature has never died. That is natural, for nowhere in the world is nature more worth loving.

The house is not a fort against nature with one narrow door like a drawbridge to the outside world, and narrow embrasurelike windows smothered with curtains, mustily challenging the outside freshness, "Come no farther!"

The house is a continuation of the garden.

And the garden is a continuation of the distant scene. For every tree, bush, hillock, and rock in the garden is placed to harmonize with those trees that tower beyond the garden and those mountains in the distance. From one house we rented we looked out on one side over a river valley to a range of mountains; on another side, over terraced rice fields; on another, up a heavily wooded mountain slope; and on the fourth, over a bay of the sea to peerless, towering Fuji, snow-crowned. In each case the designer of the garden had used his skill to make the near view blend with the far.

I have seen a gardener plant and replant a small tree six times, taking a whole day for it although he was paid by the job, not by the hour; standing back after each planting to view the effect from every angle. It reminded me of Lafcadio Hearn's observation as he watched two gardeners at work: "These two old men are composing a mysterious thought with their little trees, changing them, transferring them, removing or replacing them, even as a poet changes and shifts his words, to give to his verse the most delicate or the most forcible expression possible."

In the two-thousand-year development of the art, each tree used in garden composition has acquired a philosophical meaning, a special purpose, and a name of its own. The gardener does not think merely in terms of pines, maples, and willows. The trees to him are the "Tree of Upright Spirit" which must be straight and aspiring, the "View-Perfecting Tree," the "Tree of Solitude" which gives a solitary wooded aspect, the "Cascade-Screening Tree" suited for use beside the waterfall, the "Tree of the Setting Sun" to interrupt the glare of the setting sun, the "Distancing Pine" suggesting a faraway forest, the "Stretching Pine" which knows how to sprawl its branches over water, and so on.

One lesson from the Japanese garden is avoidance of bilateral symmetry. That applies also in Japanese interiors. Never is there anything resembling the regular, paired-off pattern of the western rug, wall paper, curtain, ceiling, or formal flower bed.

The garden also illustrates the relative unimportance of flowers. Of course the Japanese are fond of flowers and use them in their gardens—but always give them a secondary position where their early demise will not disturb the general effect. For the garden must be a thing of beauty not only during a brief flowering season, but throughout the winter. Therefore all sorts of evergreen plants, shrubs, and trees are combined with artistically molded miniature hills, valleys, watercourses, bridges, stepping stones, lanterns, to form an intimate landscape pleasing to the eye in any season.

Water is always introduced when possible, perhaps in the form of a brook and waterfall. There may be a tiny lake of irregular outline surrounded by rocks and shrubs.

If water cannot be had, then association of ideas is used to suggest water. The twisting brookway may be so deep and overhung with shrubbery that the absence of water in it is not noticeable; the dry waterfall is still beautiful because of the rocks which compose it, and the tiny pond is floored with creamy beach sand half concealed by the shrubs and rocks along the shore.

Rocks! A flat garden can be transformed by the artistic use of rocks. Beautiful rocks (and they can be gray boulders from some riverbed and still be beautiful) are in great demand among the Japanese. Frequently the rocks in a garden will cost more than the house! A water-worn rock is sometimes placed on a rich pedestal in the *tokonoma* as an object of art.

I have noticed announcement of a gift from Japan to the

University of California. It consists of a load of rocks! As if California, land of stony canyons, did not have enough rocks! But this flinty cargo is a very costly and beautiful gift—we may only hope that it will be appreciated. The shipment is accompanied by a landscape blueprint drawn by Jiro Harada of the Imperial Museum, showing how the assortment of boulders, stepping-stones, and pebbles may be used in conjunction with a stream flowing through the campus.

Irregular stepping-stones, harmonious but never matched, form the paths in the Japanese garden. Of course, no path is straight. The shortest distance between two points is of no interest to the wanderer in a garden.

At the garden limit there is no sharp disillusionment in the way of an iron or wire fence, or even a stone fence built of artificially hewn blocks. A bamboo fence preserves the natural effect.

All this time that we have been in the garden we have not left the house. And whenever we turn our eyes within we are conscious of the fact that here too care has been taken to preserve the flavor of nature. The outdoors has come in, not only in such obvious guises as the flowers in the vase, the singing cicada in the bamboo cage, and the twenty-year-old pine tree a foot high growing in a tray—but, more important, in the sincerity of the natural wood used throughout the house.

Many of the graces of Japanese character can be traced to the influence of nature.

Some people are surrounded by beauty without responding to it, notably certain wild tribes in tropical lands. But on the whole, the human race likes nature when nature is likeable. In Japan, it is. Take the adoration of the cherry blossom. Looking at our own cherry blossoms, we have difficulty in understanding how anyone could be ravished by them, drink wine to them, attach poems to them. But Japanese cherry blossoms are not like ours. When the foreigner stands amid a sea of that pink bloom, he may not write a poem, because he has never learned how, but he will want to.

The average Occidental responds instantly to the beauty of a Japanese garden, however remote it may be from anything he has ever seen at home. And he will return home with a quickened sense of appreciation.

I well remember the ineffable relief of arriving among the cool lovely hills of Nagasaki at the end of a world trip. After simmering in Egypt, sweltering in India, stewing in Sumatra, sizzling in Singapore, broiling in the Philippines, and baking in South China, the cool air of late May in Japan was like the hand of a Red Cross nurse.

But I shall be making prospective visitors expect too much. Let it be said then that the winter is damp and chilly (though not cold enough for snow), there are occasional winds during the spring, and the *nyubai* or rainy season in July is an unmitigated curse.

The best seasons are spring and autumn. And the loveliest months of all are October, November, and December. But there is not a month in the year that does not have its compensations, and doctors testify that the climate is unusually healthful.

The energy of the Japanese as compared with other Asiatics is largely due, in the opinion of climate researchers, to the temperate-zone climate of Japan as regulated by the surrounding seas.

Japan is beautiful because it is so worthless. Eighty-five percent of it is too rugged to be cultivated. Its mountains crowned with snow, its hills topped with picturesque shrines in groves of quaint trees, give unending variety to the landscape.

Add to this the fact that anything grows. There are few plants, whether from the arctic, the temperate, or the tropical zone, that may not be found in Japan. And the Japanese are most conscientious about preserving their forests, or renewing them when denuded.

As for flowers, they pass through the seasons in gorgeous succession: plum, camellia, cherry, peach, quince, dandelion, violet, wisteria, crape myrtle, mountain lily, morning glory, chrysanthemum, and a hundred more. And in autumn, the incredible colors of the maples.

Man has, as is his wont, marred nature's beauty with railroads and industrial plants. There are too many billboards advertising Merry Milk, Chicken Sauce, Calpis Drops, Lion Toothpaste (there being no *l* sound in Japanese, "Lion" is rendered in *kana* as Ra-i-on), Kirin Beer (Bi-ru), Milk Caramels (Mi-ru-ku Ki-ya-ra-me-ru), and Johnny Walker Whiskey (Ji-yo-ni O-ka U-i-su-ki).

But there is much of Japan that is undisturbed by American-style ballyhoo and untouched by war. The deer in the park at Nara, the temples of Nikko, the stone lanterns and *torii* of Miyajima, the thousand undercut isles of Matsushima, the reflected Fujiyama in the still surface of the Fuji Lakes, do not know that there has been a war.

Inheritances from the long past, very much alive today include:

Kabuki, medieval drama.

Noh, ancient drama.

Bunraku-za, drama with nearly lifesize puppets.

Shinto, origin lost in time, perhaps seventh century B.C.

Bukkyo, Buddhism, from Korea in A.D. 552.

O-Bon, feast of the dead, 1,500 years old.

Tappitsu, calligraphy, ornamental writing by brush. From China in the seventh century.

Cha-no-yu, the tea ceremony, began who-knows-when.

Katama, sword-making, from the tenth century.

Geisha, delight of men for five centuries.

Bonsai, growing of dwarf trees less than a foot high to great age, often a hundred years, the most aged recorded said to be five hundred years old.

Bonkei, complete miniature landscape in a tray.

Ike-bana, flower arrangement, a purely native art.

O-hana-mi, cherry-blossom-viewing, the first half of April.

Lango-zaka, chrysanthemum festival in autumn.

O-mushi-kiku, insect-hearing festival.

Hotaru-gari, firefly-catching.

O-tsuki-mi, moon-viewing festival.

Hi-matsuri, fire festival to the goddess of Fuji, dormant volcano.

Setsubun, demon-dispelling day.

Tanabata, two stars, representing two lovers, condemned to meet but once a year.

Tango-no-sekku, boys' festival, ancient.

Jomi-no-sekku, time-honored girls' festival.

Shichi-go, children's festival four hundred years old.

Ebisu-ko, day when tradesmen entertain customers to make amends for cheating them the rest of the year.

Higan, day of the equinox, when the sun whirls round and round at sunset.

Bon-odori, ancient dance of rejoicing for souls liberated from hell.

Judo, kendo, arts of self-defense.

Ken-jutsu, art of handling the sword.

Sumo, Japanese wrestling.

Kemari, Japanese football, a thousand years old.

Oibane, battledore and shuttlecock.

Go, eighth-century game faintly like checkers.

Soroban, the abacus, anciently from China. In small stores it has not yet been supplanted by the cash register.

Tanka, thirty-one-syllable poem.

Haiku, seventeen-syllable poem.

Ukiyoe, color prints.

Koto, samisen, biwa, shakuhachi, ancient instruments still played.

Skills of fishing by use of cormorants, breeding of cocks with twenty-foot tails, production of fine silk, brocade, bronze, ceramics, cloisonné, Satsuma, damascene, lacquerware.

And hundreds of other arts, crafts, festivals, customs of long ago still revered and practiced.

27

THE PERIL

Not all of Japan's heritages from the past have been utterly gracious.

One is Japan's recurring ambition to expand at the expense of her neighbors.

This ambition, temporarily dulled by defeat, is stirring once more. That it will revive in full force is as certain as that day will follow night. We have already seen that the ways of the past are not easily abandoned. This is the great virtue of Japan—and can be her fatal curse.

The urge for expansion of the Empire began at the beginning, with the rescript of the first emperor, Jimmu Tenno, 660 B.C.

"We shall build our capital all over the world and make the whole world our dominion."

This rescript and the philosophy back of it have been thoroughly ground into the Japanese mind for twenty-five centuries. It would be naive to assume that it has now been permanently eradicated.

Time and again it has been repeated until it has become as demanding as hunger.

•

Expansion is a Japanese passion. In A.D. 110 young Japan subdued the island of Kyushu. In the year 200 the Empress Jingo invaded Korea. In 660 Hokkaido was annexed. In 1592 Korea was again invaded. In 1609 the Ryukyu islands were assimilated. In 1874 a punitive expedition took over Formosa. In 1875 the Kuriles were acquired. In the same year the Bonins were occupied and China was ousted from Okinawa.

In 1895 Japan took the Liaotung Peninsula and the Pescadores from China. In 1897 she sought to wrench Hawaii from the U.S. In 1904 she tackled the Great Bear and won Saghalien and South Manchuria. In 1905 she made the third, and this time successful, attempt to seize Korea.

In 1914 she preempted three million square miles of the Pacific (equal to the area of the United States) and became master of the two thousand islands of the Marianas, Carolines, and Marshalls. In 1918 she grabbed part of Siberia, and, in 1931, the vast plains of Manchuria. In the 30's she took over North China. In 1935 she acquired large areas of the Philippines. In the same year she tried to take control of South China. In 1936 she undertook to dictate to Egypt, Siam, and the Dutch East Indies. In 1937, Inner Mongolia fell to the Japanese. In 1937 Shanghai was taken after thirteen weeks of heroic Chinese defense; then Nanking, Hangchow, and the Yangtze Valley.

In 1941 came the Pearl Harbor attack and occupation of Guam, Wake, the Philippines, Malaya, Hong Kong, the Gilberts, New Guinea, the Solomons, the Bismarcks, New Britain, New Ireland, Indochina, Siam, Burma, Borneo, Tarakan, Celebes, Timor, Bali, Ceram, Sumatra, Java, and the Aleutian islands of Kiska, Attu, and Agattu.

•

Considering such a record, can anyone seriously imagine that Japan will forever observe the promise she made under MacArthur's compulsion "never again to resort to arms"? In exchange for this promise, America guaranteed to protect her against all enemies.

One might suppose that Japan would be eternally content with such an arrangement. But the Japanese are a proud people. They are already showing signs of dissatisfaction with their humiliating position under the American umbrella.

A growing minority want to rid Japan of American bases and troops. They have their reasons. Air accidents have destroyed property and killed civilians. American soldiers who have made trouble cannot be tried in Japanese courts. Japanese young men resent the attention of GIs to Japanese girls. Jet noises distress residents near American bases. Test firings have wounded civilians. Coastal fishing fleets are struck by stray bullets. These incidents, though rare, are magnified in the Japanese press.

Having suffered nuclear disaster in Hiroshima and Nagasaki and near Bikini when a Japanese fishing boat was caught in atomic fallout, the Japanese are understandably sensitive about nuclear power. The administration reluctantly consented to the presence of nuclear submarines in Japanese ports, but the people didn't like it. The *Gensuikyo* (Japan Council Against A- and H-Bombs) is actively anti-American. The presence of nuclear weapons and poison gas on Okinawa adds fuel to the fire. The Japanese want these weapons removed, and the Yanks along with them.

And now Japan's neighbor, China, is turning out bombs. The Japanese have no intention of lagging behind. They are not, as this is written, making bombs, but they know how.

They have built atomic reactors "for peaceful purposes" and constructed nuclear-powered ships. Atomic power stations distribute electricity. Japanese army officers insist that Japan must have her own nuclear weapons.

•

"Never" is a slippery word. Japan's postwar constitution dictated by America required that "land, sea and air forces, as well as other war potential, will never be maintained." That "never" lasted three years. In 1950 when the U.S. went to war in Korea, she wanted Japan's help, which Japan politely refused, pointing out that she was bound by the "never" clause.

The U.S. about-faced and argued that there was nothing in the constitution that forbad self-defense. (Just how warring in Korea could be interpreted as self-defense was not explained.) Japan, while still declining to take part in the Korea tussle, nor, later, in the Vietnam war, took advantage of the new loophole and began to reinstate ground, maritime, and air forces.

She has been actively encouraged by her former enemy to rearm with modern weapons. The U.S. has given Japan a billion dollars in military aid since the war ended. The object is to enable Japan to share with the U.S. the responsibility of policing the Pacific—regardless of the fact that Japan's attempt to do exactly that led to Pearl Harbor and four years of war.

Japan has taken the bait. Now her heavy industry is embarked on an extensive armaments boom. The Army's "Self Defense Force" already numbers 171,500 troops, 24,000 reserves, 276 armed aircraft, 720 tanks. The Navy's "Self Defense Force" has 36,000 men, 214 vessels including destroyers, escorts, subs, torpedo boats, and minesweepers—together with 194 fighting aircraft, 48 helicopters, and thousands of mines three times more powerful than the 500-pound mines used by the U.S. Navy. The air "Self Defense Force" has 40,703 uniformed personnel and 1,104 aircraft, mostly jets.

"The Japanese," writes Edwin Reischauer, former Ambassador to Japan, "have a nagging worry that they cannot be influential unless they are a militarily powerful country, and that may even mean nuclear weapons. They know if they depend upon American military protection, they cannot be equal to us. This will be the big question for Japan in the next few years."

Japan today commands more firepower than in World War II. She is about to start construction of 105 Phantom jets under license from the U.S. A new submarine fleet is planned. That these plans and figures will grow there can be no doubt. They are stimulated by the rampages and riots of students who rebel against American patronage. In 1968 alone anti-American disruptions occurred on 54 campuses and three thousand arrests were made. Tokyo University, the country's greatest, was totally paralyzed.

Every visitor to Japan has heard the classic witticism: One Japanese asks another, "Have you read the new constitution?" The other replies, "No, I can't read English."

The constitution is, of course, in Japanese, but, having been translated from English its conceptions and phraseologies are so alien that its foreign origin is painfully apparent.

The constitution of a nation is something almost sacred. So at least we regard our own constitution. We respect it because it has worked. Those who framed it were highly idealistic but practical as well and put into it nothing that would not work. The Japanese have a constitution which they cannot respect since it obviously will not work. It invites circumvention and fraud. Japanese legal authorities are now reinterpreting the Renunciation of War to mean just the opposite of what it obviously does mean. Saying that it does not preclude "defensive" war, they open the gate wide since any sort of war can be called defensive. Japanese militarists claim that their attack upon Pearl Harbor was defensive.

Having found a way around one article of the constitution, apologists worked to undermine other articles. Once the worms get in, they are hard to stop. The responsibility for this corruption and chicanery goes back to those who compelled the acceptance of a document so unrealistic that it made evasion necessary.

While the effort to disarm Japan for all time was merely ridiculous, the pressure to rearm Japan is positively dangerous.

The common people, with their native wisdom, realize this. They have been through a war too recently to want another. They have suffered too severely at the hands of their own militarists to wish to see them restored to power. Yet every day the new militarism of Japan takes on more of the color and character of the old.

Some seventy thousand purged nationalists and militarists have been restored to full citizenship rights. War criminals sit in the Diet, the cabinet, and the imperial court. Military men are revising textbooks, running newspapers, producing moving pictures, operating radio stations. Japan's war guilt is denied and Tojo is made a hero.

The new soldiers use U.S. army-type equipment; they train with mortars, bazookas, machine guns, antiaircraft guns, howitzers, and U.S. tanks. The United States is supplying most of the arms until the Japanese munitions industry gets into full swing. The goal for the next few years is a 300,000-man army of fifteen divisions, a 1,500-plane air force and a 300,000-ton navy. To start the navy the United States transferred fifty landing craft and eighteen frigates to Japan's Coastal Safety Force. Concerning this transfer *Time* remarked:

"The news created hardly a ripple in either country, though in 1942 any U.S. serviceman in the Pacific would have been laughed down had he predicted such a turn of events in one decade."

Ever since the Korean war began, Japan's prewar munitions makers have been turning out armaments for the American forces and are therefore fully prepared to make them for Japan's own use.

Expansionist ambitions are once again emerging. The tremendous revival of Japanese export trade calls for markets. The markets most desired, outside of China, are Indonesia, the Philippines, Malaya, Thailand, and Indochina. If obstacles are placed in the way of Japan's trade—and this is already happening—Japan will be strongly inclined to use force. The militarists and the big industrialists will join hands as they did before Pearl Harbor. There will be a new attempt to make Asia a "co-prosperity sphere" under Japan.

The seeds of the new fanaticism are already being sown. Voices are demanding the return of Japan's far-flung territories. State Shinto with its slogan of "All the world under one roof" is being revived. The Rescript on Education of the Emperor Meiji, which declares that the Way of the Gods is "infallible for all ages and true in all places" and which was used by the ultranationalists as proof that the power of the emperor should be extended to "all places," is still read and venerated in the schools. The constitution of a new political party, the Working Masses Party, declares, "The emperor is the source of all," and "Let the universe be a single house ruled by the emperor."

The emperor, at the behest of SCAP, gave out in 1946 a statement disavowing divinity. This was publicized throughout the world and was hailed by the American public, who supposed that it would mean a complete change in the thinking of the Japanese people.

For very simple reasons, this did not happen. The Japanese suspected that the statement had been ordered by SCAP. In the second place, the statement as it appeared in Japanese was worded rather ambiguously and could easily be misinterpreted. In the third place, the fact that the emperor would belittle his own worth was taken as proof of his modesty and further endeared him to his people.

Proof that their emperor was "sacred and inviolable" was the fact that the invaders had not dared to lay hand on him. War criminals were arrested while the emperor not only went free but was accorded the most profound respect. Great care was taken in the war-guilt trials not to involve the emperor—and this in spite of the fact that everyone was perfectly well aware of the responsibility of the emperor for the war. As commander-in-chief he was responsible for the acts of his subordinates. He had been fully informed of all war plans and, although he did not approve of the war, he did not use his extraordinary powers to prevent it. If he had publicly warned his people of the plot of the militarists the people would have risen in protest and there would have been no war.

Weak-kneed apologists say, "But that would have cost him his throne, or even his life." It is true that it might have meant abdication, even assassination. But was that too great a price for a man to pay if by paying it he could save the lives of hundreds of thousands of his countrymen?

•

Premier Sato visiting Washington in 1969 referred to Japan as "the guardian of Asia."

"The time is approaching," he said, "when Japan will play the leading role in matters relating to Asian security, while the United States will cooperate from the sidelines. . . . My countrymen will have to shoulder new and expanded responsibilities, not only for their own defense but for the security of Asia."

This is as polite a statement as the prewar declarations that

Japan, out of the goodness of her heart, must convert all Asia into a "co-prosperity sphere." We saw, in World War II, how she went about this task.

Asia fears Japanese guardianship. What the Japanese call a "hate-Japan wind" is rising in Asia. Once Asia spoke of the "ugly American." Now, says a Japanese correspondent in Thailand, it is the "ugly Japanese." "The people feel that we are being invaded," says Thailand's Economic Affairs Minister, "this time economically."

In 1969 Japan sold nearly five billion dollars' worth of goods to East Asia, but bought only half that much. "No one can compete with the Japanese salesman," says a Chinese businessman in Taiwan.

As is true of Americans, Japanese are better behaved at home than abroad. Let loose in Asia, they tend to be uninhibited and arrogant. They have an insatiable appetite for drink and sex. Says a *Time* correspondent, "Several Tokyo magazines carry frank whoring guides to Southeast Asia, complete with price lists." The hottest new Japanese film is *Sexpo 70*.

Adam Malik, Foreign Minister of Indonesia, believes that Japan will be "a more vexing problem than Communist China" in the coming decade. "Japan, through its big and overwhelming economy, cannot but be an object of envy, suspicion and fear among its Asian neighbors, since the experience of almost all the Asian countries with Japan during the war was none too happy."

•

You can understand Japan's point of view. Goods are rolling from her factories. She must sell them. Whatever gets in the way of this selling campaign must be removed. Customs barriers must come down—if not by persuasion, then by force. It is a matter of life and death. She must export to live. She has already edged Britain out of Australia. A Sydney correspondent reports, "Japan has achieved a position in the Australian economy that many observers here consider dangerously dominant."

Japanese oilmen are sinking money—and striking oil—in the Persian Gulf. Mitsui invests in Cambodia. Mitsubishi is deep in Malaysia and the Philippines. China looms large on the Japanese economic horizon: eight hundred million potential customers—think of it! Both mainland China and Taiwan are buying heavily. Two-thirds of Japan's foreign trade is with Pacific nations, including the United States. The instinct to protect and expand such trade is overwhelming.

Riches are dangerous. Japan will be unable to avoid playing the major role in Far Eastern affairs if only because she will be so rich.

As early as 1951 another war was in the wind. Public sentiment was bitterly antiwar, therefore plotters met in secret.

During our junk journey down the Inland Sea we visited the island of Onigashima, Isle of Devils, chief wonder of which is a great cave in the mountaintop. The junk captain and I explored it. We were on the way out through the labyrinth of passages when we heard voices.

Peering around a sharp corner, we saw about twenty men seated on the rock floor under oil lanterns while one stood on a stone platform to address them. He was too far away and my ear for formal Japanese was too poor to catch all he had to say, but I got words and phrases. They were expressions that I had often heard in militaristic Japan before the war but that had supposedly been wiped out by Japan's defeat and her regeneration as a peace-loving nation.

"Japan can only be saved," cried the speaker, "by *fukko.*"

Fukko means return to old ways. He called for the revival of *bushido*, the spirit of the samurai warrior. He declared that Japan must rid herself of foreign tyranny. He had much to say about *yamato damashii*, the soul of old Japan. Japan must turn her back on western ways, which were enfeebling the nation. Democracy was not for Japan. Japan had fallen by the sword, it could be redeemed only by the sword. Japan must not forget her dream of a co-prosperity sphere embracing all Asia.

I retreated into the shadows and drew Yasuhiro back with me. It was the same old, bitter story, the story that we hoped had been ended by the surrender and the Occupation. There had been reports in the newspapers of these secret gatherings of dyed-in-the-wool militarists who itched to regain power and lead Japan into new and bloodier adventures. And it was in the Japanese tradition to use a cave for such plottings, if a cave were handy. During the Satsuma Rebellion in 1877 the great cave beneath the island of Enoshima was the rendezvous of northern conspirators in league with the southern rebels. As for the Cave of Devils, it was easily reached by boat from the cities of the mainland a few miles away. A landing could be made on the side of the island away from the village so that no villager need be aware of it.

It would be just as well to keep out of the way of these hyperpatriots, especially since some of them seemed to have had a bit too much sake. Probably among their number were men who had been purged by the Allied Occupation for their part in Japan's military adventure, and this public disgrace would make them less than friendly toward foreigners. One speaker followed another, whipping the malcontents up to a higher and higher pitch of excitement.

There was nothing to do but wait for the end of it. Giving up all thought of our good bed, we stretched out on the rocky floor. The men were shouting, cheering, and chanting now and our uneasiness lest they might take a notion to explore our passage made sleep impossible.

The night seemed endless and the floor, which was smooth enough at first, developed points, humps, ridges, and razor blades.

When at last the voices died away we stole out and found the council chamber empty. Not far beyond it a patch of daylight indicated the exit. We came out on the mountain side. To see the sky above us and breathe the fragrant morning air was like emerging from a bad dream.

Trampled weeds showed where the men had descended the steep slope to their boat. We followed the path down the opposite slope to our own craft.

Yasuhiro kept muttering, *"Dame desu! Dame desu!"* It is hard to translate, but it expresses deep dissatisfaction. "Those men and what they want to do—take us into more wars. I was only fifteen when I was drafted. They sent me to New Guinea. It was bad. I have a little boy—sixteen months old now. I hate to think he'll ever have to go through anything like that."

•

Perhaps it won't come that soon. Perhaps it will be Yasuhiro's grandson. Who can say? The Japanese people are strongly opposed to war. But so they were before World War II. If the issue had been submitted to popular vote there would have been no war.

Even a poll of the army would have meant peace. But a small group of officers were war-minded and their spokesman was the premier, General Tojo.

In the final analysis, it took only two men to start the war —Tojo and the emperor. Tojo instructed the emperor to issue a declaration of war, implying that if he refused he would face abdication. The emperor yielded. The people, conditioned by two thousand years of obedience to authority, obeyed their emperor.

It will happen again—not immediately—perhaps forty years from now. That is not a long time.

One of the decisive factors will be the need for more room. Japan's empire was reduced from a wartime high of five million square miles to 148,000, about half the size of Texas.

In this land are crowded 103 million Japanese. And the picture is rendered much worse by the fact that, because of mountainous terrain, only 15 percent of the land can be cultivated.

Japan has drastically cut its birth rate by contraceptives and abortion. Yet the population increases by a half million a year. But the land does not increase. It is obvious that the world's greatest population pressure must lead to an attempt to enlarge the Japanese living space.

Such expansion is rationalized as a religious duty—a duty necessary not only for the good of Japan, but the salvation of the world. As General Araki once said,

> It was the will of our Ancestress [Amaterasu, the sun goddess] that a paradise should be made of chaos. She directed her imperial descendants to organize expeditions against those who would not submit to good rule. Japan is the messenger of peace. It is Japan's mission to glorify the Imperial Way to the end of the four seas. Our imperial morality must be preached and spread over the whole world. We Japanese cannot but turn back to teach the Europeans and Americans. This is no longer the time for importations from Europe and America but exportations from Japan. The Nipponese race must rise from its slumber to embrace the universe as its state.

The day our Occupation forces began to land in Japan a Japanese policeman was seen tearing down a poster.

An American officer snatched it from his hand and called an interpreter.

"A Hundred-Year War" was the caption in large characters sprawled down the right side of the poster. Then, in vertical columns, reading leftward:

"Never has Great Nippon known defeat. The present difficulty is but a stepping stone to the future. Rallying around the Imperial Throne, fight on, for this is a HUNDRED-YEAR WAR."

For two years before surrender, according to Swiss observers who remained in Japan during the war, Japan had been building up the hundred-year war psychology.

"Those posters," said a Swiss resident, "and others like them have been displayed everywhere. Also there have been huge painted signs using billboard space contributed by manufacturers. The newspapers have carried hundred-year war announcements in display advertising space, also in news stories and editorials. There have been hundred-year war films. Popular songs have been written on the theme. And radio commentators have been continually harping on it."

Envisaging possible defeat, Japan's militarists were laying their bets on the long future. Japan was being conditioned to lose one conflict but to prepare for another—and another and another, for a hundred years if necessary, until Japan's program of conquest is fulfilled.

It is not a new idea. When I was in Japan before Pearl Harbor I had a revealing conversation with a young officer in the Japanese army.

He showed me a paragraph in his army textbook referring to the "imperial century."

"That is the coming century of war," he said. "At the end of it our emperor will rule the world."

"You look a long way ahead," I remarked.

"Not at all. Our country is 2,600 years old. To us a century is a short time. Of course in our first war we may be beaten—but we can be patient."

•

Radical right-wing organizations, anti-American and pro-expansionist, remained underground for seven years after the war. Now they are active and outspoken. They include the Revolutionary Chrysanthemum Alliance, the New Mass Party, the Daiwa Party, the Young Men's League for the Liberation of Japan (from the American yoke), the Japan

Farmers' Union, the National Rebirth Movement, the Institute for National Defense, the Federation for Deliverance of Japan, the National Defense Corps, the Cooperation Party, the Alliance for Self Defense and Neutrality, the House of Growth, the Veterans' Association, and as many more.

It is important to remember that both Shinto and Japanese Buddhism are expansionist. Shinto, of course, is based upon the rescript of the first emperor declaring that Japan must make the whole world her dominion.

Buddhism is generally supposed to be a nonviolent religion. But Buddhism has been employed in Japan for political and expansionist purposes. The most active party in today's Diet is the Buddhist Komeito or Soka Gakkai which with revivalist fervor condemns pro-Americans and expounds messianic schemes for a Brave New Japan that shall save the world.

From the radical groups emanate such pious shibboleths as "Within the four seas all are brothers"; "Eight corners, one roof" (meaning all people of the eight corners of the world under the Japanese roof); "Peace that every man wants will not come until the world is under one central authority"; "The great mission which Heaven has imposed upon Japan is to save humanity"; "The material civilization of the West must be rectified by the moral civilization of the East"; "Rescue must come from the Orient, for the light is always from the east"; "Overflowing with the divine spirit, we must offer a new life to other nations. Heaven has ordered us to complete this task"; "The divine mission of divine Japan"; "The great Messianic ideal which nations long for, the Japanese possess"; "Rising in the Eastern heavens is the hope of humanity, Messiah the Ruler"; "The imperial family of Japan is the parent not only of the Japanese race but of all nations on the earth"; "Our race has before it a great duty, the commission to assimilate the earth and the universe"; "Japan must be the light of the world"; "The suffering globe needs Japan"; "Japan shall go forth like an avenging fire to establish the power of Heaven on earth"; "They have been called hitherto Japan and foreign lands. Hereafter there shall be naught but Japan."

•

On my first visit to Japan in 1915 the elderly Etsu Sugimoto, daughter of one of the last of the samurai, related a childhood conversation with her grandmother.

"Honorable Grandmother," she said, pointing to a colored map in the atlas, "I am much troubled. Look—our beloved land is only a tiny island in the great world."

The grandmother adjusted her big horn spectacles and carefully studied the map. Then with slow dignity she closed the book.

"It is quite natural, little Etsu-bo, for them to make Japan look small on this map," she said. "It was made by foreigners. Japan is made large on Japanese maps."

One would suppose that this conception might have changed in a half century. But in 1970 in the book section of a Ginza department store, a Japanese countryman was overheard asking the clerk for a *chikyu*, globe.

He looked the globe over and did not find what he was looking for.

"Where is Japan?" he asked.

"Japan is there," the clerk said, pointing out a diminutive fleck of land in the western Pacific.

The customer was disappointed. "This is not the kind of globe I want."

"Just what kind do you want?"

"One with only Japan on it."

•

A globe with only Japan on it would please many Japanese. Industrially, they almost have it. Their nation, economically, is larger than any other on the face of the earth except the United States and Russia—and is increasing its gross national product five times as fast as America and three times as fast as the Soviet Union. Is it surprising that this astounding success should encourage Japan to dream of a far greater future?

INDEX

Abortion, 268
Agriculture, 4, 27, 120, 184, 188, 217
Ainu, 10
Aircraft, 206
Akihito, Prince, 20, 235
Alcock, Sir Rutherford, 79, 92-3, 234
Amaterasu, 7, 150
American bases, 323
Ancestor worship, 14
Animism, 13
Araki, General, 154, 161, 333
Architecture, 25, 27, 120, 134, 298ff.
Area, 294, 332
Armed forces, 324ff.
Army, 130ff., 141ff., 156ff.
Art, 280ff., 309
Asama, Mt., 192ff.
Assassination, 81ff.
Atomic bomb, 179-180, 323-4
Automobile industry, 3, 13, 205, 226

Bath, 286ff., 303-4
Beds, 299, 301, 305-7
Beppu, 195

Besshi Mine, 207ff., 225
Birth control, 266ff.
Bismarck, 16
Brazil, 274
Buck, Pearl S., Foundation, 250
Buddhism, 12, 13, 29, 276, 335
Business methods, 2, 224ff.

California, 217
Camera industry, 4, 211-2
Censorship of news, 164ff.
Chamberlain, Professor B. H., 17
Characteristics, 5ff., 12-3, 20ff., 107ff., 174-5, 189, 202, 218-9, 293, 307ff.
China, 11, 15, 26ff., 120, 140, 289, 323
Choshu, Prince of, 102, 107
Christianity, 12, 34ff., 59-60, 130, 148-9
Christian Science Monitor, 165
Cloissoné, 281
Clothing, 25, 238
Constitution, 138, 325-6
Copper mine, 207, 225

Damascene, 282
Democracy, 168ff.
Divorce, 187
Dutch, 35

Earthquakes, 190, 195-7
Education 6, 140ff., 289
Electronics industry, 4
Embroidery, 283
Emigration, 274
Emperor worship, 8ff., 21-2, 128ff., 140ff., 327-8
Europe, 3
Expansionism, 118ff., 321ff.
Expense accounts, 2
Expo 70, 4, 221, 297

Factories, 114ff.
Farmers, 183, 217
Fillmore, President, 37, 49
Fire, 198
Fishing, 4, 178, 216-17
Fleischer, Wilfrid, 129
Floods, 197
Flower arrangement, 27
Food, 25, 301-3, 305
Formosa, 119
Francis Xavier, St., 34, 311
Fuji, Mt., 191

Gardens, 27, 300, 315ff.
Geisha, 1-2, 240
Germany, 17
G.I. marriages, 240-1, 246-7, 251
GNP, 3, 337
Gods, 6-9, 11, 13
Government, 28ff., 171ff.
Grew, Joseph, 21

Halfbreeds, 249ff.
Harris, Townsend, 54ff., 92ff.
Hayama, 127, 131ff.
Health, 263-4
Hearn, Lafcadio, 312, 315
Heusken, Henry, 54ff., 89ff.
Hideyoshi, General, 32ff.
Hiroshima, 179ff.
History, 6ff., 149ff.
Hokkaido, 10, 126
Hot springs, 195

Ideographs, 289ff.
Imabari towel factory, 215-6

Imperial Rescripts, 145ff., 327
Indonesia, 329
Industrial growth, 3-4, 112ff., 203ff., 221ff.
Infanticide, 121-2
Inheritances from past, 319-320
Inland Sea, 6, 330
Inns, 303ff.
Inventions, 220
Ise Shrine, 12
Isolation, 36
Ito, Count, 16, 21, 138-9
Izanagi, 6-7
Izanami, 6-7

Jimmu, Emperor, 9-10, 321
Jingo, Empress, 322

Kahn, Herbert, 222
Karuizawa, 192
Kimono, 238
Kojiki, 9-10
Korea, 11, 29ff., 119, 322, 324
Kurile Islands, 119, 322
Kyushu, 322

Labor force, 113
Lacquer, 280
Land reform, 184ff.
Landscaping, 27, 300, 315ff.
Language, 26, 289ff., 312
Legends, 6, 19, 99, 190
Literacy, 4, 26, 289ff.
London, 4
Love of nature, 13

MacArthur, General, 162ff., 224, 241, 272-3, 313, 323
Malaya, 25
Manchuria, 139
Marriage, 235-6, 240
Medical practices, 253ff.
Medley, A. W., 128-9
Meiji, Emperor, 108, 136, 327
Micronesia, 120, 322
Mikimoto, 279-80
Militarism, 120ff., 324, 330-1
Missionaries, 34, 130, 148-9, 247
Mongols, 24
Motion picture industry, 4, 212, 285
Motorcycle production, 3, 206
Music, 285-6

Index

National Geographic Magazine, 286
Nationalism, 8ff., 130ff.
Natural disasters, 190ff.
Navy, 102ff., 324
New York, 4
Nihongi, 9–10
Nitobe, Dr., 290

Occupation of Japan, 162ff., 224, 238–9, 241, 270
Oil discoveries, 330
Okichi, 55ff., 94ff.
Okinawa, 323
Opening of Japan, 37ff.
Osaka, 296–7

Painting, 283–4
Patric, John, 313
Pearl Harbor, 130, 322
Pearl industry, 277ff.
Perry, Commodore, 37ff.
Phallic worship, 14–6, 262
Poetry, 82, 284–5
Political parties, 171
Population, 4, 178, 269ff., 294, 333
Portuguese, 34
Prices, 2, 295
Prostitution, 122, 126, 183, 187–8, 241ff.
Proverbs, 293, 310
Publishing industry, 4

Racial origins, 15, 19, 24ff.
Radical organizations, 330, 334
Radio production, 4, 213, 285
Railroads, 4, 206, 296
Rearmament, 324ff.
Reischauer, Professor Edwin, 273, 325
Religion, 11ff., 121, 276
Rescript on Education, 145ff., 327
Respect for age, 311
Restoration of emperor, 108
Riots, 325
Roosevelt, F. D., 130
Roosevelt, Theodore, 4, 277
Russia, 3
Russo-Japanese War, 119

Sams, Brigadier-General, 270–1
Samurai, 2, 8

Sato, Prime Minister, 221, 328
Satsuma, Prince of, 100, 108
Satsuma ware, 282
SCAP, 162ff., 185, 270, 291, 327
Seiji, Shimidzu, 83ff.
Sewing machine production, 4
Shimoda, 54ff., 97ff.
Shinto, 11ff., 121, 335
Shipbuilding, 3, 204, 223
Shogun, 35, 76
Siberia, 139
Silk industry, 123, 126, 214
Smog, 295
Soldiers, 154ff.
Steel industry, 205–6, 223
Suicide, 194, 248, 254
Superstitions, 257ff.
Susanoo, 8, 18
Swords, 8

Taxation, 124, 184
Television production, 4, 213, 285
Textiles, 214ff.
Thailand, 329
Tidal waves, 199
Tojo, General, 332
Tokyo, 4, 294ff.
Toynbee, Arnold, 189
Toyoda loom, 215, 220
Trade in Asia, 327, 329
Treaty of 1858, 78
Typewriter, 290
Typhoons, 198ff.

United States, 3, 37ff., 118–9, 324, 326
United States Army, 244
University of California, 317

Volcanoes, 190ff., 248

War casualties, 177ff.
Watch production, 4, 210–11
Weather, 190
Williams, Wells, 39, 42ff.
Women in industry, 113ff., 237
Women, position of, 229ff.
World War II, 23

Yedo, 74ff.
Yokohama, 79ff.
Yoshiwara, 2, 200, 240ff.

Zaibatsu, 224ff.